NATIONAL
PARKS OF THE WORLD

VOLUME 2

AFRICA / ASIA / AUSTRALASIA AND OCEANIA

by

KAI CURRY-LINDAHL

and

JEAN-PAUL HARROY

Under the general editorship of
VERA R. WEBSTER

Original Project Editor: HERBERT S. ZIM

An official publication of the International Union for
Conservation of Nature and Natural Resources (IUCN)

GOLDEN PRESS · NEW YORK
Western Publishing Company, Inc.
Racine, Wisconsin

National parks and equivalent nature reserves play an important role in the scientific, educational, economic, and recreational activities of many countries. For the traveler and nontraveler, this two-volume set, *National Parks of the World,* is an introduction to those havens of refuge for threatened wildlife and beauty that make sensible use of the world's natural resources. It includes over 200 of the most important national parks or equivalent reserves of some 73 countries of the continents of the world. Volume 1 includes Europe, North America, Central and South America; Volume 2 includes Africa, Asia, Australasia and Oceania. Countries having similar ecological conditions have been grouped together instead of being arranged alphabetically. The authors, Kai Curry-Lindahl and Jean-Paul Harroy, are internationally known conservationists who have been closely connected with IUCN's official documentation and supervision of threatened areas and world wildlife.

The majority of the photographs have been gathered from all over the world by the International Commission on National Parks in Brussels, chiefly through the efforts of Miss Jacqueline Henricot. The rest were secured from various agencies or from individual photographers. All acknowledgments are found under the title of Photo Credits.

Dr. Herbert S. Zim planned this book with Professor Frank Brockman at the first World Conference on National Parks in 1962. Later, they asked IUCN and Dr. Kai Curry-Lindahl to take over the project, and the material then on hand was turned over to IUCN. Dr. Zim remained in charge of the project until 1970, working with the author here and in Europe. After preliminary material was submitted, Dr. Zim prepared a detailed outline and layouts and worked out suggestions for illustrating and editing the manuscript before he relinquished active control.

VERA R. WEBSTER
General Editor

CONTENTS

Maps From *The Odyssey World Atlas*, © General Drafting Co., Inc.

Alpine Africa: tree heath zone in the Ruwenzori Mountains, at about 3,700 m, Albert National Park, Zaire.

PREFACE

The importance of national parks as a sensible use of natural resources has been recognized by the United Nations, which in 1959 invited the International Union for Conservation of Nature and Natural Resources (IUCN) to assist the U.N. Secretariat in preparing an official list of national parks and equivalent reserves of the world. The IUCN accepted this task and in 1961-1962 a first list was published in two parts. In 1962, the First World Conference on National Parks was held in Seattle, Washington, where the desirability was expressed of publishing further editions of the list, in which the selection of areas should be based on certain criteria.

In 1963, the Secretary General of the United Nations asked the International Commission on National Parks of the IUCN to prepare in this spirit a second edition of the list. This assignment was undertaken and in 1967 the "United Nations' List of National Parks and Equivalent Reserves" appeared in French, as a result of the efforts of Professor Jean-Paul Harroy, Chairman of the International Commission on National Parks. An English version was published in 1971.

While I was working on a research project in the Everglades National Park in 1964-1965, Dr. Herbert S. Zim, then of Western Publishing Company, suggested that I write a book on the national parks of the world for the "Field Guide Series." In view of IUCN's interest in national parks and my own close relation to IUCN it appeared natural that such a book should be associated with IUCN. The organization accepted this idea and recognizes this book as an official IUCN publication.

In this way, the preparation of this book became a part of the activities of IUCN's International Commission on National Parks. Therefore, it was quite natural for me to ask its Chairman, Professor Jean-Paul Harroy, to contribute to the preparation of this book. Numerous visits to national parks on all continents have given us the advantage of personal experiences from most reserves described in this book. We divided our work in the following way. Professor Harroy contributed the text that concerns the history and organization of national parks in each continent and country as well as data on location, acreage, accommodations and facilities in each national park, while I am responsible for the ecological introductions to the continents and the descriptions of the natural history (general character, climate, topography, geology, flora, and fauna) of each national park.

The IUCN is most grateful to all photographers and institutions who have very generously put their pictures at its disposal. The IUCN and the authors would also acknowledge the persons who have read parts of the text in manuscript. We are particularly grateful to Professor W. A. L. Fuller, Canada; Rocco Knobel, South Africa; Fred Packard, U.S.A.; Professor V. Puscariu, Romania; and Dr. A. Zahavi, Israel. I would also like to express my appreciation for the cooperation of Vera Webster, general editor; Priscilla Hiss, editor; and Joe Trautwein, art director, for bringing this work to completion.

KAI CURRY-LINDAHL, Vice Chairman
International Commission
on National Parks

Before introducing to the public more than two hundred national parks or equivalent reserves of the world, it might be useful to give some brief particulars on the origin of these protected areas, their present meaning, and the problems raised on all continents by their creation, management, and proper use.

To accord a few unique natural areas special protective measures is one of the ways in which applied ecology tries to conserve nature and natural resources. Since the demographic expansion that began in the nineteenth century and accelerated due to scientific and technical "progress," the natural resources of this planet have been increasingly depleted and the environment increasingly polluted.

The destruction and deterioration of resources, deforestation, erosion, the drying up of ground and other kinds of water disequilibriums, and the disappearance of wildlife are the disastrous results of the over-exploitation of natural resources. Air pollution, fresh- and sea-water pollution, the poisoning effect of toxic chemical products, the proliferation of undesirable species, the destruction of natural beauty and the encroachment on the countryside by uncontrolled industrialization and urbanization are the main manifestations of the increasing deterioration of our "environment."

Conservation of nature and natural resources is therefore the science — unfortunately until recent times the Cinderella of public opinion and governments — whose purpose is to investigate and to fight these threats to our natural environment. Apart from the general measures taken in almost every country to restore or to preserve resources and habitats by afforestation, rural engineering, or control of hunting, fishing, and pollution, a way of applying this science of ecology is to choose in each country a few beautiful outstanding examples of unspoiled nature to be set aside as natural sanctuaries where exploitation can be restricted to the minimum. This volume is an attempt to describe some representative examples of such national parks and reserves.

The first natural sanctuaries were created by princes keen on hunting who saw their game becoming scarcer as a consequence of the first early "advances" of humanity: demographic expansion and improvement in arms, traps, and hunting methods. During the 19th century, game multiplication was controlled by royal or domain guards in many "game preserves," for instance, the forests of France, the United Kingdom, Italy, and central Europe. A similar royal preserve can be mentioned for central Africa, in Rwanda, where only the Mwami was allowed to hunt in his royal preserve.

In the 19th century the ever-growing deterioration, pollution, and spoiling of natural beauty resulted around 1870 in the appearance in the U.S.A. of a new concept: the moral duty for every generation to take measures to preserve some parts of the country of outstanding beauty or interest from such over-exploitation, and to set these parks aside for the benefit of the entire nation. In 1872, Yellowstone, the first national park, was created. The first attempt to fight the encroachment of "progress" on the natural environment was made.

Later on, the term "national park" came to have two further connotations: (1) that it is important for natural scientists to have such areas at their disposal — modern biologists call them ecosystems — protected against human interference so that the study of normal biological cycles can proceed under the best possible conditions; (2) that it is also of vital social importance for people in urban or industrial societies, who live hectic lives in a noisy and polluted environment, to have the opportunity of acquiring new strength in peaceful and green surroundings in the fresh air and beauty of "natural" scenery. The first to see the scientific value of nature reserves were the Swiss, then the Belgians in Africa. In every industrialized area after World War II the basic importance of national parks and reserves for the physical and moral welfare of its citizens asserted itself simultaneously — in North America, western Europe, the USSR and the neighboring socialist republics, and in Japan, Australia, New Zealand, and South Africa.

The recreation aspect recently became so imperative for countries with megalopolitanism that voices were expressed in favor of reconsidering the former national park concept and inducing the authorities to define as national parks not only parts of nature protected from human exploitation but also any green tracts of land where rural activities, from cultivation and cattle breeding to lumbering, hunting, and fishing, would be permitted. This is, in fact, a distortion of the term "national

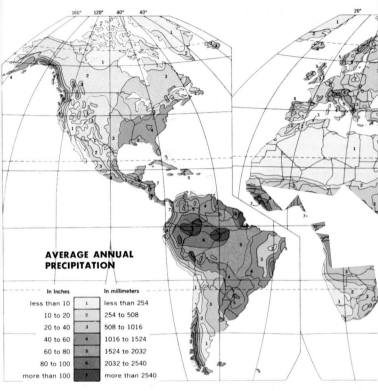

The world's vegetation zones are directly related to the annual precipitation and the map above gives an overall view of the ecological domains that have

park," which was born in 1872 in Yellowstone. The United Nations confirmed for the International Commission on National Parks that only areas with sufficient size, effective management and supervision, and those enjoying a general protective status against human exploitation and occupation would be included in the United Nations List of National Parks and Equivalent Reserves. (The name "national park" should therefore not be applied to an area where agriculture, breeding, forest exploitation, hunting or fishing are still permitted.)

From the above it can be inferred then that in the sense approved by international organizations, a national park is an area generally remarkable for its natural features, which on a relatively large territory offers one or several ecosystems left

WORLD
VEGETATION
ZONES

evolved. Vegetation maps have been used throughout to pinpoint parks having similar life zones.

untouched, or almost untouched, by human exploitation, protected by a central government where its nationals and visitors from every other country in the world are permitted and even encouraged to stay for recreation, education, or cultural purposes — part of the world's total heritage to be enjoyed.

Besides the national parks, there are, in the sense given by the UN List, equivalent reserves — protected areas offering the same characteristics of severe status as the national parks but where (1) the authority in charge of their creation and administration is not the central government, for instance state parks and provincial parks, private reserves, etc., and (2) wherein some tourism is not permitted (strictly scientific reserves) and only naturalists are allowed.

This brief definition leads us to a statement of the measures which generally had to be taken to create these national parks and make them effective. The first task is the choosing of an area, one of biological interest, uninhabited or sparsely inhabited, with few exploitations or none. Then the existing occupation and exploitation rights are acknowledged by juridical and administrative formalities, which usually involve expensive purchases and transplantations. The park's boundaries are carefully drawn and marked, sanctioned on the spot by demarcations and signposts.

Administrative and supervisory staff have to be hired and housed, and equipment, especially vehicles, purchased.

Sometimes a complex organization has to be established for scientific research with the building of laboratories and field lodges. In recent years there has been an expansion of facilities for tourists to facilitate travel and accommodation as well as to provide the necessary educational and recreational facilities, museum staff, interpretative material, etc.

Obviously the problems to be solved in creating such national parks were not the same in every country and under all latitudes. In fact where deterioration and pollution are most threatening and where the need for ecosystems free from any human interference is the most pressing, the difficulties of finding and especially safeguarding such areas are the greatest. Urban and industrial regions need large national parks; generally they have only small ones which seldom offer the spectacle, so much appreciated, of animals that can be seen close by in natural surroundings. There are a few exceptions: the countries where, early in this century or during the last century, far-sighted men followed the example of the pioneers of Yellowstone. For instance Switzerland has its Swiss National Park, set aside in 1914, and the Netherlands, the most populated country in the world, has a remarkable network of protected areas thanks to a few private persons who devoted themselves to active work as early as 1905.

The national parks in the world can therefore be logically subdivided into a few large categories, depending on geographical, historical, and economic factors.

The New World can be divided into two very distinct zones: the North, where the superindustrialized United States and

10

Canada have already succeeded in setting aside, many years ago, an exceptional network of national parks and equivalent reserves; and, on the other hand Latin America, where, with the exception of Argentina, initiatives are relatively recent and at times scarcely developed.

In western Europe, great national parks are rare and situated only in outlying countries (Sweden, Italy, Spain), whereas in eastern Europe their number is much higher.

Asia, with a few exceptions, shares the lot of Latin America. The national system of land tenure and rural economy makes it difficult for governments that have to face serious food problems to create and safeguard effectively great natural sanctuaries where human exploitation is forbidden. Japan, in spite of its overpopulation and powerful industrialization, is of course an exception since the volcanic nature of the countryside helped to solve many difficulties.

In Australia and New Zealand, conditions and therefore achievements are similar to those in Canada.

And finally Africa, the continent that is the paradise for national parks with its vast and sparsely inhabited areas and wonderful fauna, needs our consideration. Chiefly between the years 1925 and 1960, wise governments were able to create and effectively safeguard a precious network of national parks and equivalent reserves in Africa. More than fifty of these African parks will be described in Volume 2. The African national parks are in sharp contrast to other regions on the African continent where big game has almost entirely disappeared in a period of less than a hundred years. These national parks vividly demonstrate by contrast the present destructive power of man and the primary necessity of taking rapid and strong steps to stop the disastrous effects that are practically beyond repair. As a matter of fact at the beginning of this very century Africa belonged to and was the domain of its big animal wildlife, and man lived in small islets, which he left only with great caution. Seventy years later, the situation is quite opposite: the wild game live in the islets of the national parks and when they leave them, they are immediately slaughtered. Let us therefore thank those who were able in time to set aside these islet sanctuaries and let us also thank the present African governments who are managing to preserve them and increase their number.

The elephant is a dominant member in many of the African parks. Amboseli, Kenya.

AFRICA

Immense Africa, the second largest continent, spans a wide range of natural regions and climatic types. There are subtropical coastal belts as well as mangrove marshes; there are deserts, of which the Sahara is the world's largest and the Namib perhaps the oldest. Africa has salt pans and arid, steppelike subdeserts; vast savannas of grassy plains, bushvelds, and woodlands; deciduous open forests with dense underbrush, equatorial lowland rain forests with a closed canopy shadowing the soil, and montane rain forests; alkaline lakes, soda lakes, freshwater lakes as large as inland seas, and enormous swamps, nourished by a network of rivers and drained by several mighty rivers, of which the Nile, the Congo, the Niger, and the Zambesi are the longest.

The continent has extinct and living volcanoes, high mountain ranges and impressive rock massifs, of which the three highest—Kilimanjaro, Kenya, and Ruwenzori—are permanently snow-capped. These mountains climb from the humid tropics through temperate zones past the timber line on up to the icy world of snow and glaciers.

The natural regions that have been mentioned are really only broad divisions because each of them in turn is divided into a number of distinct habitats containing characteristic plants and animals.

Africa is the richest of all continents in animals. More vertebrate species, with the exception of those in the oceans, live there than anywhere else in the world. The density of large mammals on some of Africa's savannas is unequaled.

Broadly speaking, Africa's vegetation belts may be divided from north to south into eleven regions: Mediterranean coastal strip with macchia vegetation (chaparral) and temperate forests; deserts; subdesert steppes and bushlands; savanna grasslands; savanna woodlands; equatorial lowland rain forest, grassy and wooded savannas; temperate and subtropical grassland (high veld); karoo steppes and subdeserts; coastal strips of "Mediterranean" vegetation; montane rain forests and associations of higher altitudes.

The boundaries between various natural regions are usually not sharp. A mosaic pattern of savannas and woodlands is characteristic over large areas of the savanna belts both north and south of the equator—a pattern often broken by topographical features such as swamps, lakes and rivers, and high plateaus. (Permanent water is almost everywhere fringed by gallery forests or other kinds of vegetation even when it is situated in the middle of a desert.)

Madagascar, biogeographically quite distinct from continental Africa, has been separated from the African mainland for at least 20 million years. Indeed, it is doubtful whether Madagascar has ever had a land connection with either Africa or Asia. Madagascar's present animal population does not necessarily require such an explanation, though the fact that dinosaurs once lived there makes the land connection likely. Whatever its early history, animal life on Madagascar is almost as peculiar as that of Australia, and its flora is unmatched.

Man has long influenced and modified his African environment, chiefly by fire, but it was not until the arrival of the Europeans about three hundred years ago that the harmony was broken. Habitat destruction and the large-scale slaughter of animals took place. Moreover, progress in medicine and veterinary medicine reduced the mortality of human beings and of livestock, which both increased to such an extent that they locally destroyed the environment that was vital to their existence. Cattle and goats in excessive numbers are particularly unadapted to the tropical environment, where the vegetation and the soil cannot support overgrazing and overtrampling. This has led to monumental destruction of lands that were previously highly productive and able to support a large population of wild animals that are marvelously adapted to the habitats where they have evolved. For example, the savannas of the Albert National Park in the Zaire Republic and the Queen Elizabeth National Park in Uganda without any investment produce more meat per square mile in the form of large hoofed wild animals than any other region in Africa, and the land does not deteriorate—not the case in most African lands where cattle graze.

Africa is now undergoing a drastic change, perhaps more rapid than in many other regions of the world. The original ecosystems are being increasingly undermined by man, and yet this change does not work in favor of the human beings living there.

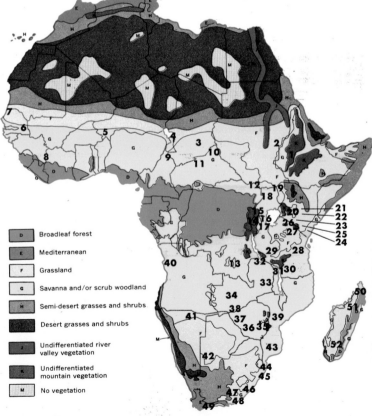

D Broadleaf forest

E Mediterranean

F Grassland

G Savanna and/or scrub woodland

H Semi-desert grasses and shrubs

Desert grasses and shrubs

J Undifferentiated river valley vegetation

K Undifferentiated mountain vegetation

M No vegetation

Fortunately, eclogists and conservationists have energetically worked for a better understanding and utilization of the living natural resources of Africa. The enormous bioproductivity in the healthy environment of some of the national parks drew attention to the fact that "farming" of wild animals is often the most economic form of land use.

According to the UN List of National Parks, nine of the 46 African countries and territories have no nature reserves that conform to its selective criteria: Burundi, Gambia, Lesotho (former Basutoland), Liberia, Libya, the United Arab Republic, Sierra Leone, Portuguese Guinea, and French Somaliland. Lesotho established its first national park in 1971.

In the remaining thirty-seven countries and territories mentioned in the UN List, there are 162 national parks and equivalent reserves. Twenty-one of these are in fourteen countries or territories that it has not been possible to include in this volume: Algeria (with 2 reserves), Congo (Brazzaville) (1), Equatorial Guinea (2), Gabon Republic (2), Ghana (1), Ivory Coast (2), Mali (1), Mauritania (1), Mauritius (2), Morocco (1), Nigeria (1), Somalia (1), Swaziland (1), Togo (3), and Tunisia (1).

The first national park set aside in Africa was the Albert National Park in the Zaire Republic, created in 1925, and in 1926 the Kruger National Park in South Africa was established. Before World War II the Belgian Congo and South Africa were the chief countries to continue to set aside national parks. After the war other countries followed their example, and it is particularly encouraging that many African govern-

Giraffes, one of Africa's many extraordinary animals. Serengeti National Park, Tanzania.

The impala is a characteristic antelope of southeastern Africa.

ments have steadily continued this policy. Tribute must especially be paid to Kenya, Tanzania, Zambia, and Zaire, the countries with most foresight in this field.

An assembly of African states meeting in Algeria in September 1968 adopted the African Convention for Conservation of Nature and Natural Resources, which emphasizes the value of the fauna and the need to protect all major habitats. (No other continent has such a conservation convention.) In effect since July 17, 1969, after ratification by Upper Volta, Swaziland, Kenya, and Ghana, the Convention has received ratification from other signatory governments.

There is now a network of national parks and nature reserves in Africa covering a wide range of habitats in various regions. Their chief characteristics are their great size and their spectacular fauna, contrasting sharply with immense neighboring regions that through overuse have been almost entirely deprived of their vegetation and animals. These parks and reserves provide a unique ground for photography and filming. Facilities for visitors to ensure access, their accommodation, and animal viewing are becoming more comfortable and less expensive.

Fifty-eight such areas are described here. Only the northern part of the continent, including the Sahara, is poorly served by national parks. Most desert animals are nomadic and therefore hard to protect.

17

Tree heaths and St. Johnswort form thickets above 2,600 m in Menegasha National Park.

ETHIOPIA

Area: 1,035,710 km²   **Population density: 20/km²**

Menegasha National Park, described below, was planned as a national park in 1958 and is Ethiopia's only accredited national park on the UN List. Although it is called a national park, in fact it is still only a forest reserve. In 1969, creation of the Awash National Park was announced, and in 1970 the Semien National Park was gazetted. The latter covers about 100,000 ha and has been set aside to protect the Walia ibex and a spectacular landscape.

With some international assistance the Ethiopian Government has created a staff and is actively preparing to set aside several national parks and game reserves, an enterprise that will require the eventual removals of some village populations. Planned projects are the Bale Mountains N.P., the Omo N.P., and the Rift Valley Lake National Park.

MENEGASHA NATIONAL PARK

Near Addis Ababa and easily accessible, this park is situated on the slopes of the volcanic cone of Mt. Wochocha and embraces montane habitats of elevations from 2,435 to 3,425 meters. Some virgin stands of forest still exist

18

Location: 53 km W of Addis Ababa
Area: 3,000 ha
Access: from Addis Ababa; difficult, even impossible, in the rainy season
Accommodation: available in the park

GEOLOGY AND TOPOGRAPHY A lava substratum prevails in the area, locally intermingled with sandstone and partly covered with soil that is subject to erosion; the soils under forest cover have a thick humus layer.

The slopes of Mt. Wochocha are wrinkled by deep gorges, carved by rivers and streams.

CLIMATE Temperate and, up to an elevation of about 2,600 m, rather humid; the upper parts are cold and dry (average temp.: 12–14°C). Rainy periods: mid-March to mid-April, mid-June through Sept.

FLORA Vegetation zones divide into almost perfectly horizontal belts around the volcano. At lower elevations: plantations of eucalypts.

A semihumid zone (2,400–2,500 m) has a beautiful forest of cedars that rise to a height of 35 m and podocarps with some *Pygeum, Olea,* and *Albizzia.* (The cedar is a relic from the cedar forests that once covered vast montane areas in Ethiopia.) Above 2,600 m, kusso-trees take command with some highland elements: tree heaths and St. Johnswort. In the montane savanna are found Abyssinian musk rose and such grasses as fescues and bent grasses. Unfortunately, the upper levels of the reserve are cultivated and their original habitats have been destroyed.

MAMMALS Menegasha's forests are populated by guerezas, vervets, gelada baboons, black bushbucks, duikers, leopards, caracals, and wildcats.

BIRDS Among the rich avifauna the white-cheeked touraco is noteworthy.

Leopards often spend the day resting in a tree.

SUDAN

Area: 2,515,500 km²   Population density: 5/km²

The Republic of the Sudan has three national parks: Dinder N.P., Southern N.P., and Nimule N.P., and, in addition, some ten game reserves where the protective status is less severe—all administered by the Ministry of Animal Resources, Game and Fisheries Department, Khartoum, which can provide further information. The political situation in the south of the country may make access to protected areas such as Southern and Nimule national parks difficult and even dangerous.

DINDER NATIONAL PARK (created 1935)

Situated around the Dinder River east of the Blue Nile and not far from the Ethiopian border, Dinder N.P. covers a semiarid steppe and bush at an elevation of 600–800 meters, ecologically a transition zone between desert and savanna. Despite low rainfall and poor vegetation, the national park supports impressive herds of herbivorous mammals. Rains fall May–Oct. and change the cotton soil into swampy ground, making travel even on camels impossible or very difficult.

A proposed irrigation canal running from Roseires Dam into the Rahad River poses a serious threat to this national park and the adjacent Rahad Game Reserve. Such a canal would constitute an uncrossable barrier for animals migrating northward from the national park in the wet season and might have catastrophic effects on the mammal populations.

Location: eastern Sudan
Area: 650,000 ha
Climate: hot, especially Jan.–May when the river beds dry up
Protection: total, except for some controlled game cropping in W sector; staff of 40 units; car road runs from NW to SW through the park; ten other roads to spots where game concentrates; observation sites
Accommodation: tourist camp at Galegu (50 beds); three camping sites—run by safari and tourist agencies

FLORA The bush is dense. Trees include acacias (Acacia fistula and A. seyal), desert date, and combretums. Scattered widely these usually give little shade, but along the river beds doum palms provide lush patches in an otherwise arid landscape.

MAMMALS During the dry season many animals concentrate around pools and swamps holding permanent water. To be found there: waterbuck, reedbuck, bushbuck, oribi, greater kudu, tiang, hartebeest, roan, Soemmering's gazelle, giraffe, buffalo, warthog, lion, honey badger (ratel), red monkey, vervet, baboon, porcupine, and others.

BIRDS Over 115 species recorded; most conspicuous: ostriches, storks, egrets, herons, and vultures.

Area: 1,288,958 km²   Population density: 2/km²

The United Nations List includes two areas in the Republic of Chad: Zakouma National Park, described below, and Manda National Park (110,000 ha). Another reserve, Siniaka-Minia Faunal Reserve with its most interesting fauna that includes the black rhinoceros, is also described below although the reserve did not meet the criteria of the UN listing. (This reserve was to have been upgraded into a national park in 1965, a project that up to the present has had to be postponed.) The national parks and game reserves are administered by the Direction des Parcs Nationaux et Réserves de Faune, from which information may be obtained at B.P. 905, Fort-Lamy.

ZAKOUMA NATIONAL PARK (created 1958, 1963)

The region of the Parc National de Zakouma shows many features indicating the proximity of northern Africa's vast desert. Steppes and savannas here are of relatively dry types belonging to the Sudanese semi-arid zone. The national park protects abundant animal life.

Crowned cranes (*Balearica pavonina*) on a drying meadow in Zakouma National Park

Sacred ibis and common egrets.

pools hold permanent water even in the drier parts of the area.

FLORA The vegetation of the western half of the national park consists of open forests and savanna woodlands of acacias and combretums, with *Hyparrhenia* the dominating grass; the eastern half, wherever it is not bare, has but poor vegetation of scattered thorn bushes and meager grass.

MAMMALS The abundant animal life is, of course, richest in the western part of the park. Altogether there are 30 species of larger mammals in the national park. Giraffes and buffaloes are common; elephants occur in sizable numbers only during the dry season (many of them leave the park during the rainy period).

Other herbivores: red-fronted gazelle, tiang, duiker, roan, hartebeest, waterbuck, kob, bushbuck, reedbuck, oribi, and warthog. Zakouma National Park also shelters some black rhinoceroses and greater kudus, but hippopotamuses do not occur there.

Among the predators, the lion is common and also, though not so often seen, the leopard. The cheetah dwells only in the northern part of the park. Other carnivores: serval, caracal, wildcat, spotted hyena, striped hyena, wild dog, banded mongoose, civet, and genet.

Baboons are numerous; red monkeys and vervets are also present.

BIRDS River lagoons and the swamps, particularly in the dry season, collect spectacular gatherings of birds; among the most conspicuous: storks, herons, egrets, crowned cranes, and birds of prey.

The latter are also found in other habitats in the park together with ostriches, bustards, bee-eaters, guineafowl, francolins, Abyssinian ground hornbills, secretary birds, and others.

OTHER VERTEBRATES Crocodiles are common.

Location: Salamat district, about 250 km NE of Fort-Archambault
Area: 297,200 ha
Protection: total, except for a village scheduled to be evacuated; staff of 80 units; car tracks for tourists within the park
Access: by road, and by plane (airstrip accessible to DC3 planes within the park, 7 km from Bahr Tinga Camp)
Accommodation: most comfortable at Bahr Tinga Camp (seven new bungalows with 56 beds); total accommodation 80 beds; running water, electricity; two air-conditioned restaurants

TOPOGRAPHY In this relatively flat area, topographical variations are provided by the beds of the Salamat and the Korom rivers in the east and by two conspicuous rocky outcrops in the west, the Bone and the Ibir, rising to 300 and 150 meters, respectively, above the plain. Large areas of the eastern part consist of bare lands, flooded by rains in the wet season (June–Oct.). The only watercourse carrying water throughout the year is the Salamat River, but some smaller

SINIAKA-MINIA FAUNAL RESERVE (created 1961, designated a "controlled hunting area" in 1967)

The Réserve de faune du Siniaka-Minia is located in an immense plain, which has some minor mountain ranges and is drained by meandering rivers. During the dry season in November—May (annual rainfall: 800–1,000 mm), these rivers dry up but keep water in a series of surrounding lagoons that are most important for wildlife. This is an area where tsetse flies are common.

Location: southern Chad, E of Melfi, about 100 km NW of Fort-Archambault
Area: 426,000 ha
Protection: supervision by ten units; area at present inhabited by some 500 people, who will have to be evacuated
Accommodation: area considered unsuitable for tourism because of the dense vegetation

FLORA The vegetation of the northern part of the reserve consists chiefly of a thornbush savanna or steppe, which changes gradually southward into a wooded savanna with combretums, then develops into woodlands with khayas and daniellias.

MAMMALS Most of the antelopes of this part of Africa are to be found in Siniaka-Minia Reserve.

Elephants, buffaloes, and warthogs are well represented; rock hyraxes live on the rocky hills. Giraffes, aardvarks or antbears, and hippopotamuses also occur in this park. The black rhinoceros numbers about 15. Baboons are very numerous. The largest carnivores: leopard and lion; others: jackal, wild dog, and spotted hyena.

BIRDS Birdlife includes many species of waterfowl, storks, egrets, and pelicans, as well as guineafowl and the ostrich.

Male buffaloes are among the most impressive African mammals.

Three lionesses dozing in the sun

DAHOMEY, NIGER, UPPER VOLTA

Areas:
  113,056 km² (Dahomey)
  1,271,891 km² (Niger)
  275,159 km² (Upper Volta)

Population densities:
  23/km² (Dahomey)
  3/km² (Niger)
  19/km² (Upper Volta)

The very beautiful park named "W," described below, is located along a reach of the Niger River that makes a double turn in the form of a W-shaped bend. It is situated in three contiguous countries: Dahomey, Niger, and Upper Volta; creation of an international agreement by the three concerned governments is under consideration.

In the UN List of National Parks and Equivalent Reserves the "W" National Park is the only park mentioned for Niger and for Upper Volta, but Dahomey has one other national park, the Parc National de la Pendjari (275,000 ha).

THE "W" NATIONAL PARK OF NIGER (created 1954 simultaneously in three countries)
Administratively, the area of the Parc National du W du Niger is divided into three national parks having boundaries in common—the largest portion of the park is in Dahomey. Close or contiguous are the Parc National de la Pendjari and nine nature reserves and hunting reserves, protecting an area of over two million hectares. The "W" National Park is one of the most important wildlife reserves in West Africa.

Location: bordered in the NE by the Niger River

Area: 1,132,000 ha (Dahomey: 502,000 ha; Niger: 300,000 ha; Upper Volta: 330,000 ha)

Climate: temperatures of 35°C in the dry season

Protection: one visitor's permit gives access to the three parks; Dahomey: 11 guards, Niger: staff of seven, Upper Volta: 14 guards; four fifths of park uninhabited; many car tracks, forming an international circuit: 48 km in Dahomey, 272 in Niger, and 320 in Upper Volta; tourism increasing; entrance to park impeded in rainy season (May–Nov.)

Accommodation: Dahomey: a room available in Keremou, in SW area of park; Niger: camp of the Tapoa, NW limit of park (lodgings for 20 persons); Upper Volta: camp hotel at Diapaga, 20 km W of western boundary of park

---

GEOLOGY AND TOPOGRAPHY

Situated on a peneplain of lateritic soils, into which the Tapoa and Mékrou rivers have eroded deep gorges, the area is a lowland (average elevation: 259 m). There are some granite and sandstone formations, rocks, and hills. Across the park runs the Atacora chain, a low mountain range. The park consists of wooded savannas and is a part of the Sudanese semi-arid zone crossing Africa from Mauretania in the west and reaching to the Nile Valley in the east.

The Niger makes an enormous bow, fed by a great variety of sources and streams, many rising in the south. Water holes remain in some areas during the long, pronounced dry season (Nov.–April). Local rains fall June–September, with some rain also in May and October. Large tracts are flooded from early July to the end of September.

FLORA The area is a transition zone between desert and savanna; parts in the north have a Sahelian aspect with semi-arid vegetation and grassy shrublands, shifting to Sudanese wooded savannas southward, while in the most southerly part moister woodlands of a Guinean type appear. Dense gallery forests fringe the watercourses.

Acacias dominate the trees. Among the tall, thick grasses are *Sporobolus*, *Cenchrus*, and *Chrysopogon*. The gallery forests are composed of *Kigelia*, *Cola*, and *Borassus* palms.

MAMMALS The park abounds with large numbers of antelopes: species like the roan, western hartebeest, and kob roam the savannas, while the sitatunga, waterbuck, bohor reedbuck, oribi, and red-fronted gazelle stay near aquatic

The warthog is the only purely diurnal species of the African pigs.

Hippopotamuses spend a great deal of time in the water.

habitats; topis graze on the northern plains near the Tapoa River. The duiker also occurs.

Warthogs, elephants, and buffaloes are found all over the park, as are hippopotamuses along the rivers. Baboons, vervets, and red monkeys are often encountered.

The carnivores include the many lions, striped hyenas, side-striped jackals, and sand foxes. Cheetahs are found mostly in the northern part of the area. Also common, though seldom observed: leopards, caracals, and wildcats.

BIRDS Migratory aquatic birds visit the region when the rivers leave their beds and flood the surroundings (Dec.—May): geese, ducks, cormorants, pelicans, waders, ibises, storks, herons, and egrets. Guineafowl, Abyssinian ground hornbills, and secretary birds inhabit the wooded savannas; frequently seen are vultures, brown harrier eagles, fish eagles, martial eagles, and swallow-tailed kites.

Vast grasslands provide food for an abundance of seed-eaters: doves, finches, and weavers, Denham's bustards, pipits, and larks.

REPTILES The most conspicuous are crocodiles, monitor lizards, pythons, and turtles.

Four stilts and a spur-winged plover—both species breed in Africa.

Topis are antelopes belonging to grassy savannas of equatorial Africa.

SENEGAL

Area: 96,950 km²   Population density: 19/km²

The Republic of Senegal has three national parks, Niokolo-Koba, Djovol, both described below, and Basse-Casamance. The country also maintains a botanical-reserve, Noflaye, in the neighborhood of Dakar, and in addition Senegal has a special faunal reserve, N'Diaël Reserve. The national parks are under the authority of the President of the Republic.

NIOKOLO-KOBA NATIONAL PARK (created 1962)

The Parc National du Niokolo-Koba with three contiguous game reserves is situated in a region where two climatic belts meet. South of the Sahelian climatic belt and on the edge of the Guinean belt, this uninhabited country has diversified floristic and animal life. Birds are abundant. Dakar University conducts important scientific research within the national park.

Location: SE corner of Senegal, near the border with Guinea
Area: 813,000 ha
Protection: total; supervised by ten motorized units; 500 km of tracks in park; airstrip at Simenti used twice a week during tourist season

Access: by the Dakar-Tambacounda-Kédougou road
Accommodation: hotel at Simenti; camps at Niokolo and Bady

GEOLOGY Part of the basin of the upper Gambia River, the na-

27

The kob inhabits savannas and flood plains.

tional park is located on a pre-Cambrian shield of gneisses, quartzites, and schists with tracts of sandstone covered by lateritic soils. At the end of the Ordovician and again at the end of the Cretaceous periods, the region was submerged by the sea.

TOPOGRAPHY Plains with scattered trees and woodland savannas dominate, but in the eastern section the land rises to a high plateau and mountain ridges. Some pools of the Niokolo-Koba and Gambia rivers contain permanent water, but most of their tributaries carry water only from June to November, progressively drying by December–January. Highest point: 311 m.

CLIMATE The annual temperature is 28°C and precipitation 1,000–1,300 mm. (The rains fall May–Oct.)

FLORA Dry tree savannas and woodlands constitute the chief vegetation. Vast plains are covered by tall grasses but with much variation of plant cover. Trees include combretums, African watertrees, bombax with orange flowers, West African padauks, terminalias (2

species), and many others, mingling with associations of herbaceous plants like bluestem grass, lovegrass, and many species of *Lepicagathys*. There are also groups of bamboos and palms (*Raphia, Phoenix,* and *Helaeis*).

Large mushroomlike termite stacks dot some tracts. Other areas almost bare become green after a few days of rain.

In contrast to the relative poverty of the savanna, tall trees grow in the gallery forests. These include several species of rubber or fig trees and kapoks or ceibas.

MAMMALS The following are relatively widespread: buffalo, kob, bohor reedbuck, oribi, bushbuck, waterbuck, roan, hartebeest, topi, duiker, redflanked duiker, black duiker, blue duiker, hippopotamus, warthog, red monkey, vervet, baboon, bush baby, porcupine, spotted hyena, striped hyena, side-striped jackal, wild dog, wildcat, serval, lion, leopard, caracal, and civet.

The elephant, however, is rare, most easily seen during the dry season in the proximity of water.

The park is the periphery of the giraffe's range, this animal visiting irregularly in the dry season. The giant eland, largest of antelope species, is rare in the park. The bushpig, a typical species for the Guinean savannas, is numerous.

BIRDS Savanna species are abundant: guineafowl, francolins, bustards, and larks, but there is also a great variety of woodland and aquatic birds (the Simenti pool is a favorable spot for watching water birds as well as mammals). The magpie mannikin, a weaver almost exterminated in Senegal and Gambia, has a refuge here in Niokolo-Koba. 328 species recorded.

REPTILES Among the reptiles, the crocodile, python, cobra, and four species of turtles and tortoises should be mentioned.

DJOVOL NATIONAL PARK (created 1962, upgraded 1971)

The Parc National du Djovol is a strict nature reserve particularly important for aquatic birds in the delta of the Senegal River close to the border with Mauritania. When birds migrating from Europe and Asia fly across the Sahara Desert, it is the first permanent water they find.

An immense wetland, a labyrinth of islands, islets, and marshy banks, rice fields, and floating prairies of grasses, the area can nourish enormous quantities of birds.

Location: northwestern Senegal
Area: 3 ha
Protection: strict enforcement; entrance permitted only to scientific staff

TOPOGRAPHY The ancient alluvial beds are arid and steppelike during the dry season but inundated in autumn. In the Richard-Toll region a depression runs across the Senegal Valley connecting the basins of the Rkiz and Guiers lakes. Great littoral dunes block the river outlet forcing the river to turn southward. Pools of the wetlands are fresh, brackish, or weakly saline.

CLIMATE Tropical, with a very long dry period (7-10 months).

FLORA Salt-loving plants such as glasswort and thistles abound, but there are also grasses like witchgrass or panicum and signal grass. In the seasonally inundated area the floating prairies are composed of *Echinochloa stagnina*, *E. pyramidalis*, *Diplachne fusca*, and *Polygonum senegalense*.

There are also extraordinary riverine forests of *Acacia nilotica*, *Symmeria panicula*, *Cola laurifolia*, *Ficus capraefolia*. These are subjected to complete submersion for about a month and are without water for nine or ten months.

MAMMALS The delta flood plain is inhabited by warthogs, probably Africa's densest population.

BIRDS Gathering birds use the reserve and the entire surrounding area. Herons, egrets, storks, ibises,

The wood ibis, despite its name, is a stork.

pelicans, gulls, and terns are present in great numbers; ducks and waders are still more abundant. The estimate of black-tailed godwits numbers several hundreds of thousands; reeves and wood sandpipers are even more numerous.

Other palaearctic waders wintering in astonishing numbers: green sandpiper, greenshank, redshank, spotted redshank, ringed plover, little ringed plover, little stint, snipe, and black-winged stilt.

Aerial estimates indicate about 150,000 ducks, many garganeys; also pintails, shovelers, teal, pochards, and ferruginous ducks.

Large flocks of great flamingos and many avocets are present in a saline area of the reserve.

Migratory birds tally about 100 species, native species about 200. Among the latter are colonies of cattle egrets, with some 4,000 nests, and the red-billed quelea finches, very numerous in rice areas.

Areas: Population density:
247,411 km² (Guinea)   16/km² (Guinea)
331,552 km² (Ivory Coast)   13/km² (Ivory Coast)
111,800 km² (Liberia)   10/km² (Liberia)

About three fourths of the Mount Nimba Reserve, described below, lies in Guinea, with almost all of the remaining part in the Ivory Coast, but the mountain range also stretches across the boundary of Liberia; there has been some consideration of extending Mount Nimba Reserve farther into that country.

In Guinea there is no other protected area. The Ivory Coast, containing about a quarter of Mount Nimba Reserve, has a second protected area: the Bouna Reserve (900,000 ha), open part of the year to visitors. Liberia at present has no protected areas except forest reserves, but, as indicated above, a plan to extend Mount Nimba Reserve has been contemplated, as are three other projects: Mount Wutivi National Park, Bokoma National Park, and Tiempo National Park, with a total of about 22,000 hectares.

THE MOUNT NIMBA RESERVE (created 1944)

The Réserve Naturelle Intégrale des Monts Nimba covers an isolated mountain range with an astonishingly high number of endemic animal species. (The area of the whole massif is treated below as a complex and independently of the national boundaries.) Very important as a key area for evolutionary research, this territory with further exploration will certainly yield more biological surprises.

Location: at the boundaries of the three countries
Area: 18,000 ha (13,000 ha in Guinea)
Protection: strict nature reserve; visitors prohibited; staff of 37 persons; park threatened on Liberian side by iron ore mining operations but negotiations under way to extend protection

GEOLOGY AND TOPOGRAPHY Nimba is an isolated inselberg (40 km long and about 12 km wide) rich in iron ore, lying in the rain forest of tropical west Africa; a forest covers both sides of the steep, abrupt ridge, but the highest parts have savannas extending down the slopes, and some patches of grasslands are scattered in the forest.

BIOGEOGRAPHY Habitats are quite different from those of the surrounding lowland forests and savannas. At present it is difficult to say whether the high number of endemic animals (some 200 are known) is because Mt. Nimba functioned as a refuge for animals that were more widely distributed during previous pluvial periods, or whether these animals, through geo-

30

graphical isolation, have evolved from their ancestral forms into local races and species. Probably both factors have played a part. But even if most of the endemics are relics, Mt. Nimba is extremely important for speciation studies.

CLIMATE Typically humid (but moisture decreases in dry season: Dec.–Feb. or March). A dense cloud cover hangs above 850 m much of the year. Conflicting air currents create tornadoes March— April.

FLORA Though the surrounding plain is covered by savannas and lowland rain forest, the markedly increased rainfall on the mountain is reflected in zones of vegetation. Lower slopes (450–850 m) have a mixed rain forest of genera like *Bussea, Chlorophora, Entandophragma, Lophira, Parkia, Piptadenia,* and *Terminalia* (constituting a transition type of rain forest between lowland and montane).

At 800–900 m, a change marks the cloud line and brings a "mist forest" of *Parinari excelsa,* the dominant tree, completely covered with a thick layer of filmy fern and mosses.

In the valley bottoms the wet ground supports riverine forests: small stands of raphia palms and treeferns.

The origin of the upland savannas of Mt. Nimba, grasslands of bluestem and *Loudetia,* has been much discussed as perhaps the remnants of man's activities: burning, clearing, and grazing of livestock— a plausible supposition. But further study gives the impression that at least many of these grasslands are old, natural savannas that probably correspond to a vegetational climax. They give the impression of being an ancient type of habitat, and a great number of animal species are found there that do not occur elsewhere.

Treeferns in a rain forest at the bottom of the Iti Valley of Mount Nimba

The most remarkable plant on Nimba is the endemic *Blaeria nimbana,* an ericaceous species.

MAMMALS Chimpanzees, locally rather common in the Guinean part, are extremely rare though increasing on the Liberian side. There are many other species of monkeys.

The bongo, forest buffalo, Jentink's duiker, the pygmy antelope, and the pygmy hippopotamus are all known to have been in the area formerly, but, if still existing there, are very rare. Other small antelopes in the park are two species of duikers (bay, and black) and bushbucks, and there are also water chevrotains and tree hyraxes.

AMPHIBIANS The most famous animal of the Nimba range is a small viviparous toad, *Nectophrynoides occidentalis,* the only endemic vertebrate of the area. Seemingly adapted exclusively to the high savannas of Nimba, and to adjacent woods, it has not been found on savannas at the foot of the mountain. Its nearest relatives live in trees on mountains in East Africa more than 4,800 km from Nimba.

Area: 447,311 km^2 Population density: 9/km^2

The UN List has credited the Federal Republic of Cameroon with three national parks: Waza National Park, described below, Boubanjidah National Park (220,000 ha, with one hotel), and Benoué National Park (180,000 ha, with five camps). These areas are administered by the Water and Forest Department under the Secretary of State for Rural Production, Yaounde. Information office is in Garoua.

WAZA NATIONAL PARK (created 1936)

The Parc National de Waza, in the corridorlike part of the country stretching northward between Nigeria and Chad, has a wealth of animals spectacular both in number and species. Established as a forest and game reserve in 1934 to protect the numerous giraffes and large herds of antelopes that characterize this part of Cameroon, it was created a national park in 1968. The eastern parts of the park are inundated from November to March.

Location: northern part of Cameroon
Area: 170,000 ha; protection general, staff of 22; 420 km of car tracks within the park
Access: by plane (airstrip)
Accommodation: one hotel (60 beds)

GEOLOGY AND TOPOGRAPHY The national park lies within the basin of Lake Chad, which formerly covered a much larger area than it does today. The lake, nourished by the Logone and Shari rivers and minor tributaries, has seasonal floods.

CLIMATE These northern savannas are influenced partly by the harmattan, a dry wind blasting from the nearby desert, and partly by a moister type of climate. Rainy period: June to October.

FLORA Two main kinds of vegetation prevail in the park: the western half: woodland or woodland savannas with acacias predominating; the eastern half: vast grassy plains, the so-called "Yaérés," where the grasses include such genera as *Chrysopogon, Aristida,* and *Sporobolus* (with stems usually more than two meters high). By the end of the floods (February—March), the grasses become dry and are invaded by fires, but regenerate quickly, offering fresh pastures to a multitude of ungulates migrating eastward from the western woodlands.

MAMMALS Herbivores, as well as predators, thus move regularly between the two halves of the national park. Roughly between March 15 and June 1, almost all the larger animals are in the eastern, treeless savanna part. (Some giraffes and elephants can be found there too, but since these species are browsers, most of them remain in the woodlands.)

Large agglomerations of animals concentrate, particularly March—June, along the desiccating water holes, of which only about 20 are permanent (there are no rivers in the park). In May new rains fill the water holes again. Drinking time: midday, when sensational gather-

Male kobs are territorial and have a remarkable ability to withstand the heat of the sun when standing guard.

ings of antelopes may be seen: kobs, topis, roans, bohor reedbucks, and waterbucks. (The park contains altogether some 40,000–50,000 antelopes.) One species not often seen in African national parks is present: the red-fronted gazelle.

Among the carnivores are lions, leopards, cheetahs, caracals, striped hyenas, spotted hyenas, servals, and sand foxes.

BIRDS In or beside the water are found impressive numbers of birds such as pelicans (two species), crowned cranes, ibises (seven species), storks (four species), herons (eight species), geese, ducks, waders, gallinules, and many other groups.

The ostriches, vultures (at least four species), and eagles (six species) should also be mentioned.

Particularly important for both mammals and birds is Tchikam, a marshy area situated in the southeastern part of the park.

A roan in the Waza National Park

REPTILES Both the African python and the ball python live in the park, as do the desert monitor and the Nile monitor.

Area: 614,362 km²   Population density: 2/km²

The UN List of National Parks notes four national parks or equivalent reserves in this country, under the administration of the Service des Eaux, Forêts et Chasses, Bangui.

SAINT-FLORIS NATIONAL PARK (created 1933) and ANDRÉ FÉLIX NATIONAL PARK (created 1960)

These two parks of the upper basin of the Shari River protect large numbers of animals and spectacular flocks of birds. They cover savanna plains, inundated during the rainy season and transformed into marshes. Game reserves, one of which is in Chad, surround both national parks.

Location: northeastern Ubangi-Shari

Areas: Saint-Floris: 100,700 ha
André Félix: 170,000 ha

Protection: about six guards assigned to these parks from the staff of Game Inspector of the Northern Central sector, based at Ouadda; plans under consideration to organize facilities for tourists

FLORA Though these two parks are located within the woodland savanna belt, which is here of the Sudanese type, the Saint-Floris National Park chiefly consists of a treeless, grassy plain with some stretches of dry type forests.

MAMMALS Great numbers of larger mammals congregate in both parks: buffaloes, roans, oribis, hartebeests, topis, kobs, waterbucks, reedbucks, duikers, giraffes, hippopotamuses, warthogs, bushpigs, lions, leopards, and spotted hyenas; in addition, the cheetah can be found here. The elephant migrates seasonally through these areas.

BIRDS Aquatic species concentrate in enormous numbers at the permanent lagoons during the dry season. Herons and egrets of various species gather in spectacular thousands. The most remarkable bird in the area is the whaleheaded stork, which has here perhaps its only locality in West Africa.

Marabous, wood ibises, and white pelicans on bank of Shari River

BAMINGUI-BANGORAN NATIONAL PARK (created 1960) and VASSAKO-BOLO STRICT NATURE RESERVE (created 1940)

The Resérve Naturelle Intégrale de la Vassako-Bolo is entirely enclosed within the Parc National de Bamingui-Bangoran, which in turn is surrounded by three game reserves. The area described below is a complex with rich fauna (including the largest population in West Africa of the black rhinoceros). Many aquatic birds concentrate in the lagoons and in the grassy marshes, flooded during the rainy season.

The two areas are now under the same administration, but in the strict nature reserve visitors are only admitted by special permit. The three contiguous game reserves are Bribingui-Bamingui; Koukourou-Bamingui; and Miaméré-Miadiki, their total area comprising 900,000 hectares.

Location: north central Ubangi-Shari, headquarters at Ndele
Area: Bamingui-Bangoran: 1,000,000 ha
Vassako-Bolo: 150,000 ha
Climate: relatively moderate rainfall and severe dry seasons
Protection: staff of 20 guards, considered sufficient in this sparsely inhabited area.
Tourism: establishment of car tracks and tourist camps in the process of being organized

GEOLOGY AND TOPOGRAPHY

The area of these reserves is a vast peneplain (elevation 400—500 m) with granitic-gneissic outcrops, so-called "kaya," rising from 30 to 100 meters above the plain.

FLORA The landscape is dominated by wooded and open savannas, interspersed with gallery evergreen forests along the watercourses and patches of dense closed woodlands of a dry type, which seems to be the climax vegetation of the vicinity.

These savannas of the area form a transition zone between two types of vegetation: the Sudanese and the Guinean savannas. The woodlands consist chiefly of *Isoberlinia doka, I. dalzielli, Daniellia,* and *Anogeissus*.

MAMMALS The fauna is rich in individuals and species. Mammals include (except for the cheetah) same species listed above for Saint-Floris National Park and André Félix National Park. In addition the black rhinoceros and the giant eland can be found here, and numerous species of monkeys, such as olive baboons, colobi, vervets, mangabeys, red monkeys, and dwarf galagos.

Giant eland

Area: 2,345,364 km^2 Population density: 6/km^2

From their beginnings the three largest national parks in this country, Albert N.P., Garamba N.P., and Upemba N.P., were directed toward scientific research under an autonomous institute with adequate financial means. After the year 1933 many scientific missions were organized: collecting missions and, later, ecological investigations. An enormous amount of material was gathered, sorted, and studied by specialists from the entire world and many publications were issued by the Institut des Parcs Nationaux du Congo (placed under the Minister of Agriculture when the Congo became independent in 1960). In 1969 it was transferred to the Presidency of the Republic and named Institut National Congolais pour la Conservation de la Nature. In 1970 four new parks were created: Kahuzi-Biega N.P. (120,000 ha), Kundelungu N.P. (120,000 ha), Maiko N.P. (1,000,000 ha), and Salonga N.P. (3,000,000 ha). The country's name became the Zaire Republic in 1971.

GARAMBA NATIONAL PARK (created 1938)

The Park National de la Garamba has boundaries contiguous with the Sudan in the northeast and with a game reserve in the southwest. Originally it was established to protect the populations of the square-lipped rhinoceros, one of the rarest mammals in Africa, and of the giraffe, which occurred in great numbers and has here its last Congolese refuge in this area. What has happened in this national park, once sheltering a very impressive concentration of animals, is a frightful example of how vulnerable the large mammalian fauna becomes when war breaks out in a region.

Though the park did not suffer much from the turbulence of 1963 and 1964, during the next few years about three quarters of the big game was slaughtered by rebel *simba* gangs, by Sudanese refugees, by national Congo soldiers, mercenaries from many countries, and poachers to meet the illegal demand for rhino horns and elephant ivory. A census of wildlife in 1966 showed a catastrophic decrease.

By now the protection of animals in this park has been resumed, and if it can be continued the populations will certainly slowly increase to their former numbers.

Garamba National Park is white rhino country.

Location: Uele district, NE Zaire
Area: 492,000 ha
Climate: tropical: semimoist in rainy season, arid in the long dry period (Nov.—March); tsetse flies absent
Protection: staff of 100 guards (in 1963) temporarily reduced but being reconstituted; visiting possible but difficult
Accommodation: to be available at Gangala na Bodio (station for elephant domestication) or at Nagero

GEOLOGY AND TOPOGRAPHY

An ancient peneplain, the region of this park is a vast undulating plateau with a few isolated hills (inselbergs); elevation: 710–1,061 meters.

FLORA Woodlands, wooded savannas, and enormous treeless grasslands (annually swept by fires) form a forest—savanna mosaic, with important gallery forests fringing the Garamba River.

Grasses are chiefly *Loudetia arundinacea* and *Hyparrhenia* that reach in June a height of more than two meters. Tallest grass: *Urelytrum thyrsoides*, over 5 m.

Human locomotion in such a sea of tall grass is not easy, of course, and the visibility is difficult.

In the woodlands are bauhinias, dombeyas, erythrinas or coral trees; in the gallery forests: *Irvingia smithi*, date palms, khayas, fig or rubber trees, water-berry trees, and flambeau trees.

MAMMALS Originally the park contained about a third of the world population of the square-lipped rhinoceros and more than half of the northeastern race of this species. The park was also the home of thousands of elephants (in herds up to 600 animals, largest known in the world in the present century). In 1963 there were 1,202 square-lipped rhinos, 5,594 elephants, and 4,677 buffaloes (in 1966 the census of these species tragically gave: only 100 square-lipped rhinoceroses). Giraffes, hartebeests, kobs, waterbucks, and hippopotamuses have also decreased.

Other mammals: chimpanzees, olive baboons, colobi, vervets, and five other species of monkeys, as well as wild dogs, otters (two species), mongooses (five species), golden cats, leopards, lions, warthogs, bushpigs, giant forest hogs, and seven other antelope species not listed above (including roans).

37

Miombo woodland with *Isoberlinia* trees and dense under-vegetation in the Upemba National Park

UPEMBA NATIONAL PARK (created 1939)

The Parc National de l'Upemba, second largest reserve of the Zaire Republic, is located in the Katanga in the tropical southern savanna belt. Its diversified habitats range from lakes, swamps, and savannas to woods, forests, and highland prairies, a diversity arising from its situation at the border of two biogeographical regions: the Guinean and the Zambesian. The park offers vast landscapes with far-off horizons.

The park suffered great damage from the fighting of 1960 and 1961 and also from the slaughtering of game by soldiers and by professional hunters during the war years between 1961 and 1963.

An investigation in 1967 revealed that the southern sectors were practically emptied of their fauna, that villages had been settled in the northern sector, but that the center of the park, some hundreds of thousands of hectares, remained intact with a great number of animals more or less undisturbed. The villages have now been evacuated.

Location: Katanga, SE Zaire Republic
Area: 950,000 ha
Protection: (see above); staff of 130 units, mainly guards
Visiting: never systematically fostered, now possible, though difficult; accommodation now provided at Lusinga camp

GEOLOGY AND TOPOGRAPHY

The two high plateaus of Kibara in the north and Biano in the south, relics of an ancient peneplain covering an immense area of Katanga, are today separated by an extensive geologic fissure, part of the Graben of Kamolondo.

This N.P. is characterized by the Lake Upemba depression with many lakes and swamps drained by the Lufua R. and by the Lualaba R. (which, on its way to the Atlantic Ocean, changes its name to Congo R., recently renamed the Zaire River).

CLIMATE   In general, temperate on the high plateaus, diversified by elevation differences (500—1,860 m).

FLORA   The lowlands comprise aquatic habitats, with papyrus, joint vetches, and cattails; grassy savannas fringing lakes and swamps; gallery forests with khayas (mahogany) and fig or rubber trees along river courses; lowland bushy or wooded savannas of miombo type with uapaca trees, bark-cloth trees, palmyra palms, sansevieria, hyparrhenia grass, sat-in-tail grass and panicum or witch-grass. Somewhat higher are gallery forests with raffia palms and bamboos and the open Katangese forest, one of the most beautiful in Africa, dominated by bark-cloth trees and *Isoberlinia*.

The highlands have aquatic habitats; marshy savannas and wooded savannas with satin-tail grass; gallery forests along rivers; and primary savannas of the high plateau with a great variety of herbs.

MAMMALS   Species chiefly frequenting lower areas: hippopotamuses, waterbucks, buffaloes, and elephants; on the high plateaus are roans, elands, Lichtenstein's hartebeests, and zebras; sable antelopes are found in the forests.

Among other mammals in this national park: monkeys (six species), lion, leopard, cheetah, spotted hyena, wild dog, bushpig, warthog, and eight species of antelopes other than those already mentioned.

BIRDS   Water birds gather in fabulous numbers in the lowlands. There are 31 species of raptors in the reserve.

REPTILES   include two crocodiles (*Crocodylus cataphractus* and *C. niloticus*) and ten species of chameleons.

High plateau savannas intersected by gallery forests, Upemba N. P.

Tree heaths, orchids and other flowering plants, mosses and lichens on the slope of Ruwenzori at about 3,100 meters

ALBERT NATIONAL PARK (created 1925, enlarged 1929, 1934, and 1935)

The most famous of this country's national parks, originally created as a reserve to form a sanctuary for the mountain gorilla, Albert National Park extends from the volcanic shores of Lake Kivu in the south to the rain forests around the middle Semliki River in the north; that is, it lies on both sides of the equator.

Its territory covers an extraordinary diversity of habitats, ranging from the equatorial lowland rain forest at 800 m up to the permanent snow and glaciers on the Ruwenzori at 5,119 m, an altitudinal range that gives a representative series of different types of climate and a variety of vegetation zones. In this remarkably rich complex of habitats there are many plant and animal species with endemic or restricted distribution, the best known being the mountain gorilla, which lives in the Virunga volcanoes.

The park has a tremendously high biomass per square kilometer, far superior to that of cultivated pastures. It is sufficiently large to be considered as "bioindependent" so long as its water supply, coming from rivers outside the reserve, remains untouched by man. Although in the past the savannas were modified by man's burning, the area is still a kind of virgin landscape, and consequently, it is vitally important to keep the national park intact.

The great value of the Albert National Park is that it can be regarded as an ecosystem where man does not interfere. As such it is unique and has immense scientific importance, and also eventually can prove to be of economic benefit. It helps us to understand how in tropical Africa man can, in an ecologically sound way, cooperate with nature instead of fighting it.

Location: Kivu province, eastern Zaire
Area: 800,000 ha
Protection: a strict nature reserve; staff of about 420 persons including about 200 guards; certain zones open to tourists; several hundred kilometers of tracks, permits required to visit, guides compulsory; possibility of ascending some volcanoes on foot (requiring several days)
Access: by plane to Goma, south of the park, then by road (about 160 km from Goma to Rwindi Camp); chalets at Tshango are available in the northern sector.
Accommodation: Rwindi Camp (for 100 persons, restaurant) between Rutshuru and Lake Edward

---

GEOLOGY The Albert N.P. is part of the western Rift Valley. Of the eight large volcanoes of the Virunga chain, two are still active with frequent eruptions: Nyamuragira (3,058 m) and Nyiragongo (3,471 m). Old and recent lava fields cover the high plains between the two active volcanoes and the extinct volcanoes in the eastern sector: Mikeno (4,427 m), Karisimbi (4,507 m), Visoke (3,711 m), Sabinio (3,634 m), Gahinga (3,474 m), and Muhavura (4,127 m). The giant snow-capped Ruwenzori (5,119 m), third highest mountain in Africa, is a horst and much older than the Virungas, which probably originated during the Quaternary.

During recolonization of the vegetation on the lava slope of volcano Nyamuragira, a satellite crater erupted in the flank of the volcano.

Buffaloes are common in almost all habitats of the Albert National Park from savannas and marshes to forests and mountain plateaus.

TOPOGRAPHY Straddling the equator, the park embraces large and small lakes at various levels, marshes, bogs, rivers, different types of savannas and forests, all montane vegetation belts, extinct and living volcanoes, hot springs, lava plains, and nonvolcanic mountains (Ruwenzori).

The two largest lakes of the park belong to different water systems: Lake Kivu to the Congo basin and Lake Edward to the Nile system.

CLIMATE Altitudinal differences have a strong influence on temperature, rainfall, humidity, and evaporation at various levels of the reserve. There are no pronounced dry or rainy seasons.

FLORA The park covers all of the main habitats of tropical Africa (except deserts, semideserts, and marine biotopes).

The plains surrounding Lake Edward and the Rwindi, Rutshuru, and Semliki rivers are savannas of different types: some covered by grasses (species belonging to genera like *Themeda, Heteropogon, Imperata, Cymbopogon, Hyparrhenia, Sporobolus*) with patches of bush—acacias, combretums or bush-willows, and maeruas; other savannas have euphorbias scattered over vast areas; the plains north of Lake Edward are dominated by acacia forests.

Mountain rain forests with a wealth of plants and animals cover the lower slopes of the Virunga volcanoes and the Ruwenzori. Above the montane rain forests, extending up to 2,300–2,500 m, there are belts of bamboos, hagenia or kusso forests, heaths or ericaceous species (*Erica and Philippia*), dense growths of St. Johnsworts, afro-alpine species of lobelias and groundsels, and finally grasses, mosses, and lichens. On Ruwenzori, glaciers fill the uppermost zone.

MAMMALS These open grasslands and tree savannas offer views of most of the larger ungulates of the park. Elephants and buffaloes are very numerous; among the antelopes, species like the kob, the topi, and the defassa waterbuck are the most common, but reedbucks and bushbucks occur. Warthogs are common while their relatives, the giant forest hog and the African bushpig, chiefly nocturnal, are common though seldom seen.

The spotted hyena is the most often encountered of the larger carnivores. Lions and leopards are common but not so easily seen since they rest during the day. Among other carnivores of the savannas: the side-striped jackal, banded mongoose, greater gray mongoose, African civet, African wildcat, and serval. Olive baboons and vervet monkeys are characteristic animals on bush and tree savannas.

Rivers are lined with wild date palms and inhabited by thousands of hippopotamuses (Albert N.P. has Africa's densest population), which are also common along the shores of Lake Edward. Though they may also graze in the daytime, they leave their water refuges chiefly at night to graze on the plains, mostly on the panicum grass.

The transition zone between the enormous equatorial lowland rain forest and the mountain rain forest has a remarkably high number of plant and animal species, the most interesting being the okapi, the bongo, and the chimpanzee.

Above the montane rain forest belt the most famous and interesting animal in this park is the mountain gorilla that lives in the hagenia forests of the Virunga volcanoes at an elevation between 3,000 and 3,500 meters.

BIRDS Passerines, pigeons, vultures, eagles, kites, waders, francolins, and many others are seen almost everywhere.

Marshy river deltas and many bays of Lake Edward, which has abundant fish, are extremely rich in birds, particularly during September—April with a multitude of migratory waders and herons and also large numbers of purely African birds such as pelicans, storks, ducks, gallinules, and birds of prey.

Mountain gorillas in the *Hagenia* forest, which is located in the saddle between the volcanoes Karisimbi and Mikeno

Eternal snow and glaciers are found on the equator: the Stanley glacier on Ruwenzori, at about 4,600 m. The big plants are giant groundsels.

RWANDA

Area: 26,432 km²   Population density: 110/km²

There are two national parks in Rwanda: Kagera National Park, described below, and part of Albert National Park (see p. 40), recently named "Volcanoes National Park" (23,000 ha), both administered by the Ministry of Agriculture, Kigali.

KAGERA NATIONAL PARK (created 1934)

The Parc National de la Kagera lies south of the equator in the northeastern part of Rwanda where that country adjoins Tanzania and Uganda. The park is bordered on the east by the Kagera River and the enormous swamps, representing extremely interesting habitats, which separate Rwanda from Tanzania. As a savanna landscape, the park is one of the most beautiful in Africa with abundant mammals and interesting birdlife.

Location: northeastern Rwanda
Area: 251,000 ha
Protection: total in about three fourths of the area, an uninhabited, strict nature reserve where even most traffic is forbidden except for a few tourist tracks; remaining part (72,000 ha) contains 1,500 families engaged in

agriculture and cattle breeding but all mining, hunting, lumbering operations forbidden; staff of 110 persons; network of tourist tracks

Accommodation: guest house at Gabiro

Best visiting: dry season (May—Aug.); roads in July, though dry, have annoying dust and luminosity, bad for filming; in November there is no dust, light is bright, but tracks, although practicable, are often slippery; much rain in March—April and traffic can be impossible

GEOLOGY AND TOPOGRAPHY

The park is part of an upland plateau (elevation: 1,300—1,400 m) between two great tectonic grabens (Rift valleys) of Africa. A succession of large valleys resembling undulating plains are separated by hills, ridges, and mountains.

The Kagera depression, the deepest valley of the area, harboring the Kagera River, several lakes, and vast marshes, was once part of an enormous inland sea, of which the present Lake Victoria is a fragment.

CLIMATE Relatively little rainfall (802—1,048 mm) and a rather long dry season of three months (June—August).

FLORA The park's area lies within the Sudanese-Zambesian flora region. Four kinds of savannas may be distinguished by the dominating grasses and trees: (1) *Hyparrhenia collina* and *Loudetia arundinacea;* (2) *Hyparrhenia lecomtei* and *Themeda triandra;* (3) *T. triandra* and *Bothriochloa insculpta,* and (4) *Acacia nefasia* savannas.

Woodlands are dominated by *Croton dichogamus* and *Euphorbia dawei;* the swamps and marshes occupying such a large area of the park are chiefly colonized by papyrus.

MAMMALS Antelopes, zebras, and buffaloes are the most often encountered of the larger mammals. Zebras frequent the acacia savannas of the Uruwita Plain, while buffaloes are found throughout the reserve. Most interesting antelope of the park is the sitatunga with a fairly large population in the Kadjumbura marshes. Antelopes usually observed are topi, duiker, black-fronted duiker, oribi, roan, waterbuck, reedbuck, impala, eland, and bushbuck.

Other grazers and browsers of the park are hippopotamus, warthog, and bushpig.

Baboons also graze but they are almost omnivorous, frequenting aca-

Treeferns in the montane rain forest of Ruwenzori; Butahu Valley at about 1,800 m. Albert National Park.

Male lion

cia savannas as well as woodlands. Vervets are common in the park.

Lions are rather common; leopards, servals, wildcats, spotted hyenas, and side-striped jackals also occur. The carnivore most often seen is the banded mongoose, or mungo.

The black rhinoceros once occurred in the area. It disappeared but was reintroduced in 1958 from the other side of the Kagera River in Tanzania, which provided five of these animals. Since then they have reproduced.

BIRDS The most famous bird of the swamps is the whale-headed stork. Other marsh birds include numerous species of herons, egrets, storks, ibises, gallinules, and rails. Around the lakes and on the islands: white-faced tree ducks and Egyptian geese. Darters and white-necked cormorants nest on the islands.

Among the many birds of prey to be seen on the savannas are the pale harrier, eagles (long-crested hawk, bateleur, martial, tawny, black, and fish), African kite, black-shouldered kite, and six vultures (Rüppell's, lappet-faced, white-headed, white-backed, Egyptian, and hooded).

REPTILES Apart from the numerous crocodiles, pythons and cobras are the most noteworthy reptiles.

Zebras almost always keep together in herds.

Cormorants, a wood ibis and Egyptian geese in Queen Elizabeth N.P.

UGANDA

Area: 236,949 km^2 Population density: 40/km^2

There are seven protected areas in Uganda, four of which are described below. The others are Toro, Aswa-Lolim, and Lumunga game reserves. The Board of Trustees of the Uganda National Parks administers the national parks; game reserves are under the Game Department of the Ministry of Animal Industry, Game, and Fisheries.

Information on these areas can be obtained from the Ministry of Information and Tourism, P. O. Box 142, Kampala.

QUEEN ELIZABETH NATIONAL PARK (created 1952)

The Queen Elizabeth National Park, situated on both sides of the equator, lies between Lake Edward and Lake George. Boundaries of the reserve include the littorals of both lakes, which are in turn connected by the Kazinga Channel (32 km) lying within the national park. In the north on clear days from the terrace of the Mweya Safari Lodge can be seen the snow-capped massif of the Ruwenzori (Mountains of the Moon). To the west, beyond glittering Lake Edward, rise the Mitumba Mountains in the Zaire Republic, the western escarpment of the western Rift Valley.

Contiguous with this national park is the Zaire Republic's Albert National Park. Together with the Albert N.P., the Queen

Elizabeth National Park covers one of the scenically most spectacular regions of Africa, both national parks literally filled with mammals and birds. The Queen Elizabeth N.P. is renowned for its numerous elephants, large herds of buffaloes, thousands of hippopotamuses, and multitudes of aquatic birds.

Location: southwestern Uganda
Area: 220,000 ha
Protection: total, except for a few fishermen's villages; staff of 150; game control of hippopotamuses; 480 km of tracks within the park; excursions by launch on Kazinga Channel; entrance fee
Access: by road and by air
Accommodation: Mweya Lodge (100 persons)

GEOLOGY AND TOPOGRAPHY

The area lies in the western arm of the Rift Valley. During the last half of the Pleistocene period earth movements and volcanic eruptions created the actual landscape, and some dramatic geological events were even more recent. An extremely violent eruption occurred NE of

Lake Edward probably about 7,000 years ago and many holes were blown through the crust of the earth. This region with its 78 explosion craters at the foothills of Ruwenzori covers about 208 square kilometers. (The craters vary in depth, 15–150 m, their walls shrouded in forest.)

Lake Edward once covered a much larger expanse; hence the soils in this park derive from lacustrine deposits and volcanic tuffs, ejected from the nearby craters.

This national park chiefly contains open undulating grasslands, bush and acacia savannas, and swamps. In striking contrast to the great open plains, is the Maramagambo Forest in its SE part.

CLIMATE The Lake Edward region has two not very pronounced rainy seasons, March—May and August—November; the climate always allows visits to various parts of the park. (Annual rainfall at Mweya: 650 mm, in nearby Katwe: 950 mm.) Wettest month: Oct.; driest: Jan.

FLORA Grasses of *Themeda* and *Imperata* dominate the savannas, often mixed with shrubs and trees, particularly red thorn acacia. Euphorbias (*Euphorbia candelabra* and *E. dawei*) are locally common, particularly on the Mweya Peninsula. Thickets of wild olive and *Sansevieria* occupy large areas. On the shores of rivers and lakes: *Acacia mildbraedii*; in the Kihabule Forest, west of Katwe: *A. sieberiana*.

Maramagambo Forest, the only closed forest in the national park, has Uganda ironwood mixed with warburgias, and uapacas.

About 4,000 elephants live in Queen Elizabeth N.P.

Lions in the Maramagambo Forest in the Queen Elizabeth National Park frequently rest in trees.

A tree savanna with figs and albizzias occupies the most southern part of the park. Swamps harbor papyrus, cattails, Nile cabbage.

MAMMALS About 14,000 hippos, 18,000 buffaloes, and 4,000 elephants live in this national park.

On the open plains and in the thickets are herds of waterbucks, topis, Uganda kobs, as well as groups of bushbucks, bohor reedbucks, warthogs, and giant forest hogs. Among the carnivores: lions, famous here for their tree-climbing ability, and spotted hyenas are common; with luck, the leopard, serval, honey badger (ratel), spotted-necked otter, and civet may be seen. Other common animals are olive baboons, vervets, red-tailed monkeys, large-spotted genets, mongooses.

The Maramagambo Forest gives sanctuary to the chimpanzee, colobus monkey, blue monkey, duiker, red duiker, blue duiker, tree hyrax, bushpig, Cape pangolin, and others.

BIRDS Some 543 birds have been recorded. The astonishing tally lists among others: herons (15 species), storks, (14 species), the lesser flamingo, birds of prey (50 species), pigeons and doves (13 species), cuckoos (14), rollers (four), kingfishers (12), bee-eaters (eight), hornbills (four), swallows (17), shrikes (18), and sunbirds (16).

REPTILES The most common reptiles: the Nile monitor lizard, the rock lizard, skinks, geckos, chameleons, the python, the puffadder, cobras, the boomslang, sand snakes *(Psammophis)*, slender green bush snakes *(Philothamnus)*, the house snake, the marsh snake, and some turtles, terrapins, and tortoises.

FISHES Lake Edward, Lake George, and the Kazinga Channel are very rich in fish. The Nile ngege is the prime wealth of the lakes. Other fish personalities: mudfish, catfish, the barbel, and a lungfish.

Spotted hyena

A view from the Kigezi Gorilla Sanctuary with the Virunga volcanoes in the background

KIGEZI GORILLA SANCTUARY (created 1952)

Along Uganda's border with the Zaire Republic and north of the Virunga volcanoes (see the Albert National Park, the Zaire Republic, p. 40), an escarpment rises abruptly from the valley floor and forms a rugged forest-covered mountain. This beautiful rain forest was first designated in 1958 the Kayonza Sanctuary (also officially called the Impenetrable Central Forest Reserve), and in 1961 was named an animal sanctuary, the Kigezi Gorilla Sanctuary. (The area of Kigezi Gorilla Sanctuary should not be confused with another more northerly area called the Kigezi Game Reserve!)

An uninhabited area, famous for the beauty of its forest, the sanctuary is primarily intended to give protection to the rare apes living there. Situated geographically only about 56 km from the Queen Elizabeth National Park (p. 47) and even closer on the map to the Zaire Republic's Albert National Park, the sanctuary is much farther from them by road.

Visitors for the first time will see much more in the forest if they are accompanied by the Batwa as guides. These people, pygmoids about five feet in height, are forest hunters living in the vicinity of the Kayonza Forest.

Mountain gorilla with young

Location: Kigezi district, SW Uganda
Area: 33,000 ha
Protection: severe; staff of 35; grazing
  forbidden, hunting strictly controlled
Tourism: to be organized; nearest town
  by road: Kabale, Uganda (40 km)

TOPOGRAPHY A steeply undulating region of numerous ridges and valleys, and many small streams, the sanctuary lies at an altitude of 1,524–1,676 meters.

CLIMATE At these altitudes the air is chilly at night, day temperatures ranging from 12°C to 25.5°C at 2,283-meter level. Rainfall is rather high and so is the humidity.

FLORA The Kayonza Forest is not so impenetrable as its second name suggests, but very steep slopes make climbing difficult. At higher elevations there is a pure montane rain forest, not so heavily moist as forests on the Zaire Republic side.

Trees reach a height of 37–42 meters, forming a dense canopy though some light penetrates here and there. Tree genera such as *Pygeum, Olea, Chrysophyllum, Olinia, Polyscias, Newtonia,* and *Podocarpus* are common, as are stands of treeferns. In unshadowed valleys are dense shrubs, herbs, and vines.

MAMMALS The mountain gorilla is the chief zoological feature of the Kayonza Forest. About 150 gorillas probably live in the reserve, isolated from the main population in the Virunga volcanoes.

The chimpanzee occurs here as well as several monkeys: Hoest's monkey, blue monkey, red-tailed monkey, and black-and-white colobus. Elephant, buffalo, duiker, bushbuck, and bushpig also occur.

BIRDS Inconspicuous in the dense forest, birds make the air alive with their calls; touracos and hornbills are often seen.

About nine tenths of the mountain gorilla population live in Zaire.

The Victoria Nile cascades through the narrow gorge at the Murchison Falls.

MURCHISON FALLS NATIONAL PARK (created 1952)

Situated 2° north of the equator, this is the largest of Uganda's national parks. The Albert Nile which flows from Lake Albert forms the northwestern boundary of the national park. Ninety-six km of the Victoria Nile flow westward within this reserve, which also contains the famous Murchison Falls and the delta where the Victoria Nile runs into Lake Albert, a vast papyrus swampland.

Daily launch trips on the Victoria Nile are arranged from the Paraa Safari Lodge to the Murchison Falls—a comfortable way to see the spectacular birdlife and to watch animals along the shores of the river: crocodiles basking or swimming in great numbers, schools of hippopotamuses, elephants bathing and drinking.

This national park is a relatively flat land, covered chiefly by grassy or bushy savannas, swamps, scattered woodlands, and a few patches of high forest. South of the national park is the Budongo Forest, which is harvested but still represents one of the finest rain forests in Uganda. Chimpanzees live there.

Location: Acholi and Bungoro districts, northwestern Uganda

Area: 384,000 ha

Protection: total, though game control exists (because of absolute necessity of checking the number of elephants and hippos); staff of 300 persons; 288 km of tracks within the park; entrance fee; many visitors (38,000 in 1968/1969); launch trips on the Victoria Nile

Access: by road from Kampala (304 km, via Masindi); by air from Entebbe

Accommodation: Paraa Safari Lodge (160 beds), Chobe Safari Lodge (70 beds)

GEOLOGY AND TOPOGRAPHY

The soils of W half of this N.P. derive from relatively young lacustrine and volcanic deposits; in the E half, soils are formed from the underlying ancient pre-Cambrian rocks. However, much of the N.P.'s soils are lateritic.

The average elevation of the national park is 730 meters, the highest point being Rabongo Hill (elevation 1,292 meters) rising in the eastern part of the national park.

As the Victoria Nile flows westward across the park, it cascades through the Karuma Falls, then descends in a series of rapids to the Murchison Falls. It then flows majestically into Lake Albert at the N end of the park, not far from the Lake's outlet into the Albert Nile. One of the main attractions is the Murchison Falls, where the immense Victoria Nile narrows its course through a gorge eroded in the rock about 7 meters wide, and tumbles tumultuously down in a fall that is a drop of 43 meters.

CLIMATE Temperature is rather uniform, oscillating from 70°F at night to 85°F at midday. The "long rains" occur chiefly from April through June; "short rains": Sept.—Oct., with occasional rains in August and November. Annual rainfall varies: 1,000—1,250 mm a year.

There are some 12,000 to 14,000 elephants in the Murchison Falls N.P.

The Nile crocodile formerly occurred in thousands in the Murchison Falls National Park; at present there are only about 600.

FLORA Tall grass savannas, where the dominant genus is jaragua grass associated with Guinea grass and lemon grass, and mixed tree and shrub savanna, mainly composed of acacias, terminalias, and combretums, dominate the vegetation of this national park.

The woodlands, almost entirely consisting of *Terminalia glaucescens*, continue to be greatly damaged by fire and by elephants to such an extent that the vegetational change from woodlands to grasslands may in the long run be a threat to the welfare of the elephants themselves.

The Rabongo Forest, with Uganda ironwood the commonest tree, is a remnant of a much larger forest and was probably once contiguous with the Budongo Forest. Beautiful riparian forests of mahogany may be seen at Wairingo, and of *Trichilia roka* on the southern bank of the Victoria Nile between Murchison Falls and Paraa.

Papyrus covers vast areas in the delta of the Victoria Nile at Lake Albert and elsewhere around the shores of Lake Albert.

MAMMALS Launch trips for viewing animals have been mentioned, but animals may be seen almost everywhere in this national park. The principal mammal is the elephant, whose population of about 9,000 represents an overpopulation that is modifying the vegetation; the 12,000 hippos are also a management problem. The park's 30,-000 buffaloes seem to be more in equilibrium with the environment.

The Uganda kob

Buffaloes and egrets

Antelopes like Uganda kob, waterbuck, bohor reedbuck, bushbuck, and oribi abound and so does the warthog. Giraffes are numerous. Both black and white rhinoceroses occur (the latter is introduced).

Among many other mammals are bushpig, olive baboon, grivet, red-tailed monkey, black-and-white colobus, black-backed jackal, wild dog, spotted hyena, honey badger (ratel), civet, lion, serval, leopard, duiker, red forest duiker, blue duiker, aardvark or ant bear, Cape pangolin, and crested porcupine.

BIRDS The checklist of birds contains 423 species, among which herons (14 species), the whale-headed stork, falcons, (eight species), eagles (11 species), cranes (two), kingfishers (seven), bee-eaters (ten), hornbills (four), and sunbirds (11) may be mentioned.

On some slippery rocks in the middle of the rapids just above Murchison Falls, one may usually see a few white-collared pratincoles.

REPTILES Some 41 species have been recorded though there must be more.

FISHES include Nile perch (two species in Lake Albert: *Lates niloticus*, an inshore form, and *L. macropthalmus*, an offshore form), two species of tiger fish, electric catfish, and Nile ngege.

Fishes belonging to the Nile fauna are to be found below the Murchison Falls but not above, with the exception of *Lates niloticus*, introduced in Lake Kyoga in 1956, which have since found their way into the Victoria Nile above the Falls. Above the Falls the waters are populated by Lake Victoria fishes, which include two native tilapia species.

Goliath Heron

KIDEPO VALLEY NATIONAL PARK (created 1963)

This national park, in Karamoja with a common frontier with the Sudan, is in one of the wildest and most remote parts of Uganda, situated on a high plateau and surrounded by hills and rugged mountains. The larger part consists of arid savannas waterless for most of the year with mammal populations that move seasonally within the reserve. The narrower, western part of the area contains more water, moist habitats, and most of the animals. Despite the dry climate and the small size of the reserve, the vegetation and the animal life of the national park are surprisingly rich both in species and individuals. The area is heavily infested with tsetse flies.

Location: northeastern corner of Uganda
Area: 125,000 ha
Protection: total; total staff of 124; 2,000 visitors (1970)
Accommodation: rest camp (30 beds); (100 bed lodge under construction)

TOPOGRAPHY The altitude varies between 1,300 and 2,250 meters. The Kidepo River, running westward with most of its length in Sudan, is dry for most of the year. There are permanent waters in some streams, swamps, water holes and springs, important to the animals, particularly in the dry season. Hot springs occur.

CLIMATE Daytime temperature high. A prolonged and severe dry period starts in Sept.—Oct. and ends in March—April. Wettest periods: April—May and July—August. (Average rainfall in W part: 750—875 mm, in eastern sector: 625—750 mm.) Intensely dry winds make the plains vulnerable to fires that sweep through grasslands and bushes.

FLORA Main vegetation of the Kidepo Valley N.P. is an arid woodland savanna consisting of *Lannea*—*Acacia* trees and thickets. Palms fringe the river courses.

Mountain slopes and valleys are clad in a forest-savannah mosaic, dominated by *Protea* and *Faurea*, and lush gallery forests.

MAMMALS The N.P. has 21 species of ungulates including zebra, giraffe, eland, roan, Chandler's mountain reedbuck, bohor reedbuck, Bright's gazelle, dik-dik, klipspringer, greater kudu, lesser kudu, hartebeest (most common antelope of the area), oribi, duiker, waterbuck, bushbuck, bushpig, and warthog. Elephants, buffaloes occur; about 60 black rhinoceroses known.

An impressive number of predators: lion, leopard, and cheetah, caracal, serval, civet, mongooses (five species), striped hyena, spotted hyena, aardwolf, and bat-eared fox. Side-striped and black-backed jackals are common. Wild dogs appear periodically.

Other mammals include vervet, red monkey, blue monkey, olive baboon, bush baby (galago), rock hyrax, aardvark, crested porcupine, and pangolin.

BIRDS 480 species known to occur.

REPTILES Nile crocodile, monitor lizard, other lizards, snakes, and tortoises.

Black-backed jackal

Thousands of lesser flamingos in Lake Nakuru National Park

KENYA

Area: 584,896 km^2 Population density: 18/km^2

Kenya has 15 protected areas, seven of which are described or mentioned below. The others are Malindi and Watamu marine national parks, Meru N.P., Isiolo Buffalo Spring, and Samburu Uaso Nyiro game reserves, South West Mau and Mount Elgon nature reserves, and Marsabit National Reserve.

The national parks are administered by the Trustees, National Parks of Kenya, and visits of tourists are generally organized by the office of "Kenya National Parks." In the County Council Game Reserves, visiting is under the management of the county councils, with the assistance of the Game Department; the nature reserves under the Forest Department.

LAKE NAKURU NATIONAL PARK (created 1968)

This national park is a bird sanctuary embracing a soda lake on the plain of the Great Rift Valley, about a two-hour drive from Nairobi on a good road. Enormous flocks of flamingos congregate there—the pink hordes extending for several miles along the shore or flying against the blue sky. Such a fabulous concentration of flamingos is unsurpassed anywhere else in the world. Countless other birds occur (nearly 400 species have been observed at Lake Nakuru).

57

Location: N of Nairobi; Nakuru town 48 km
Area: 4,660 ha
Climate: similar to that of Nairobi
Protection: staff of 13, plus volunteer guards, provides strict protection; a track runs along part of lake; increasing numbers of visitors
Accommodation: available in Nakuru but none within the park

TOPOGRAPHY This shallow lake has been steadily shrinking in size, probably a long process since the end of the last pluvial period. There are variations in level with exceptional rains. During the 1960's the water was again high.

Throughout the 1950's when the lake was almost dry, the water became more alkaline but the birds remained. In such a drying situation, sodium salts increase in high enough concentrations to make the water lethal to drink.

MAMMALS In the acacia forest surrounding Lake Nakuru are waterbuck, bushbuck, reedbuck, leopard, serval, civet, and mongoose.

BIRDS The flamingos frequenting Lake Nakuru are of two species: the greater flamingo and the lesser flamingo, the latter congregating in larger numbers. Estimates of more than three million lesser flamingos were made in 1972. Their food consists of blue-green algae and diatoms; the productivity of this shallow lake is so high that it could surely support even larger flamingo populations. Though they are to be found at this lake over most of the year, flamingos have never been known to breed there. They alternate seasonally between the different saline lakes of the Great Rift Valley.

Migrants from Africa, Europe, and Asia congregate at Lake Nakuru together with species resident in the area: grebes (13 species), pelicans (two), herons (10), storks and ibises (11), ducks and geese (17), birds of prey (39), rails and gallinules (eight), crowned cranes, bustards (two), waders (32), gulls and terns (six), and many others.

The forests encircling the lake, chiefly feverthorn trees, are also full of birds: pigeons and doves (six species), cuckoos and coucals (11), rollers (four), kingfishers (three), bee-eaters (five), hornbills (four), hoopoes (two), owls (nine), nightjars (four), barbets (four), honey guides (four), woodpeckers (six), swifts (five), and nearly 200 passerine species.

Strips of acacia forest border Lake Nakuru.

ABERDARE NATIONAL PARK (created 1950)

Situated in an isolated tropical mountain range, the park offers from the saddle spectacular vistas of African landscapes: rugged mountains in the east, immense plains in the west.

The home of many mammals, the park contains much-visited Treetops, a world-famed game lookout.

Location: between the Great Rift Valley and Mount Kenya
Area: 59,050 ha
Climate: temperate and wet; periods of heavy rain: March or April to May
Protection: supervision insured by staff of 138; a road and tracks lead through the park; many visitors
Accommodation: Treetops; Arch Hotel (new)

GEOLOGY AND TOPOGRAPHY

The isolated Aberdare range, about 100 km long, is of volcanic origin and rises from the surrounding plain. Its gently undulating highlands and numerous ridges are separated by valleys and by streams and waterfalls. Altitude: 2,286–4,000 meters.

FLORA The road crossing the Aberdares, highest in Kenya, climbs through a montane rain forest (2,200–2,400 m), the bamboo forest (2,400–3,000 m), the kusso tree–St. Johnswort forest (about 3,000–3,400 m), and finally, at about the same elevation, runs across alpine moorlands.

Only on this mountain can a high moorland be easily reached with its rolling ridges covered by waving tussock grass, heath bushes, St. Johnswort, and flowers of many species like gladioli, everlastings, and violets.

Above this plateau follows a zone of bamboo and one of kusso tree–St. Johnswort, and then still higher, an alpine moorland with giant groundsels, some lobelias, and other alpine plants.

MAMMALS The range shelters many mammals; in the rain forest: the giant forest hog, bongo, several duikers, colobus, and the galago; on the grassy moorlands and open scrublands: the eland, bushbuck, waterbuck, and reedbuck. Elephants, black rhinoceroses, and buffaloes roam everywhere.

Treetops, the small but celebrated hotel built at tree-top height, is connected with the forest by a "wildlife corridor," 19 km long, 3–11 km wide. Most mammals, large and small, that visit Treetops live in the main forest, not in the outskirts of Treetops, but visit at night to lick the artificial deposits of salt, phosphates, and other minerals important for herbivores; they are also attracted by a pool.

Sometimes as many as 300 elephants appear together; other species visiting Treetops include black rhinos, buffaloes, bushbucks, waterbucks, reedbucks, bongos, giant forest hogs, Syke's monkeys, colobus, bush babies, leopards, large-spotted genet cats, wild dogs, spotted hyenas, mongooses, and hares.

Black rhino and waterbucks

MOUNT KENYA NATIONAL PARK (created 1949)

This mountainous reserve (elevation: about 3,300 m to 5,194 m) comprises the upper highlands up to the summit of Mt. Kenya, Africa's second highest mountain, capped all year round by snow and glaciers despite its situation on the equator, which runs across the northern slopes. Wildlife is abundant, in general similar to that of Aberdare N.P. (p. 40).

Location: central Kenya
Area: 58,790 ha
Climate: high annual precipitation (about 2,700 mm on the NE slope at an elevation of 1,700 m)
Protection: strict; 138 guards, who also patrol Aberdare N.P.; few visitors
Accommodation: no lodgings but Mountain Club of Kenya maintains a hut

GEOLOGY Mt. Kenya is an ancient volcano. In the past, glaciation was extensive and reached much lower down (to about 3,000 m, revealed by moraines); lower slopes consist of volcanic ash.

TOPOGRAPHY From the central peaks, numerous big U-shaped valleys (most beautiful is the Teleki Valley on the western slope) radiate in various directions and are separated by pinnacled ridges. At higher valley levels are numbers of lakes and tarns. The mountain's northern slopes (less steep) are chiefly covered by a vast plain.

FLORA Cutting, burning, cultivation, and heavy grazing have destroyed parts of the montane rain forest, formerly extending down to 1,370 meters but now not reaching below 1,830 meters. Tracts of magnificent forests still exist of wild olives, camphors, podocarps, and cedar, decorated with lichens. Above are mountain bamboos up to about 3,400 m, then a belt of tree heaths, but on the northern slopes a narrow belt of rain forest gives way to a kind of glade with kusso tree—St. Johnswort and other trees before highland grassy savannas

Flora on the northern slopes of Mount Kenya.

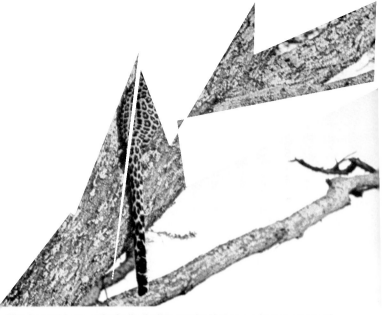

The leopard is an ecologically flexible species that occurs in many types of habitats, even high up in the mountains.

and moorlands take over and continue upward for miles to the alpine belts. These have giant groundsels, (*Senecio brassica, S. keniodendron*), giant lobelias, tussocks of fescue and carpets of *Alchemilla*.

MAMMALS Wild life is abundant in the montaine rain forests and glades of Mount Kenya: elephants, buffaloes, black rhinoceroses, bongos, bushbucks, duikers, waterbucks, elands, giant forest hogs, leopards, servals, and many smaller mammals and numerous birds. Many of these species are also found on the vast montane savannas (3,500—4,500 m) of the northern slopes, together with kongoni (Coke's hartebeest), steenboks, zebras, and wild dogs. Leopards and spotted hyenas are common in these grassy highlands where there are also six genera of rodents and three of shrews, an astonishingly large number for the high elevation.

Alpine heath of sedge (*Carex monostachya*) with groundsels (*Senecio brassica*)

BIRDS Various birds of prey are very common, among them the magnificent crowned eagle and even the secretary bird (a lowland species).

The impala is one of the most graceful antelopes of Africa.

NAIROBI NATIONAL PARK (created 1946)

It is amazing that this small park, a few minutes by car from the center of the country's capital, can offer such a variety and high number of wild African fauna, both species and individuals, living in a natural state. The rather poor vegetation of the plains—the result of overgrazing and overstocking—cannot support the huge number of browsing mammals, but these also utilize other areas of the Athi–Kapiti Plain, particularly the Ngong National Reserve, a contiguous and very much larger refuge.

Location: a short distance from Nairobi
Area: 11,400 ha
Protection: total; staff of 120 persons; 160 km of car roads; visitors very numerous
Accommodation: none within the park, which is, however, in close proximity to the capital.

TOPOGRAPHY The park is part of a high plateau, its flatness broken by a hilly forested area, a shallow escarpment, and deep river valleys. A stretch of the Athi River

Secretary bird is a common sight in Nairobi National Park.

Dik-dik, a small antelope

flows through the park, and there are also small water pans and artificial water supplies.

FLORA Open grasslands alternate with tree savannas. Grass cover consists of *Digitaria macroblephara, Pennisetum mezianum, Bothriochloa insculpta,* and *Themeda triandra* with scattered shrubs and acacias. Riverine vegetation along the Athi River is mainly *Acacia xanthophloea, A. kirkii,* and *Ficus sycomorus.* Semi-evergreen forests on the park's western border include wild olive and *Croton megalocarpus.*

MAMMALS Mammalian fauna of the park include Thomson's and Grant's gazelles, impala, waterbuck, eland, bushbuck, steenbok, suni, Kirk's dik-dik, duiker, kongoni (Coke's hartebeest), black wildebeest (white-tailed gnu), buffalo, zebra, giraffe, black rhinoceros, warthog, olive baboon, vervet, Syke's monkey, lion, leopard, cheetah, spotted hyena, black-backed jackal, mongoose, and other smaller mammals.

Hippopotamuses occur in the Athi River and surrounding pools.

BIRDS The secretary bird can almost certainly be seen, as well as ostriches, vultures, francolins, guineafowl, bustards, hornbills, and many others.

REPTILES Crocodiles occur in the river. Pythons are rather common.

Kongoni (hartebeest), Grant's gazelle, and warthogs

Zebras grazing in the Tsavo National Park

TSAVO NATIONAL PARK (created 1948)

This national park is the most important faunal reserve in Kenya and one of the largest in the world. Some zones of the park provide dramatic exhibits of animals from lookout vantage points. Its arid, wild and rugged country contains much of the atmosphere of remoteness and peace of yesterday's Africa. The park covers a large section of the subdesert, thornbush steppe country, the so-called "nyika," but despite this rather meager vegetation the area supports large populations of large mammals. It is the stronghold of game in Kenya and reveals the surprisingly high productivity of the arid bush when utilized by wild grazers and browsers.

The park is contiguous with the West Chyulu Conservation Area, proposed as an extension of the Tsavo Park. On the boundary with Tanzania, Tsavo National Park borders directly on the Mkomazi Game Reserve.

Location: midway between Nairobi and Mombasa

Area: 2,080,000 ha

Climate: warm throughout the year, varying according to the altitude; rain periods in April–May, Nov.–Dec.

Protection: total, except for some mining operations and the collecting of water from Mzima Springs for Mombasa; supervisory staff of 205 persons; 1,280 km of car tracks, many airstrips

Accommodations: five safari lodges: Kilaguni, Ngulia, Voi, Aruba, and Kitani

GEOLOGY The greater part of the area consists of gneisses and schists probably more than 600 million years old. Much later volcanic eruptions gave rise to the Chyulu Range and the Yatta Plateau, the most scenic features. Volcanic cones and lava flows characterize the western area, including Mzima Springs, the main source of the permanent Tsavo R.

TOPOGRAPHY The elevation of Tsavo ranges from about 335 to 1,825 meters. Three rivers flow across the sandy undulating plains: the Tsavo, Galana, and its tributary, the Athi River. From a narrow gorge the Lugard Falls of the Galana thunder down beside rocks fantastically shaped by erosion.

FLORA The dry season presents an arid country of brown-yellow landscape with leafless acacia thornbush and sparse grass—though the desert rose, a succulent shrub, is in full bloom—but with the first rains in April, the country bursts into fresh greenness and delicate flowers.

The bushlands are dominated by acacia and myrrh trees with baobabs conspicuous and two strange species of euphorbias. Highest tree of the plain is *Melia volkensii*.

Among the flowering shrubs: *Thunbergia affinis* with dark bluish-purple gloxinialike flowers, *Cassia longiracemosa* with sprays of golden flowers, and *Ruttya fruticosa* with red or yellow flowers. The common climbing flame lily with orchidlike yellow and purple flowers is considered Kenya's most beautiful wild flower.

In the woodland savannas *Piptadenia hildebrandtii* is fairly common; *P. buchanani*, in gallery forests or around oases, grows to almost 30 m, together with coral trees, *Erythrina abyssinica* (coral-red flowers), and *E. webberi* (flame-colored flowers).

Drastic vegetation changes—trees replaced by grasslands due to fires started by poachers and charcoal burners—have taken place in the last few decades. The baobabs have particularly suffered. Fires prevent regeneration of trees and push elephants to damage and to feed on the remaining trees.

MAMMALS The large elephant population is estimated at 20,000 animals. Buffaloes are numerous too, and black rhinoceroses number about 2,000.

Many species of antelopes occur in various habitats: waterbuck,

The baobab is a conspicuous tree in many parts of Africa.

Vervets playing in an acacia

cat, civet, mongoose (six species), Cape clawless otter, honey badger (ratel), and genet.

The lions of Tsavo became famous at the end of the last century for defying construction of the Mombasa-Nairobi railroad.

Especially fine areas for visitors to watch animals: Mzima Springs for hippos and crocodiles; Roaring Rocks to see animals moving in the valley below; "Poacher's Lookout" at Ol Turesh for black rhinos (also a view of Kilimanjaro); Mudanda Rock, north of Voi, with nearby pool attracting hundreds of elephants in dry season; lakes Kadetcha and Aruba near Voi in dry season for buffaloes, rhinos, elephants, and other mammals, also many open-bill storks; Kilaguni Lodge, with water hole attracting many animals.

bushbuck, bohor reedbuck, steenbok, Kirk's dik-dik, duiker, red duiker, Grant's gazelle, impala, gerenuk, hartebeest, klipspringer, lesser kudu, oryx, and eland. There are also the giraffe, zebra, hippopotamus, and warthog; also hyrax (two species), the aardvark (antbear), and the porcupine.

A large number of carnivores include wild dog, bat-eared fox, black-backed jackal, spotted hyena, striped hyena, aardwolf, caracal, cheetah, leopard, lion, serval, wild-

BIRDS About 500 species recorded, of which the following might be mentioned: eagles (five species), vultures (four), bustards (four), guineafowl (three), sandgrouse (three), and hornbills (six).

OTHER VERTEBRATES Among the numerous reptiles are African python, cobras (two species), puff adder, Nile crocodile, monitor lizard and agama lizards (two species). Aruba Lake contains tilapia and catfish.

Elephants in the Tsavo N. P. number about 20,000 and are, since the 1960's, heavily damaging the baobab tree.

The black rhinoceros is the outstanding animal of the Amboseli Game Reserve.

MASAI AMBOSELI COUNTY COUNCIL GAME RESERVE
(first protective measures in 1948)

This world-famous Amboseli reserve, a photographer's paradise, which is situated in southern Kenya below the northern slopes of Kilimanjaro, contains many Masai living with their cattle and goats within the boundaries. (The reserve was not included in the UN List because of the concessions that have had to be made to the Masai populations, grazing, etc., threatening to game.) Negotiations are underway to give a more severely protected status. A presidential decision of 1970 will lead to upgrading of the reserve and evacuation of people and livestock.

Overgrazing by cattle occurs and vegetation is damaged; in dry years livestock competes seriously with the wild animals for water—a tragic situation in many parts of Africa. The area nevertheless shows an amazing richness of wild animals, which have become so adapted to visiting cars filled with tourists that not even a shy species like the black rhinoceros objects to being approached closely.

The landscape with the magnificent backdrop of Kilimanjaro makes the area particularly attractive.

A unique series of springs at Amboseli maintains conditions of existence for the vegetation and the animals during the dry season.

Location: southernmost Kenya

Area: 326,000 ha

Protection: two zones set aside in 1961 already have absolute protection: Ngong, 17,845 ha, and West Chyulu, 37,550 ha

Accommodation: at Ol Tukai Lodge (24 persons)

GEOLOGY, TOPOGRAPHY, AND CLIMATE

Amboseli is largely situated on volcanic soil; the area is chiefly flat with some hills.

The name comes from an ancient dry lake bed that contains surface water only in seasons of extremely high rainfall. In dry seasons (June–Oct., and Jan.–March) it produces enormous clouds of dust with remarkable mirages formed by the heat haze.

Around Ol Tukai, in the eastern part where the animals concentrate, there are swamps and a series of springs. In 1958 the water of the main swamp of Ngoni Naibor or Ngong Narok rose, probably as a result of an earth tremor, and overflowed into the Simek River. There it spread out to form a channel 12 km long, all the way back into the ancient Amboseli lake bed. Vegetation regenerated and animals increased, an effect still prevailing.

FLORA A part of the East African grasslands, Amboseli is characterized by tracts of shrubs, thickets, and open woodlands of thorny trees, acacias and myrrh dominating. Among the grasses are *Sporobolus, Aristida, Chrysopogon.* Swampy area has parklike glades.

MAMMALS The reserve is famous for its black rhinos and elephants, of which there are large populations; other mammals occurring: buffaloes, giraffes, herds of zebras, wildebeests, Grant's and Thomson's gazelles, kongoni (Coke's hartebeest), oryxes, lesser kudus, elands, bushbucks, waterbucks, gerenuks, lions, leopards, cheetahs, spotted hyenas, and many smaller species.

Long-toed lapwing

Area: 945,641 km^2 Population density: 14/km^2

Tanzania has six national parks, five described below and one park (Tarangire) recently opened, and one conservation area: Ngorongoro. A Board of Trustees administers the national parks, and information may be obtained from the Director of Tanzania National Parks, P.O. Box 3134, Arusha.

SERENGETI NATIONAL PARK (Tanzania), NGORONGORO CONSERVATION AREA (Tanzania), MASAI MARA GAME RESERVE (Kenya)

The Serengeti plain and the adjoining Togoro and Ndabaka plains SE of Lake Victoria extend from Lake Eyasi and Ngorongoro Crater in the south to the Mara River and the Loita plains and hills in Kenya in the north. In the west a corridor area includes the Nyakoromo Range and almost reaches the Speke Gulf of Lake Victoria. The Ngorongoro Conservation Area, the Serengeti N.P., and the Masai Mara Game Reserve are administered separately and located in two countries, but here treated as an ecological unit.

This large reserve area of 22,594 square kilometers is frequented by vast herds of ungulates that migrate seasonally from one part to another, often covering distances of 500 kilometers. The migrating animals also utilize regions outside the reserves—the total area involved in these seasonal migrations is about 33,800 square kilometers. Lions are very common and probably represent Africa's densest lion population. Leopards can be seen more easily than elsewhere in Africa around the Seronera rest camp in Serengeti N.P.

In our day no place in the world offers such fantastic scenes of mass assemblages of larger savanna mammals as the plains of Serengeti. The crater highlands of the Ngorongoro Conservation Area are also the home of many animals. The area includes the Olduvai Gorge, famous for its strata of different ages containing rich deposits of early extinct animals and prehistoric man. Finally, the Masai Mara Game Reserve in Kenya must still be considered one of the finest wildlife areas of East Africa, particularly the so-called Mara fly belt.

Important research in management of wildlife resources is carried on by the Serengeti Research Institute at Seronera.

At Olduvai Gorge man lived about two million years ago. Recently even older human remains have been found at Lake Rudolf in Kenya.

Location: northern Tanzania and south-western Kenya, east of Lake Victoria
Areas: Serengeti N.P. (created 1940, 1951): 1,450,000 ha; Ngorongoro C.A. (created 1959): 780,000 ha; Masai Mara G.R. (created 1961): 151,300 ha
Protection: Serengeti N.P.: total, except for some mining rights; guides available; road joins area with Masai Mara G.R.; Land Rovers for hire. Ngorongoro C.A.: about three quarters effectively protected, grazing and hunting in remaining area, inhabited by Masai tribesmen; staff of 12
Masai Mara G.R.: general protection of central part (64,750 ha), sheep and goat grazing permitted in remaining area; staff of 22, plus 35 part-time game scouts; roads (160 km)
Access: Serengeti: by tracks and by air
Accommodation: Serengeti N.P.: Seronera Lodge (68 beds), Ndaboka Entrance; Lobo Hotel (100 beds); camping sites
Ngorongoro C.A.: Ngorongoro Crater Lodge (94 beds); Ngorongoro Wildlife Lodge (150 beds)
Masai Mara G.R.: Keekorok Lodge in central sector (40 beds)

GEOLOGY The plains of Serengeti are mostly formed by crystalline rocks overlaid by volcanic ash particularly in E part. The most recent layer of ash has been produced by the Oldonyo Lengai volcano, which has erupted several times in the 20th century.

Geologically and paleontologically the most famous site of the Ngorongoro Conservation Area is the Olduvai Gorge, where the hitherto oldest remains of prehistoric man have been found, as well as extremely rich records of fossils of other vertebrate animals.

The Masai Mara Game Reserve has mainly volcanic and basement soils, chiefly of the same system as the Serengeti plain.

TOPOGRAPHY Serengeti's undulating plains are covered by grass but turn almost to desert during periods of severe drought. Numerous granitic rock agglomerations, so-called "kopjes," form isolated mountain islands in the open plain.

The Crater Highlands comprising the massifs of Loolmalasin (3,587 m) and Oldeani (3,168 m), are dominated by extinct volcanoes (the area is mostly covered by layers from volcanic rocks). The Ngorongoro Crater (caldera) is 16–19 km in diameter; the floor (alt.: 1,707 m) is 400–600 meters below the level of the rim.

The topography of the Masai Mara Game Reserve (elevation

Wildebeest or white-bearded gnu
(*Connochaetes taurinus albojubatus*)

range: 1,524–1,676 m) is more varied than that of Serengeti.

CLIMATE Tropical, varying greatly with altitudes and vegetation.

FLORA Vast treeless grasslands and savannas in Serengeti have occasional acacia bush. Woodlands appear around rivers and in the northern sector.

In the volcano area, montane rain forests once climbed on the upper parts. On Ngorongoro Crater these forests have been preserved and cover the steep slopes. Crater floor consists of short grass.

Open woodlands increase in the Mara region where locally there are dense forests. The Loita plain, in contrast, is a devastated area, overgrazed and heavily eroded.

MAMMALS It is in the Serengeti and Mara regions that enormous herds of ungulates (sometimes up to 400,000) are to be found, chiefly wildbeest (gnu), Thomson's and Grant's gazelles, zebra, and topi.

Other common mammals: eland, impala, bohor reedbuck, steenbok, duiker, kongoni (Coke's hartebeest), bushbuck, waterbuck, roan, oribi, klipspringer, buffalo, giraffe, warthog.

Elephants and black rhinoceroses are less frequent although also existing in large numbers, particularly in the N part of the region.

Elephants have recently invaded Serengeti N.P., where they were recorded in 1955. In 1967–1971 there were about 2,000 elephants.

In March 1966, the following were counted on the Serengeti plains: 500,000 Thomson's gazelles, 340,000 wildebeests (600,000 in 1971), 180,000 zebras, 40,000 Grant's gazelles, 39,000 buffaloes, 20,000

Serengeti National Park is the only area in the world that can offer spectacles of hundreds of thousands of wild animals migrating.

Cheetahs are diurnal carnivores and the fastest of mammals.

topis, 14,000 giraffes, and 10,000 impalas.

Around Olduvai there are also many animals, an area with a population of about 70 black rhinoceroses. The main animal migration at the end of the wet season (usually May–June) moves westwards from the central plain. The animals move from area to area following the permanent water and their particular feeding requirements. By September they are usually back in the national park.

Such a wealth of grazers and browsers attracts many predators·among the carnivores, the most spectacular are lions, leopards, cheetahs, spotted hyenas, side-striped and silver-backed jackals, and wild dogs.

Around the Mara River, hippopotamuses have a good population (crocodiles also occur).

Lions and wildebeests in close proximity; lions are aggressive only when actually hunting.

Black rhinoceros with young in the Ngorongoro Crater

On the Ngorongoro volcano, dense forests have been preserved and cover the steep slopes.

Within the Ngorongoro Crater there is a large population of wild ungulates of the same species as in the Serengeti plain (see above). There are about 10,000 wildebeests, 5,000 zebras, elands, and numerous gazelles in the crater. Black rhinoceroses (up to 110 individuals) also occur. On the high ground of the crater walls live giant forest hog, buffalo, elephant, mountain reedbuck, and leopard. **BIRDS** Ostriches roaming the plains, kori bustards, and lesser flamingos may be mentioned. The lesser flamingos may be encountered in lakes Magadi and Lagarja, often also in a lake in the Ngorongoro Crater. At least 355 species recorded in the Serengeti National Park of which 34 are birds of prey.

White-backed vultures and marabous play an important role in the ecology of a tropical landscape; they feed mainly on carrion.

ARUSHA NATIONAL PARK

Situated on the eastern slope of Mount Meru, this national park received its name in 1967 when the Ngurdoto Crater National Park (established 1961) was combined with the Mount Meru Game Reserve.

The national park offers breathtaking views of two great mountains, Kilimanjaro (5,894 m) and Meru (4,540 m), and has an abundance of mammals and birds. The best area for watching mammals is the Ngurdoto crater rim. In 1964, thanks to international assistance, the park area was enlarged by the purchase of a very interesting contiguous zone: Momela Lakes.

Location: northern Tanzania, 37 km from Arusha
Area: 31,880 ha
Climate: period of long rains: March–May; light rains in November possibly even continuing until March
Protection: total; staff of six units
Access: from Arusha
Accommodation: at Momela Game Lodge

GEOLOGY The Ngurdoto Crater is a volcano probably extinct for 250,000 years. At some period the enormous 4,500-meter eastern wall of the Meru caldera collapsed, the tremendous landslide coming to rest in the present labyrinth of hollows, dells, and hills around Momela in the N part of the national park. Before that giant avalanche the caldera walls probably enclosed a great lake.

TOPOGRAPHY The national park covers not only the almost circular Ngurdoto Crater, but also a much larger area of the Meru forests, woodlands, and grasslands including the Momela Lakes and the crater of Meru. Ngurdoto itself is a beautiful miniature crater (or, more

The Ngurdoto Crater is a natural arena showing a closed and undisturbed world of Africa in miniature.

correctly, a caldera) about 2.4 km across and about 152 m deep. Highest point of the crater rim: 2,053 m above SL. Water of the crater floor drains off through the side of the rim.

FLORA Virgin montane rain forest clothes the shoulders of the Ngurdoto crater; the inside walls are also heavily forested. In the crater is an open floor of perpetually green, rich grass, mainly dogtooth grass, moist meadows, swamps, and dense forests.

Grassy or reedy foreshores surround the Momela Lakes; thick bush and acacia woodlands occupy other tracts.

The Mount Meru part of the national park, comprising the upper part of the mountain from 1,676 meters to the summit and the crater, includes montane rain forest, bamboo forest, cedar forests of junipers and podocarps, heath forest (*Erica* and *Philippia*), and a steppe-like alpine belt.

MAMMALS From the precipitous forest-clad walls at the Ngurdoto Crater's rim there are splendid views of animals down in the crater, which seems to be a peaceful world where human beings are not allowed. Residents within the crater: bushbucks, waterbucks, giraffes (though some of these wander back and forth through dense rain forest), a great herd of about 500 buffaloes, innumerable warthogs, over a dozen black rhinoceroses, elephants (always present, often climbing up and down the forested walls). Other mammals include baboons.

Leopards frequently visit or perhaps live within the crater, while lions only come from the surrounding plains for short visits.

Since all the mammals moving back and forth to the crater have to penetrate the rain forest, they may be encountered there as well. Species frequenting the forests:

Colobus abyssinicus and blue monkey, also bushpig, civet, and duiker. Hippopotamuses have found their way to the enclosed waters of Lake Ilkek Otoito and to the small Momela Lake. Other species in the park include spotted hyena, wild dog, large-spotted genet, mongoose, vervet, reedbuck, dik-dik, steenbok, and suni. Occasionally elands pay visits to the park.

The mammals of the Mount Meru part of the park include among others: bushbuck, giraffe, giant forest hog, buffalo, black rhinoceros, elephant, tree hyrax, and colobus monkey.

BIRDS Great flocks of waterfowl rest, feed, and winter in the series of lakes. Migrants from the north include shoveler, wigeon, garganey, pintail, tufted duck, common sandpiper, and avocet. Many species also nest there, and among the African ducks are the white-backed duck, the Hottenrot teal, and the red-billed duck. White and pink-backed pelicans as well as greater and lesser flamingos occur in some lakes.

From Mount Meru the soaring lammergeier may occasionally be seen, and of course this area contains many other birds.

Lake Manyara National Park, with Lake Manyara, the woodland and the escarpment, has a very high density of large mammals.

LAKE MANYARA NATIONAL PARK (created 1960)

This national park contains one of the densest concentrations in East Africa of large mammals and water birds that occasionally include millions of flamingos. Elephants are common in the park, and it has become famous for its lions, which have a habit, uncommon for this feline, of resting in the branches of umbrella acacias during the heat of the day. During the dry season, Lake Manyara holds perennial water, making the area very important for the animals.

Set at the foot of the Rift Valley escarpment, the park stretches for 40 km along the edge of the soda and saline Lake Manyara. At an altitude varying from 960 to 1,828 meters, the area of the national park includes adjoining marshes, grasslands, forests, and about two thirds of Lake Manyara, its northwest shores, and parts of the escarpment slope. Hunting is prohibited in the area east of the lake, and north of the national park is a game controlled area so that it is surrounded by protecting buffer zones.

Location: northern Tanzania
Area: 8,550 ha (not including the lake)
Protection: total; staff of ten units; Land Rovers for hire
Access: by good road from Arusha; (117 km), on way to Ngorongoro Crater, Olduvai Gorge, Serengeti Plains; airstrip
Accommodation: Lake Manyara Hotel (100 beds, swimming pool), with good view of the lake; camping sites

GEOLOGY, TOPOGRAPHY, AND FLORA The lake is a shallow soda depression, but several rivers run from the escarpment across the national park, providing fresh water. So do the hot springs in the SW end of the park, indicating that there is still some volcanic activity going on.

A spectrum of habitats spreads out between the lake and the rift wall—such as soda flats, reedbeds, saltings, swamps, meadows, savannas, scrubs, and heavy forests.

One of the few examples of lowland water forests remaining in East Africa lies within the national park. The forest is nourished by a line of springs and has towering wild fig and mahogany trees, interspersed with open glades of grassland and acacia parkland with *Acacia usambarensis, A. spirocarpa,* and *A. albida.*

Alkaline flats around the lake are colonized and surrounded by extensive beds of sedges, an important food plant for many of the animals.

MAMMALS Many animals migrate seasonally to and from the lake, but there are also large resident populations of almost all mammals occurring within the area. During the wet season, elephants (about 350) are found throughout the park; in the dry period they congregate at the Endebash River or at the lake. There are splendid herds of buffalo (more than 800 may keep together). The giraffe and the black rhinoceros are permanent residents as well as waterbuck, bohor reedbuck, impala, Kirk's dik-dik, klipspringer, zebra, and warthog. The oryx has been seen; a few hippopotamuses occur along the lake. Other mammals: leopard, serval, spotted hyena, bat-eared fox, jackals, civet, large-spotted genet cat, mongooses, baboon, blue monkey, vervet, and bush baby (lesser galago).

A male olive baboon

BIRDS Both the lesser and greater flamingo occur, occasionally in huge numbers; there are also hundreds of thousands of pelicans. Migrating waterfowl gather in great numbers, arriving in late Nov.–Dec. and leaving in March–April.

Altogether, over 340 species of birds have been recorded in the park. Nesting species include Cape wigeon, wood ibis, crowned crane, two-banded courser, and the African pratincole. There are also many birds in the forests, in the acacia woodlands, and in the open grasslands.

REPTILES Cobras and the monitor lizard are noteworthy.

Vulturine guineafowl

MIKUMI NATIONAL PARK (created 1964)

In the bushland of the drier eastern part of Tanzania called the "nyika," this national park covers a wilderness area of extensive thorn thickets where many large mammals can be seen at most times of the year.

Location: eastern Tanzania, 308 km from Dar es Salaam

Area: 116,500 ha

Protection: total; staff of eight rangers; guides available; Land Rovers for hire; graded roads and tracks (96 km) within the park; entrance fee.

Access: by macadam road and by charter aircraft

Accommodation: at Mikumi Camp (eight double tents); camping sites

Best visiting: June to November

TOPOGRAPHY The area comprises the open Mkatu Plain (altitude: about 550 m), wooded hills, swamps, open pans, and flood plains. Beyond the park area in the east and west, rugged mountains rise to over 2,438 meters.

River beds run through extensive stretches of black cotton soil and sands. The Mkatu River provides permanent water.

CLIMATE Long periods of drought are broken in April and November.

FLORA Dense growths of acacia thornbush characterize the vegetation. There are also bark-cloth tree woodlands of the miombo type and gallery forests.

MAMMALS include giraffe, impala, wildebeest, buffalo, zebra, warthog, elephant, hippopotamus, lion, spotted hyena, jackals, and yellow baboon. Less often seen: duiker, waterbuck, bohor reedbuck, greater kudu, Lichtenstein's hartebeest, black rhinoceros, wild dog, leopard, cheetah, mongooses, thick-tailed galago, Angolan black-and-white colobus, and vervet. The sable antelope is rare.

78

RUAHA NATIONAL PARK (created 1964)

This huge national park lies between the Great Ruaha and Njombe rivers and occupies a vast area of miombo woodlands and savannas. The park was formerly the southern half of the Rungwa Game Reserve. The specialty of the national park is the greater kudu. Great numbers of this antelope occur, particularly along the rivers, but it can be seen to advantage only during the dry season when the bush is almost leafless.

Location: S. highlands of Tanzania
Area: 1,150,000 ha
Protection: total; staff of 20 persons with aircraft at their disposal; tracks; visitors strongly urged to take a guide
Access: by good all-weather road from Iringa; airstrip at park's headquarters
Accommodation: two hotels in Iringa; small safari camp close to park; Mkwawa Camp at Mbage station
Best visiting: July–November

GEOLOGY AND TOPOGRAPHY

The Ruaha N.P. is located on an elevated plateau of ancient pre-Cambrian rocks. The country between the two large rivers varies from mountains to plains dotted with hills and kopjes (alt.: 732 m in Ruaha Valley, 1,600 m on Ngalambulwa mountain). Open pans and large bogs also occur, and some parts of the plain are annually flooded. The Great Ruaha River, forming the eastern boundary of the N.P., flows throughout the year running through various habitats, from rugged gorges to undulating plateaus. Black cotton and sandy soils dominate the area.

CLIMATE Dry season: July–Nov.; temperature in daytime is about 85° F and at night, 70° F.

FLORA There is typical miombo woodland with *Brachystegia boehmii* and *B. spiciformis*, *Julbernardia paniculata* and *J. globiflora*; elsewhere there are associations of acacias and myrrhs. Doum palms and large acacias form canopies of deep shade along the river flanks much appreciated by many animals.

MAMMALS The greater kudu, and the lesser kudu are plentiful, as well as impalas, Kirk's dik-diks, waterbucks, warthogs, buffaloes, and

Impalas are abundant in the Ruaha National Park.

Greater kudu male

and Grant's gazelle exist only in small numbers. Klipspringer and bushpig are uncommon, or at least seldom observed.

Predators, spread all over the park, include lion, leopard, spotted hyena, bat-eared fox, and black-backed jackal. The clawless otter can be found in the river gorges. Cheetah and wild dog live in the park but are not common.

Other carnivores recorded: genet, civet, mongooses (five species), honey badger (ratel), aardwolf, caracal, serval, and wildcat.

Some of the other mammals in the park: thick-tailed galago, vervet, yellow baboon, tree and rock hyraxes, porcupine, hare, springhaas, squirrels, and other rodents, and bats.

elephants. Other large herbivorous mammals: black rhinoceros and hippopotamus; the giraffe and the eland are common and scattered throughout the park; also widespread: zebra, bushbuck, duiker, and steenbok.

Fairly large herds of sable and roan antelopes occur in the miombo bush, but Lichtenstein's hartebeest

BIRDS So far, a list of over 300 species for this park has been recorded. The ostrich should be mentioned.

Extremely interesting in December and January is the passage through the park in considerable numbers of the rare Eleonora falcon, a migrant from the Mediterranean region.

An ostrich male accompanies a group of young which may be his own offspring. The female of the species lays up to 30 eggs.

The zebra is one of the most common herbivores in the Malawi N. P.

Area: 93,860 km^2 Population density: 37/km^2

Malawi has one national park with two other game reserves in the process of being constituted as national parks. There are three other game reserves with an additional three in an advanced stage of constitution. All national parks and game reserves are regulated by the Forestry and Game Department under the Ministry of Natural Resources, Zomba.

MALAWI NATIONAL PARK (created 1966)

This national park is one of the largest and most striking upland areas of grasslands occurring within the southern woodland savanna belt cf Africa. Located on the Nyika Plateau, it extends over mountains, hills, and plains and has large numbers of ungulates grazing at different levels and also a great variety of birdlife.

It is planned to extend this national park to include additional grassland and possibly some of the steep escarpment that leads down to Lake Malawi.

Location: northern Malawi
Area: 84,170 ha; altitude: 2,350 m.
Protection: uninhabited area; full protection of animals and vegetation; controlled burning of grassland; some controlled game cropping; staff of one resident game ranger and ten game guards
Visiting: a visitors' camp accommodates 26 persons

81

Elands thrive in many different habitats; they have a remarkable resistance to droughts.

GEOLOGY AND TOPOGRAPHY
The plateau consists of a large intrusion of granite into beds of sediments (fine-grained and pebbly sandstones) and coarse grits of quartzite and phyllitic types with interactions of schist.

CLIMATE Though the area is barely 10° below the equator and surrounded by pure tropics, the climate is intermediate between temperate and tropical. Frosts have been regularly recorded from late May to early October. Rainy season: Dec.–April.

FLORA Grasslands chiefly occupy the plateau composed of *Loudetia simplex* and *Exotheca abyssinica,* and locally of extensive stands of *Festuca schimperiana.* (More than 50 other species of grasses include

Themeda triandra, Hyparrhenia cymbaria, Andropogon schirensis.)

Below the grasslands are dry bark-cloth tree woodlands of the miombo type characteristic for large tracts of Africa S. of the equator.

Above, at 1,676 meters, is a secondary montane forest, often swept by fires, dominated by *Hagenia abyssinica, Rapanea melanophleos,* and *Polyscias fulva.*

Unburned habitats are evergreen forests composed of *Podocarpus milanjianus* and cedars, and locally of *Entandrophragma excelsa* and *Aningeria adolfi-friederici.* Camphor trees appear in moister habitats as well as treeferns.

MAMMALS The most abundant species to be found grazing are eland, roan, and zebra; other grazers: klipspringer, duiker, red duiker, blue duiker, Lichtenstein's hartebeest, bushbuck, reedbuck, and warthog. Among the carnivores: leopard, lion, cheetah, serval, side-striped jackal, and wild dog, and of course several of the smaller species.

BIRDS Among the great variety of birds, those seen among the antelopes: ground hornbills, Denham's bustards, and wattled cranes.

Wild dogs play a useful role in animal communities.

Area: 749,138 km^2 Population density: 6/km^2

Since 1971 Zambia has had 18 national parks, of which three are described below. Before 1971 Kafue was Zambia's only national park. Of the other national parks the most important are Kasanka, Lochinvar, Lunga, Lusenga Plain, and Mweru Marsh. All of these areas are administered by the Department of Wildlife, Fisheries, and National Parks under the Ministry of Lands and Natural Resources, Lusaka, where further information may be obtained.

SUMBU NATIONAL PARK (created game reserve 1942, N.P. 1971)

This is the only national park located on the shores of Lake Tanganyika, a lake that has remarkable fish fauna. The reserve covers a considerable area of the valley plains and marshes surrounding the Lufubu River and its estuary into Lake Tanganyika. The area is rich in game, particularly elephants and various antelopes. Migrations of elephants and probably also other mammals used to occur between this reserve and the Mweru Marsh National Park, located about 80 km westward and east of Lake Moero but settlement has curtailed this. The lodges at Kasaba and Nkamba bays as well as at Sumbu are within the reserve.

The sable antelope is one of many various species found in Sumbu.

Fish eagle

mals include blue duiker (unusually common), duiker, puku, eland, roan, sable antelope, Lichtenstein's harte-beest, waterbuck, bushbuck, Sharpe's grysbok, klipspringer, zebra, buffalo, warthog, rock hyrax, lion, leopard, and spotted hyena.

Hippopotamuses frequent the shores of Lake Tanganyika.

BIRDS A rich birdlife includes many large species, among them: the palm-nut vulture and fish eagle.

The osprey, white-winged black tern, and lesser black-backed gull are migrants from Europe or Asia. Many waders pass by or rest on the shores while migrating. Dense "mateshi" thickets close to the shores hold a wealth of other birds.

REPTILES Crocodiles occur along the lake shores. The small endemic water snake and the poisonous but shy water cobra, which grows to about three meters, are common.

FISHES As many as 42 genera of fishes are peculiar to Lake Tanganyika, which reflects eons of time of evolution and also the age of the lake itself. Of all the animals living in the lake, 75 percent do not occur elsewhere in the world. The lake contains over 230 species of fish, of which at least 140 species are endemic.

Crystal clear waters give wonderful opportunities for skin diving and for watching many of the littoral fishes. The most characteristic fishes of the lake are cichlids, of which there are 94 endemic species (all these cichlids take care of their eggs and young). Commonest fish: a small clupeid species, in Swahili called "dakala." Mormyrids attract observers because of their elephantlike snouts. Also common: giant catfish, electric catfish, sangala, tiger fish, and giant tiger fish. (Many of these species weigh up to 32–45 kg.) Big game fishing at both Kasaba and Nkamba bays, almost always successful, has become a popular attraction.

Location: northernmost Zambia
Area: 200,000 ha
Climate: hot, but with a fresh breeze blowing from the lake; relatively dry
Protection: general, except for fishing rights for some hundred fishermen with villages inside national park
Access: by road from the Great North Road via Mporokoso; by boat (Tanganyika Lake); and by air (twice weekly flights from Lusaka)
Accommodation: two lodges, Kasaba and Nkamba, and a camp at Sumbu

GEOLOGY AND TOPOGRAPHY
Gigantic forces created the enormous earth fissure at Lake Tanganyika, the longest lake in the world (650 km) and second deepest (1,436 m), situated at 775 m above SL at the floor of the western Rift Valley. The surrounding mts. rise to 3,000 meters. Deltas of alluvial sediments occur at the mouths of minor streams running into the lake. Most of the shore line is rocky but there are several sandy beaches and also dunes.

FLORA The deltas support groves of acacias; close to the shore the slopes are covered by thickets of combretums and Bussea. At higher levels are woodlands formed by bark-cloth trees and Julbernardia intersected by smaller grassy plains. Extensive, seasonally wet grassland plains provide key areas for the grazing animals.

MAMMALS Elephants are numerous and often wander peacefully around the two lodges. Other mam-

LUANGWA VALLEY NATIONAL PARK (created 1938; upgraded to national park 1971)

An extraordinary variety of large mammals occurs in the Luangwa Valley National Park. During the dry season there are spectacular concentrations of animals and birds along the bends and turns of the meandering Luangwa River. The surrounding great valley offers beautiful scenes of virgin country. Unfortunately the northern and southern sectors of the park are separated by a broad corridor, a game management area with controlled hunting, through which many mammals migrate without being protected.

Location: eastern Zambia, 135 km from the Malawi border
Area: 1,290,000 ha
Climate: hot and dry; dry season, May 15–October 30
Protection: southern sector (460,000 ha); 320 km of tourist roads; fishing at certain river sites allowed; open: June–Oct.; game watching camps along the riverine strip as well as in the adjoining Nsefu and Luambe game reserves (eastern side of the river)
Access: by air and by road; airstrips at Mfuwe, the park's lodge (Fort Jameson airport, 135 km, and Lusaka, 736 km); twice-weekly scheduled flights on Lusaka–Chipata run
Accommodation: many camps; bookings through Zambia National Tourist Bureau, Box 17, Lusaka

GEOLOGY AND TOPOGRAPHY

The Luangwa Valley is a rift valley with a flat floor, bounded on the west by the steep Muchinga Mts. The Luangwa River constantly changes its course, forming oxbows and lagoons of great importance for the animals.

The reserve is relatively well watered by the Luangwa River and its tributaries during the dry season. During the rains the valley is flooded several miles back from the river, and these inundations provide favorable conditions for many species and individuals.

Thornicroft's giraffe is a special form found only in Luangwa.

Elephants are common in the Luangwa Valley National Park.

FLORA The park is divided about equally into three main vegetation types: the lower lying areas contain acacia and combretum woodland on the more recent fertile alluvial soils. Mopane woodland is also common on heavy low-lying soils, providing important forage for many browsing species. "Miombo" (*Brachystegia* and *Julbernardia*) woodland is found on the sandier, well drained sites.

MAMMALS The national park has an abundance of mammals: many thousands of elephants, hippopotamuses, and buffaloes as well as many species of antelopes.

Waterbuck and puku thrive, particularly in the wet areas along the main river where many other species may also be found: impala, roan, eland, greater kudu, bushbuck, wildebeest, zebra, and giraffe.

The valley is the last stronghold of the black rhinoceros (between 100 and 200) in Zambia. Carnivores are lion and leopard; the cheetah occurs at least occasionally. Other mammals include bush baby, vervet, blue monkey, yellow baboon, antbear (aardvark), wild dog, side-striped jackal (uncommon), spotted hyena, honey badger, otter, civet, mongoose (five species), serval, caracal, warthog, bushpig, and Sharpe's grysbok. The klipspringer is common in the escarpment.

Throughout the Valley in the foothills there are Lichtenstein's hartebeest and duiker.

BIRDS During the dry season marvelous concentrations of waterfowl and other aquatic birds gather on the pans fringing the Luangwa River: herons, storks, ibises, spoonbills, ducks, geese, rails, moor hens, jacanas, and waders of many species. Game birds such as francolins and guineafowl are ubiquitous. At least six species of eagles and four of vultures are usually seen. Carmine bee-eaters, arriving in September, nest in colonies in holes in the river's sandy banks, and often associate with the white-fronted and little bee-eaters.

REPTILES Crocodiles are common, often occurring close to the hippos.

KAFUE NATIONAL PARK (created 1959, national park status, 1961)

Kafue National Park is the third largest of the national parks in Africa. Situated in the heart of the western part of Zambia, the reserve consists of flat woodlands and open grasslands intersected by extensive flood plains and swamps. Principal rivers (all of which are tributaries of the Kafue) include the Musa, Lufupa, and the Lunga. The fauna is very rich in species and individuals. Seasonally the flood plains are densely populated with game and with an interesting range of aquatic birdlife. Between Lusaka and the Kafue N.P. lie the Kafue Flats with two nature reserves, Lochinvar and the Blue Lagoon, inhabited by great numbers of Kafue lechwe and by aquatic birds.

Location: western Zambia
Area: 2,240,000 ha
Climate: semi-arid; dry season normally from June to November
Protection: generally severe with some exceptions such as fishing rights; staff of 300; 800 km of roads within park; open May 1–Nov. 1; sport fishing allowed; occasional lectures at Ngoma Camp; booklets, maps, pamphlets available; scientific research conducted
Access: by road and by air: Lusaka, 232 km; Livingstone, 200 km, Ndola, 398 km; Lubumbashi (Elizabethville), Zaire Republic, 800 km; scheduled flights provide regular service during the dry season on some of the Lusaka–Livingstone (Victoria Falls) runs
Accommodation: Ngoma Camp and many other camps; bookings made through Zambia National Tourist Bureau, Box 17, Lusaka

GEOLOGY Seasonally flooding rivers have carved broad valleys in the plateau of the Kafue N.P., which consists of ancient pre-Cambrian rocks covered by sandy soils. In the S part are clay soils.

Miombo woodland is the dominant habitat in the Kafue N. P.

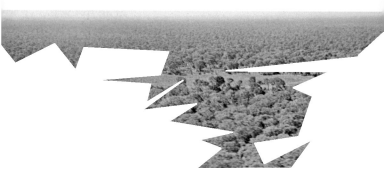

Zebras in mopane woodlands of the Kafue National Park.

TOPOGRAPHY Though large expanses of the national park are "miombo" flatlands, there are undulating plains and rolling hills. In the rainy season extensive areas of the valley plains are waterlogged, alluvial strips of grass.

The Kafue River flows within the park for approximately 160 km and forms its boundary for some further 96 kilometers. Average elevation is about 1,300 meters.

FLORA Typical miombo woodlands formed by several species of *Brachystegia* and *Julbernardia* oc-

cur throughout the national park; other parts consist of grasslands or swamps; the southeast has *mopane* woodlands. Two forest patches with *Terminalia* and other taller trees and thickets with Rhodesian teak add to the variety.

MAMMALS There are three subspecies of lechwe found in Zambia. A herd of about 600 red lechwes is preserved on the Busanga flood plains within the national park. This is one of the strongest surviving breeding herds known to exist in Zambia.

Defassa waterbucks, though fond of water, can be found far away from the nearest aquatic habitat.

Hippopotamuses are common in the rivers of the Kafue National Park.

Other antelopes to be seen: waterbuck, puku, impala, Lichtenstein's hartebeest, blue wildebeest (brindled gnu), greater kudu, sitatunga, sable, roan, bushbuck, reedbuck, steenbok, Sharpe's grysbok, duiker, yellow-backed duiker, blue duiker, oribi, klipspringer, and eland.

Other mammals include buffalo, zebra, elephant, black rhinoceros, hippopotamus, warthog, bushpig, baboon, vervet, lion, leopard, caracal, serval, cheetah, spotted hyena, aardwolf, wild dog, side-striped jackal, pangolin, ant-bear (aardvark, and seven species of mongoose.

BIRDS Among the fantastic birdlife along the flood plains the number of saddle-billed storks is particularly striking. Best areas for birds are the Busanga plain and on the river banks. Above the savannas, eagles like the bateleur and the martial eagle, as well as four species of vultures, can be seen soaring.

OTHER VERTEBRATES The rivers contain crocodiles in abundance and fishes like barbel and bream.

The vine or twig snake (*Thelotornis kirtlandii*), one of Africa's two most poisonous snakes, resembles a thin branch.

Area: 390,866 km^2 Population density: 13/km^2

Rhodesia has 14 national parks, of which four are described below, and six game reserves. These areas are administered by the Department of National Parks and Wildlife Management of Rhodesia under the Secretary of Mines and Lands, Salisbury, where further information may be obtained. The Research Branch of the Department of N.P.'s and Wildlife Management is responsible for the study of every aspect of life, conservation, management, and use of wild game. Pamphlets are available for almost every sanctuary.

CHIMANIMANI NATIONAL PARK (created 1950)

A highland wilderness area of great scenic splendor: rugged, castellated mountains, deep gorges, tumbling cascades and waterfalls, rolling grasslands, evergreen forests, crystal clear streams, deep pools, bogs and swamps—all this only a few hours by range road from Salisbury. There are few spectacular mammals in the park, but the area is rich in birds.

Location: along the Mozambique border, east of Melsetter and Chipinga
Area: 8,166 ha
Protection: general; staff of 16 persons; open all year; sport fishing permitted
Access: by road from Melsetter village
Accommodation: Chimanimani Hotel in Melsetter, and in mountain huts

---

TOPOGRAPHY AND CLIMATE South of Umtali, the area of the park includes the Chimanimani Range and is close to a lowland forest of great interest, the Makurupini-Haroni Forest near the confluence of the Haroni and Lusitu rivers.

A rainfall of 1,100 mm (even up to 4,000 mm in isolated areas of the mts.) brings a lushness and greenness in contrast with most other areas of Rhodesia.

The semi-arid bush country of the Sabi Valley beneath the Chimanimani highlands is one extreme of the wide range of habitats of this region.

FLORA Vegetation consists chiefly of montane communities. At the southern foot of the mts. (at elevation of 305 m) near the Haroni-Lusitu river junction, there is a lowland rain forest, unique because high rainfall at low altitudes is normally nonexistent in Rhodesia. Here trees like *Filicium decipiens, Blighia unijugata, Parinari,* and *Erythrophleum* form forests.

From altitudes of about 1,220 m and upward are patches of evergreen montane forests and scrub associations of *Philippia, Erica,* and *Protea.* Valleys and slopes are colorful with flowers.

BIRDS In the rain forest near the river confluence are found among many others: chestnut-fronted helmet shrike, grosbeak weaver, green coucal, and lourie.

In the upper areas, above 915 meters, are the rufous-bellied tit, the gray cuckoo shrike, Gurney's thrush, and other species.

INVERTEBRATES For butterflies, moths, and other insects, the Chimanimani Range has the reputation of being one of the richest areas in southern Africa.

A granite kopje hill in the Rhodes Matopos National Park

RHODES MATOPOS NATIONAL PARK (created 1953)

With its fantastic granite kopje hills, strange rock formations, caves with ancient rock paintings, numerous pools,
wild animals, scenic landscape, and historic memories, the
Matopos National Park offers much of interest. Human history
goes back here at least as far as the Middle Stone Age, the
numerous caves sheltering the earliest people. Bushman cave
paintings of men and animals such as elephants, square-
lipped rhinoceroses, giraffes, and kudu antelopes were made
by Bushmen, certainly before the first Bantu tribes ever took
possession of these hills.

The Matopos Hills also played an important role during
the Matabele Rebellion in 1896; Cecil Rhodes camped alone
there during his successful negotiations with the rebels.
Later he chose the Matopos as his burial place.

Location: in Matabeleland, 32 km south of Bulawayo
Area: 43,320 ha
Protection: total, but grazing rights granted to neighboring populations in time of drought; supervising staff of 69; sport fishing allowed

Access: by road from Bulawayo
Accommodation: rest huts at Meleme Dam
Of special interest: famous rock paintings; 485 ha of fully fenced game park where animals can be observed; site of grave of Cecil John Rhodes

Zebras and a giraffe are shown grazing in the Rhodes Matopos N. P.

GEOLOGY AND TOPOGRAPHY
The "kloofs" (ravines) and "kopjes" (rocky hills) are explained by the forcing upward through the schist of a great mass of granite, semifluid under great pressure. As it slowly cooled, lines of cleavage developed that, along with weather action over millions of years, sculptured the rounded, balancing boulders piled atop each other.

The park's green valleys with permanent water and well-wooded kopjes have a higher rainfall and a richer vegetation than the surrounding dry thorny bush and mopane woodlands—the area is a sort of large oasis on the northern edge of the dry bushveld.

FLORA The woodland is chiefly made up of *Julbernardia globiflora;* other trees representing eastern floral elements: *Erythrina lysistemon, Streptocarpus eylesii,* and *Calodendrum capense.* Striking winter-flowering plants are succulents of the *Crassula* group, traveler's joy *(Clematis), Pterolobium exosum,* the redwing that climbs to the tops of the tallest trees, cream-colored proteas, and four species of aloes. The meadows are covered with white-flowered habenaria and other ground orchids.

White and mauve water lilies, yellow ottelia, and treeferns grow on or near the streams and pools.

MAMMALS Areas formerly eroded and overgrazed by cattle have healed well and game animals have returned; reintroductions of animals into this park from the Wankie National Park have also brought up the numbers of animals. The following may be observed: sable antelope, greater kudu, impala, duiker, steenbok, klipspringer, eland, wildebeest, giraffe, buffalo, zebra, warthog, rock hyrax, black and square-lipped (white) rhinoceros. Troops of baboons and vervets are common. Among the carnivores: leopards are fairly common; civets and genets may also be seen.

BIRDS A very large population of the black eagle (52 pairs) is the avian glory of the hills; these large birds prey chiefly on rock hyraxes. Other noteworthy birds: African rock swallow, the little rush warbler, and the purple-crested lourie; often observed: augur buzzards, white-necked ravens, red-winged starlings, sooty babblers, mocking chats, and rock pigeons. Migrants: willow warblers, European swallows, bee-eaters, white storks, Abdim storks, and red-chested cuckoos.

WANKIE NATIONAL PARK (created game reserve 1927, N.P. 1949)

This national park, one of the most accessible sanctuaries in Africa and one of the largest, protects huge numbers of elephants, lions, and other animals. On an elevated plateau (about 914 m) with little rainfall, it is largely a semiarid, flat country having extensive woodlands and also, in the north, open grassy plains. Few rivers drain the area, but water collects in so-called pans (shallow depressions and artificial water holes) where the animals concentrate from August to November when the water supplies dry up. At certain windmills overlooking water holes, observation platforms have been erected and give visitors an opportunity of watching by day and during full-moon nights.

Location: western Rhodesia, about 112 km SW of Victoria Falls, 256 km NW of Bulawayo

Area: 1,439,080 ha

Protection: about a third of the area open to visitors year round, the rest a strict nature reserve; staff of 211 persons; 400 km of game-viewing roads; observation towers

Access: an airstrip near Main Camp

Accommodation: two rest camps: Main Camp at southern entrance, Robins Camp (120 persons) at northern entrance; also hotels on the road to Main Camp; a new Sinamatella rest camp (80 beds) in northern section under construction, also a tarmac road running from the new rest camp to Main Camp

GEOLOGY Reworked Kalahari sand about 70 m thick underlies

Buffaloes have the reputation of being Africa's most dangerous mammal, but it is only when hunted and wounded that they become aggressive.

most of the area and with the exception of the Zambesi drainage system no older rocks are exposed.

FLORA The most important habitat is the mopane woodland occupying large areas; some pans are surrounded by a savanna of *Acacia uncinata* and *Lonchocarpus nelsii.* Camel thorns are characteristic of drier savanna tracts; some parts of the park have forests of Rhodesian teak; in valley grasslands baobabs may be common.

MAMMALS The elephant population in this park (more than 5,000) is probably the largest in southern Africa; some of them keep together in herds of up to 250 animals. Buffaloes number 12,000 and as many as 1,500 have been counted together.

A great quantity of antelopes include roan, sable, wildebeest (16,000), and greater kudu are fairly generally distributed, as are giraffe, zebra, and lion.

Lions are a specialty of Wankie National Park, where they exist in such numbers that it is difficult to miss them on any visit, particularly in the northern sector of the reserve where the tsessebe (sassaby), impala, and waterbuck are also chiefly found.

The oryx usually occurs around the Ngweshla Pan in the southern sector.

Other species a visitor may see in the reserve: eland, duiker, reedbuck, steenbok, Sharpe's steenbok, bushbuck, klipspringer, baboon, cheetah, leopard, and wild dog. Rescued black rhinos from Kariba and square-lipped (white) rhinos from Natal have been reintroduced.

BIRDS The hot dry savanna vegetation harbors among others the scrub robin, the ant-eating chat, the rufous-naped lark that is almost omnipresent in African savannas, the sandgrouse (three species), kori bustard, helmeted guineafowl, francolins, the ostrich, and large birds of prey such as many species of eagles and vultures.

Other ornithological highlights are saddle-bill storks and dark chanting goshawks.

Lioness with cubs under the spiny branches of an acacia bush

The Victoria Falls, famous since Livingston discovered them in 1855

VICTORIA FALLS NATIONAL PARK (created game reserve 1939, N.P. 1952)

The Victoria Falls, largest sheet of falling water in the world, is one of the great sights of Africa and certainly one of the greatest natural wonders of the world. The grandeur of the area is still unspoiled and as enthralling as in 1855 when the first white man, David Livingstone, viewed the world's mightiest billowing curtain of water.

The national park protects part of the Falls, the gorges, the mist forest fronting the Falls, the gallery forest along the river banks, and an area of woodland savannas with a variety of animals.

On the northern bank, in Zambia, is Livingstone's Game Park, protecting antelopes, giraffes and zebras, bushpigs and warthogs. The nearest town to Rhodesia's Victoria Falls National Park is Livingstone in Zambia, with an airport only ten miles away.

Location: southern bank of Zambesi River, NW corner of Rhodesia

Area: 59,307 ha

Climate: summers hot; average annual temp.: about 68°F; annual rainfall (chiefly in summer): 600–700 mm

Protection: total, staff of 70 persons; 128 km of roads in park and two drives: Zambesi Drive of 56 km along river, and Chamabonda game-viewing drive (both open May–December, permit required from main control gate)

Access: by air, rail, and road

Accommodation: two well-equipped rest camps: Main Camp, 1.6 km from Falls, and Zambesi Camp, 6.4 km upstream

TOPOGRAPHY

The Zambesi River, rising in mts. near the Congo–Zambia border, flows through Angola and Zambia and spreads over a wide plateau area above the Falls. With a width of 1,650 meters the river drops into a fissure of basalt; below the Falls it has cut a deep and narrow gorge winding downward for about 100 km to the Zambesi-Matetsi confluence. The giant ditch clearly exposes four horizontal lava flows.

The most majestic frontal views of the Falls are obtained along a trail extending from Devil's Cataract at the western end in Rhodesia to Eastern Cataract in Zambia. At several points spray from the Falls is very heavy (particularly in Jan.–Aug.); the river is at its highest and the Falls most impressive in April–May, but clouds of spray often obscure the thundering water.

Islands divide the crest of the Falls into five separate waterfalls; greatest height (102 m): Rainbow Falls; widest span (732 m): Main Falls between Cataract and Livingstone islands. Water races over Devil's Cataract at 160 km an hour.

FLORA

The "rain forest" sustained by the mist and spray from the Falls contains tall African ebony and various figs; it continues on the west side along much of the length of the Falls. A huge baobab outside the rain forest has a 21-meter circumference.

There are various types of savannas and woodlands with patches of Rhodesia teak; tree savannas also have wild seringa and *Dialium*; bark-cloth trees dominate on tracts with Kalahari sand, and near the Zambesi there are savannas with baobabs and the doum palm.

MAMMALS

The park has impressive herds of sable antelope and eland. Along the river, elephant and hippopotamus are prevalent. Buffalo grazes in several areas. Other large species include giraffe, bushbuck, greater kudu, waterbuck, impala, reedbuck, duiker, zebra, warthog, baboon, lion, and leopard.

In the volcanic rocks of the Batoka Gorge lives a strong population of rock hyraxes.

BIRDS

Species like the African wood owl, the fishing owl, and the nicator may be seen in the riverine forest. The beautiful Madagascar bee-eater, a migrant from the east, hunts insects above the river, and trumpeter hornbills can be seen in flapping flight passing overhead.

Larger birds in the national park include Egyptian geese, kori bustards, and white-backed duck.

In the gorges the extremely rare Taita falcon has one of its few known breeding places.

OTHER VERTEBRATES

In the river are crocodiles and tiger fish, silvery-golden with black longitudinal stripes and large impressive teeth.

Kori bustard

Hippopotamuses occur in very high numbers in the Gorongosa N. P.

Area: 774,701 km²   Population density: 8/km²

A national park, Gorongosa, was created in 1960 and also several partial reserves, of which Niassa, the largest, extends over 1,500,000 hectares. Bazaruto N.P. was established in 1971. These protected areas are under the management of the Director of Veterinary Services, Lourenço Marques, Moçambique.

GORONGOSA NATIONAL PARK (created a game reserve 1921, N.P. 1960)

An abundance of mammals and the excellent opportunity of seeing them has made the Parque Nacional du Gorongosa famous. The well-known "Acampamento Velho" is a group of houses abandoned by the personnel of the Companhia de Moçambique and now inhabited by lions.

Though the area is flat or gently undulating with maximum elevation of about 600 meters, it offers varied landscapes of vast open plains, woodland savannas, lovely glades, closed woods, gallery forests along river banks, swamps, pools, and lakes. The Instituto de Investigação Agronómica de Moçambique conducts important scientific research.

Crowned crane

(the hippo population in this park is surpassed only by those of the Albert National Park, Zaire Republic, and the Queen Elizabeth National Park, Uganda).

Black rhinoceroses, however, are very rare in Gorongosa (a few live in the regions of Mt. Xiluvo and Mt. Bungo) while more than 30 square-lipped rhinos have been reintroduced.

Elephants and buffaloes are found throughout the park. Common all over the plain and the open woodlands are the blue wildebeest (brindled gnu), and the zebra. In the bush and wooded savannas are impalas, oribis, Lichtenstein's hartebeests, bushbucks, and waterbucks; reedbucks frequent savannas with moister soils or woodlands with fresh grass and bushes; elands are found in all habitats. Other antelopes in the park: two species of duikers (*Cephalophus natalensis* and *C. caeruleus*) and the southern suni.

The greater kudu and the nyala are rare in Garongosa. Warthogs and bushpigs are common. Lions and leopards roam the savannas, though the latter prefer bushlands and woods. Among other carnivores: cheetah, caracal, wild dog, black-backed and side-striped jackals, spotted hyenas, and honey badgers (ratels).

Baboons and vervets are common; in the woods are blue monkeys and two species of bush babies (galagos)—the Senegal and the bush-tailed.

BIRDS Some 339 species of birds have been recorded. Spectacular numbers of storks, crested cranes, egrets, and pelicans congregate along the Urema River.

REPTILES Crocodiles are plentiful in the Urema River, the two species in the park: the African and the small long-snouted crocodile. The python is also to be found.

Location: central Mozambique, 137 km NW of Beira, 203 km from Umtali, Rhodesia
Area: 870,000 ha
Climate: very heavy rains (Nov.–Dec.)
Protection: general; patrol staff of 132; many car tracks through park
Access: from Beira; tourism organized by the Veterinary Service and the Tourists Information Center
Accommodation: at an important and comfortable camp at Chitengo

FLORA Grassy savannas occupy large areas of the park; thorny acacias dominate the wooded savanna and open woodlands. Other savannas have euphorbias and broad-leaved trees, such as terminalias and baobabs. Doum palms and fever trees fringe open glades; dwarf palms are common. Locally, the ground is covered by sensitive plants (*Mimosa pudica*).

MAMMALS Hippopotamuses are here in almost countless numbers

(Portuguese West Africa)

Area: 1,251,513 km²   Population density: 4/km²

There are seven protected areas in Angola, of which the best known is Quicama National Park, described below. (Other areas: Iona N.P., Bicuar N.P., Azevedos N.P., Cameia N.P., and two strict nature reserves—Luando and Mupa.)

QUICAMA NATIONAL PARK (created game reserve 1938, N.P. 1957)

The Parque Nacional de Quicama bordering the Atlantic Ocean serves as a refuge for many interesting animals. Occasionally, concentrations of more than 1,000 elands may be seen, an uncommon sight in Africa.

Location: about 70 km south of Luanda
Area: 996,000 ha
Climate: relatively dry
Protection: almost total, but some habitation permitted in park's eastern area, Demba Chio; staff of 40, reinforced by state patrols; many weekend visitors from Luanda; guides
Access: by road (80 km) from Luanda
Accommodation: camp for tourists

GEOLOGY AND TOPOGRAPHY

Most of the area consists of ancient pre-Cambrian rocks hidden under sandy soils. From the coastal plains in the west, the land gradually rises to hills and plateaus.

FLORA The whole park is within the savanna belt stretching across southern Africa from the Atlantic Ocean to the Indian Ocean.

Quiçama has a coastal strip of grasslands dominated by millet, or bristlegrass; in the eastern part the savanna changes into thickets with *Strychnos* and dry woodlands with *Ptaeroxylon, Croton, Adansonia, Sterculia, Balanites, Commiphora,* and *Euphorbia.*

MAMMALS Animals are abundant; among the particularly interesting species are the eland, the cheetah, and the West African manatee, one of Africa's rarest mammals. Among other species: elephants, buffaloes, hippos, roans, reedbucks, bushbucks, wild dogs, spotted hyenas, leopards, and lions. Square-lipped rhinos were reintroduced 1969.

Vervet monkeys are common, as well as bushpigs and warthogs.

BIRDS AND REPTILES Diverse bird fauna. Crocodiles occur in the river.

Both species of eland in Africa are larger than all other antelopes.

Gemsbok in Etosha National Park

SOUTH-WEST AFRICA

Area: 826,491 km²   Population density: 1/km²
Further information on the Etosha National Park, the world's
largest game reserve, described below, may be obtained
from the Department of Nature Conservation and Tourism,
Private Bag 13186, Windhoek.

ETOSHA NATIONAL PARK (created 1958)

Situated around the Etosha Pan in Ovamboland about 480
km north of Windhoek, the huge uninhabited area of this
park with an adjoining game reserve in the Kaokoveld comprises more than 95,830 square kilometers. For its meager
vegetation the reserve is remarkably rich in animal life,
again an amazing example of how arid regions with poor
plant life support and produce high numbers of herbivores.

Both the lesser and greater flamingo breed on the Etosha
Pan, where they are seen in great numbers.

Location: northern South-West Africa
Area: 6,500,000 ha
Climate: very hot in summer; in win-
ter: warm days, cold nights
Protection: total; staff of 310; open
March 15–October 31
Access: by car, by train, or by air to
Windhoek, where cars may be hired;
regular bus service and chartered air-
craft from Windhoek to the park
Accommodation: three modern rest camps:
at Okaukuejo, Halali, and Namutoni

Best visiting: August and September, when
animals concentrate around water holes

TOPOGRAPHY Surrounded by vast
plateaus, the Etosha Pan, where
nothing grows, is itself an enormous expanse of mud deserts and
salt beds occupying an area 128
by 64 kilometers. Winds, water and

sunshine form dead flats of this kind. Flowing rivers of the past deposited coarse sand and gravel in a huge, shallow basin and in its flat surroundings, killing vegetation by an almost unending accumulation of fine silt. Where there is no outlet, as at the Etosha Pan, such a flat gradually becomes saline, preventing plant recolonization. Whirlwinds in hot temperatures carry dust and silt far away, spreading it over the ages.

The adjoining Kaokoveld reserve is a mountainous area rising to about 1,828 meters. Plateaus and hills at various levels descend to the Skeleton Coast along the Atlantic Ocean, a part of the Namib Desert, one of the oldest deserts of the world, virtually devoid of vegetation except for occasional widely scattered solitary plants.

FLORA Except for the pan itself, the Etosha National Park is covered with bush characteristic of semi-arid regions. Extensive plateaus are occupied by tropical karstveld with grasses and thorny bushes or by a mopane veld comprising mopane, marulas, tamboti, various acacias, wild apple, and wild fig.

The contiguous reserve in the Kaokoveld is a vast highveld changing to arid bushlands and semi-desert steppes at lower elevations where the extraordinary *Welwit-*schia bainesii occurs, often with *Zygophyllum stapfi*. The Namib Desert area has almost no vegetation, but along the Kunene River, forming the border with Angola, there is a lush forest.

MAMMALS Some of the grazers and browsers around the Etosha Pan are the eland, blue wildebeest, red (Cape) hartebeest, impala, greater kudu, springbok, gemsbok, giraffe, black rhinoceros, and elephant. Surprisingly, the mountain zebra occurs on the plains in impressive herds mixed with blue wildebeest, springbok, and oryx, though most of the mountain zebras (perhaps as many as 10,000) occur in the Kaokoveld highlands. (The mountain zebra of this reserve is a different race from its southern relative that survives in a few herds in the Cape Province.) The dik-dik occurs in both the Etosha Pan and Kaokoveld reserves.

BIRDS Estimates of the lesser and greater flamingos breeding on the Etosha Pan indicate numbers from 500,000 to 1,000,000.

Ostriches thrive on the open steppe. The bushland and the mopane veld have a variety of birds: kori bustard, secretary bird, francolins, sandgrouse, blacksmith, crowned plover, sociable weaver.

Springboks

Area 1,228,133 km^2 Population density: 13/km^2
South Africa has 32 protected areas, ten of which are described below. The protection covers seven national parks, four protected areas in Cape Province, 14 reserves in Natal, one in the Orange Free State, and five in Transvaal, as well as some less important reserves. The Tsitsikama Forest and Coastal National Park was created in 1964.

A National Parks Board of Trustees administers the national parks (except those in Natal) and will supply further information and pamphlets (P.O. Box 787, Pretoria). The Provincial Administrations administer the game reserves. Data on the Natal reserves is obtained from the Reservation Officer, P.O. Box 662, Pietermaritzburg.

KALAHARI GEMSBOK NATIONAL PARK (created 1931)
The Kalahari National Park, situated between the Auob and Nossob rivers, borders South-West Africa and straddles the border between South Africa and southwestern Botswana. More than half of the area lies in Botswana, but the whole reserve is administered by the National Parks Board of South Africa. Nomadic Bushmen live in the area; though they still wander a great deal, many have jobs of various kinds.

Set within the rather inhospitable desert region of the Kalahari sand veld, the park supports an amazing wealth of animals despite its aridity and meager vegetation. Again there is extraordinary evidence that wild grazers can convert poor grasses into excellent meat and protein without destroying their environment. With domestic livestock it is exactly the reverse even for rich habitats.

The normal maximum rainfall in this extremely parched landscape is only 125 millimeters.

This national park was established mainly for the protection of migratory antelopes: gemsboks, springboks, blue wildebeests, and elands. The lions of Kalahari have the reputation of having the finest manes in all Africa.

There is a surprisingly high number of birds. Acacias, and even telephone poles, harboring immense communal nests of the sociable weaver bird are a feature of the landscape of the open Kalahari.

Semi-desert and pure desert side by side—a part of desert dynamics

Location: NW corner of Cape Province
Area: S. Africa: 895,316 ha; Botswana, 2,452,400 ha
Protection: total, except for some Bushmen who live and hunt freely; staff of 10 persons; travel within park restricted to 320 km of car tracks; entrance fees
Accommodation: in cottages and huts; rest camps at Twee Rivieren (36 beds), Mata Mata (9 beds), and Nossob (14 beds); camping sites

TOPOGRAPHY The Kalahari Desert, largest of desert regions south of the Sahara, is a huge sand-filled basin. The park covers an area of sand dunes, colored red by iron oxide, and extensive plains (elevation: about 1,200 meters).

Rarely is there any surface water, the rain sinking immediately into the sands. The dry, firm beds of the Auob and Nossob rivers (which make excellent roads) are filled with water only once or twice in a century. Several bore holes have been constructed to supply animals with water.

CLIMATE Extremely arid and hot (often over 100°F in summer), with frequent strong winds. Nights can be quite cool. Winters may have long cold periods, even with frosts.

Persistent droughts are common, but abundant rains may finally interrupt and the vegetation recover.

FLORA Biologically most of the park's area is a semidesert with sparse vegetation. The dunes have become stabilized by a variety of grasses (mostly *Aristida* and *Eragrostis*) and shrubs (*Rhigozum obovata*, *Grewia flava*, and *Acacia destinens* are common).

There are even trees, forming a kind of arid parkland, including the camel thorn (*Acacia giraffae*), another acacia (*A. haematoxylon*), and the witgat.

After the rains the dunes are miraculously covered with grasses, such as gemsbokkommkommer and tsamma.

MAMMALS Thousands of gemsboks graze over the dunes keeping together in herds. The springbok appears in huge herds of 1,000 to

103

Springbok

occur in the park: red (Cape) harte-beest, greater kudu, duiker, and steenbok.

Among these antelopes live the lion, leopard, cheetah, caracal, serval, black-footed cat, aardwolf, spotted hyena, brown hyena, bat-eared fox, silver jackal, black-backed jackal, wild dog, honey badger, ant bear, and warthog.

BIRDS Conspicuous species: spotted eagle owl, chanting goshawk, secretary bird, kori bustard, and ostrich. Often seen: sparrow weaver, sociable weaver, Cape sparrow, helmet shrike, crimson-breasted shrike, Namaqua sandgrouse, several species of larks, and, soaring overhead, eagles and vultures.

REPTILES Lizards and snakes are numerous as in other semideserts.

1,500 through which one can drive for miles. The blue wildebeest (brindled gnu) appears in herds of hundreds, and the eland in herds numbering a hundred or more. Four other antelope species

Gemsboks (oryx) in excellent condition bear witness to how well-adapted mammals can thrive in harsh environments.

Giraffe in woodland savanna of the Kruger National Park

KRUGER NATIONAL PARK (created game reserve 1898, N.P. 1926)

Visitors to this park in lowveld country have many opportunities to observe a very high percentage of Africa's savanna and bushveld mammals at close range.

Situated between the Limpopo and Levubu rivers in the north and the Crocodile River in the south, Kruger National Park, one of the world's largest, occupies land that is mainly flat, varying from open plains and thick bushes to mopane woodlands and wooded hills, kopjes, and low mountains.

Location: eastern Transvaal, along the border of Mozambique
Area: 1,817,146 ha
Protection: staff of 300, reinforced in tourist season (300,000–400,000 visitors a year); entrance fee
Accommodation: main rest camps: Skukuza, Pretoriuskop, Lower Sabie, Olifants, Letaba; camping sites; restaurants; every tourist facility
Best visiting: winter (May 1–Oct. 15); northern section of park closed during summer

GEOLOGY AND TOPOGRAPHY

Granite, the oldest geological formation, underlies western half of park and is exposed as kopjes; the eastern half belongs to the Karoo system of more recent formation. The Kruger N.P. is in the lowest part of Transvaal (altitude: 150–610 meters).

CLIMATE Warm, fairly dry. Rainfall chiefly in summer months (Oct.–March), 375–500 mm a year in N part of park, 500–875 mm in SW and SE parts. Severe droughts occur irregularly. January temperature: 86°F; July: 73°F.

FLORA Regionally there are five main vegetation associations:

Around Pretoriuskop in the SW part, there is a large-leaved deciduous bush and woodland, chiefly combretums—Zulu bush willow, Zayher's bush willow, and velvet-leaf bush willow—and silver terminalia, with an understory of tall grasses.

South of Olifants River, also in SW, is an association of mixed veld with predominant red bush willow, knobthorn, marula, lowveld terminalia, and *Eragrostis superba*.

In the SE quarter lies open parkland with knobthorns, marulas, and umbrella thorns, joined in low areas by leadwood and ilala palm.

A mopane woodland has colonized the N half; near the Levubu River, stony slopes have large baobabs, graceful white seringas, and soft-wooded corkwood.

A forest in NW portion has Rhodesian mahogany, sycamore fig, Transvaal ebony, and mountain mahogany.

MAMMALS Among the many antelope species: impala in large numbers, greater kudu, nyala, bushbuck, steenbok, Sharpe's grysbok, duiker, red duiker, klipspringer, roan, sable antelope, waterbuck, blue wildebeest, tsessebe, reedbuck, mountain reedbuck, and eland.

Other grazers and browsers in this fantastic animal community: warthog, bushpig, zebra, giraffe, and buffalo. There are elephants and hippopotamuses. The square-lipped (white) rhinoceros, reintroduced from Natal with 94 animals, is multiplying well.

Major and minor carnivores control herbivorous populations: spotted hyena, brown hyena, aardwolf, wild dog, black-backed jackal, side-striped jackal, bat-eared fox, lion, leopard, cheetah, serval, wildcat, mongoose (five species: banded, slender, ichneumon, white-tailed, and dwarf), clawless otter, honey badger (ratel), civet, rusty-spotted genet, small-spotted genet. Still other mammals: bush babies (two species), chacma baboon, vervet, ant bear, Cape pangolin, porcupine, and rock hyrax.

BIRDS Some 400 species have been recorded. The three tallest ground birds most often seen are ostrich, kori bustard, and secretary bird. Other large birds include crested and crowned guineafowl, francolins (five species), hornbills (six), saddle-bill stork, vultures (five), eagles (nine), lesser birds of prey (20), and rollers (three).

OTHER VERTEBRATES There are nearly 100 species of reptiles, including crocodiles, pythons, and cobras, about 30 species of amphibians, about 50 of fishes.

Elephant in typical bushveld during the dry season

Black Umfolozi River with Masinda Hill in the background

HLUHLUWE, MKUZI, AND UMFOLOZI GAME RESERVES

These three nature reserves, here treated together, are among the oldest in Africa. Hluhluwe and Umfolozi are about 288 km, and Mkuzi is about 400 km, from Durban. (Information is obtainable from the Reservations Officer, P.O. Box 662, Pietermaritzburg.) The reserves are stocked with large mammals and again demonstrate that even heavy grazing by large populations of wild animals is less damaging to habitats than the presence of cattle and goats.

The reputation of the Hluhluwe and Umfolozi reserves is worldwide, primarily as the home of the square-lipped, or white, rhinoceros and the black rhinoceros (they exist also in Mkuzi). Both rare rhinos are threatened by extinction.

Hluhluwe and Umfolozi reserves are separated by a stretch of land called the "corridor," rich in wild animals. It is very desirable to incorporate the corridor with the two already existing reserves, which are among the most important on the continent and contain almost the whole fauna that once occurred so abundantly is this part of Africa.

Most exciting places to watch various mammals at Mkuzi are the Bube and Msinga pans, the only drinking spots in the dry season, where structures on stilts resembling "Treetops" provide comfortable watching towers.

107

Location: eastern Zululand, in Natal
Area: Hluhluwe (created 1897) 22,800 ha; **Mkuzi** (created 1912) 24,600 ha; **Umfolozi** (created 1897) 48,000 ha
Climate: Hluhluwe and Umfolozi: temperate; Mkuzi: hot
Protection: Hluhluwe: total, though a projected dam on Hluhluwe River may threaten the area; staff of 37 units; guide required to visit this reserve
Mkuzi: general; staff of 24; native game guide must accompany visitors
Umfolozi: total; staff of 60; wilderness trails; travel within reserve on foot or by car but native guide must always accompany visitors
Accommodations: huts available at each reserve but visitors must bring own food

GEOLOGY

The coastland of Natal consists of sedimentary formations chiefly from periods of marine submersion dating back to the early Cretaceous though some of the sedimentary formations are from more recent times. The present Mkuzi Game Reserve has rich fossil beds of marine animals: molluscs, seashells, ammonites, and sharks.

TOPOGRAPHY

The Hluhluwe and Umfolozi reserves are hilly and of partly mountainous terrain (altitudes 84—590 m), while the Mkuzi reserve is a relatively flat lowland plain of grassy savannas and woodlands bounded by the Lebomo Mts. and the Mkuzi River.

FLORA

The Hluhluwe and Umfolozi reserves have forested valleys, bushveld, open grasslands, and scrub-covered hills, and both have vast areas of rolling thornbush (transitional between highveld and the lowveld of the coastal strip). Gallery forests with sycamore figs line banks of rivers in each reserve.

Trees in Hluhluwe, apart from the predominant acacias of several species, include Cape chestnut, tree fuschia, red ivory, tamboti, marula, kaffirboom (three species), wild pear, and cabbage tree. *Dalbergia armata* is a characteristic climber.

The square-lipped rhinoceros has its densest population in Africa in the Umfolozi Game Reserve.

Zebras and wildebeests at a waterhole

In Umfolozi, many of the same trees occur and also gardenias and the crane flower.

Most prominent species of the Mkuzi reserve: various species of acacia, together with marula, tree wisteria, torchwood, and flame creeper. Fever trees concentrate around marshy depressions, and along the Mkuzi River are beautiful groves of sycamore figs, some of the largest in Zululand. The area is the southern limit of many species, including the South African mustard tree and the matumi.

MAMMALS The square-lipped rhino, the world's third largest terrestrial mammal (after the African and Indian elephants), is divided into two geographically widely separated races. About nine tenths of the southern square-lipped rhino population is limited to Hluhluwe, Umfolozi, and the "Corridor." Hluhluwe has 89 individuals, the "Corridor" 175, and Umfolozi 717. Both reserves shelter black rhinos.

Hluhluwe and Umfolozi reserves have an impressive assemblage of other mammals, including buffalo, zebra, blue wildebeest, nyala, greater kudu, impala, bushbuck, waterbuck, steenbok, reedbuck, duiker, red duiker, warthog, chacma baboon, and leopard. Of the two reserves, Hluhluwe alone has these species: blue duiker, qiraffe, and bushpig, while Umfolozi (but not Hluhluwe) has klipspringer and lion.

Mkuzi Game Reserve supports large populations of nyala and impala. Animal life is rather similar to that in the other two, more southern, reserves, but Mkuzi alone protects the suni and the black-backed and side-striped jackal.

Species mentioned above for both Hluhluwe and Umfolozi but missing in Mkuzi are buffalo, waterbuck, and mountain reedbuck.

BIRDS Some species to be seen at Hluhluwe include marabou, white-backed vulture, bateleur, crested guineafowl, blue quail, green pigeon (Treron australis), emerald cuckoo, narina trogon, and ground hornbill.

At least 241 species have been recorded at Umfolozi, including

109

Marabous, Egyptian geese, and white-headed vulture

black stork, dwarf goose, lappet-faced vulture, cuckoo hawk, francolins (four species), pigeons and doves (eight), cuckoos (five), rollers (two), kingfishers (four), bee-eaters (thee), and hornbills (five).

Among the birds at Mkuzi, the following are worth special mention: Reichenow's touraco, white-fronted bee-eater, greater honey guide, crowned and crested guineafowl, white-backed vulture, black cuckoo, hadada ibis, and woolly-necked stork.

REPTILES Rivers contain crocodiles.

AMPHIBIANS Frogs and toads of the three reserves include common toad, common, striped, and sharp-nosed ranas; puddle, running, forest tree, painted tree, long reed, red-banded, and mottled burrowing frogs; and platanna. Many of these amphibians are strikingly beautiful but more often heard than seen.

Warthogs and impalas drinking at Bube in the Mkuzi Game Reserve

Adult and young wood ibises and white-faced tree duck

ST. LUCIA GAME RESERVE AND PARK

This reserve stretches along the coast of the Indian Ocean, near Hluhluwe Game Reserve (see p. 107). It covers Lake St. Lucia, one of the biggest salt-water estuaries in the world, into which four rivers flow (Mkuzi, Mzenene, Hluhluwe, and Umfolozi). Unfortunately three of these have been dammed, and the last major freshwater source (the Hluhluwe River) is threatened. The delta is silting up as a result of this unwise exploitation, and if a new dam should be built the area would become a salt pan, incapable of supporting its present rich fauna.

The reserve was created in 1897 to preserve the hippopotamuses that live in the freshwater pans so essential to their existence in the area.

Birds are among the reserve's most attractive features. Great flocks of flamingos and pelicans occur.

Location: east central Zululand, Natal

Areas: St. Lucia Game Reserve (created 1897): 36,500 ha
St. Lucia Park (created 1939): 12,400 ha

Climate: hot

Protection: total; staff of 24 guards; wilderness trails; boats available; conducted launch tours, when water conditions permit, from Charters Creek and St. Lucia Estuary

Access: by road from Mtubatuba, clearly sign-posted

Accommodation: camps with huts at Charters Creek (15 beds) and Fanies Island (12 beds); open camp site at St. Lucia Estuary

TOPOGRAPHY

Biggest marine lake in Africa, St. Lucia is 72 km long with a width varying from 91 meters to 16 kilometers and an average depth of only about a meter. This vast expanse of water has great variations in salinity and thus has freshwater, brackish, and marine life forms.

Heavily wooded sand hills and a flat plain intersected by swamps and freshwater pans divide the lake from the sea. The pans are extremely important for the existence of many plant and animal species, as well as for the hydrography of the whole area.

FLORA

In addition to the aquatic vegetation with extensive reed-beds, there are coastal grasslands, scrub, woodlands and forests. Mangroves occur from the mouth of the estuary up to the Makakatam shallows; other coastal trees: flat-crown acacia, several figs, palms, Kaffir plum, and white pear. Locally there are luxuriant swamp forests containing numerous ferns. St. Lucia lilies are conspicuous on the grasslands after grass fires.

MAMMALS

The St. Lucia reserve is the most southerly concentration of the hippopotamus (population there about 250). Other large mammals around the lake: reedbuck, duiker, red duiker, suni, steenbok, bushbuck, nyala, bushpig, the rare samango monkey, serval, and the Tonga yellow-chested squirrel.

BIRDS

More than 345 species have been found within the reserve. The large flocks of flamingos and pelicans have been mentioned. The many nesting birds include African spoonbill, glossy ibis, wood ibis, herons, African white pelican, pink-backed pelican, black-winged pratincole, avocet, and stilt. In the open grasslands: pink-throated long-claws. Birds of the woods include broadbill and Reichenow's touraco.

OTHER VERTEBRATES

This park is a refuge for the crocodile. Snakes are numerous but usually invisible in the bush cover. The Gaboon viper and the black-lipped cobra should be mentioned. Frogs and toads of various species abound in large numbers.

Fishes are abundant, among them: barbel, tilapia, garrick, silver bream, grunters, and Cape salmon. Sharks penetrate into the waters of the lake.

The Nile crocodile has been much depleted due to its valuable skin.

Grasslands with scattered trees and bushes dominate the upper levels of the Royal Natal National Park.

ROYAL NATAL NATIONAL PARK (created 1916)

This national park (altitude 1,443-3,364 meters) and the adjoining Rugged Glen Nature Reserve offer magnificent landscapes of remarkable grandeur. The area includes the Mont-aux-Sources, one of the highest peaks (3,277 meters) in South Africa, and many rugged krantzes, deeply ravined foothills, and waterfalls. On clear days the summits and ridges afford fantastic views over much of Natal.

An interesting feature of the national park is provided by the numerous well-preserved Bushmen rock paintings on the walls of caves.

Location: western Natal
Area: 8,000 ha
Protection: total; staff of 14 units; travel within park only on foot or on horseback; guides available; limited trout fishing; information available from the Warden, Royal Natal National Park, Mont-aux-Sources
Access: by road
Accommodation: the modern Royal Natal National Park Hotel, with every facility; Tendele hutted camp; Royal Natal camp site

GEOLOGY, TOPOGRAPHY, AND CLIMATE The underlying rocks of the Drakensberg Mts. are of the Karoo series, mostly sandstone and basalt.

Prominent topographical features of the national park: the Eastern Buttress, the Devil's Tooth, the Inner Tower, the spectacular Amphitheater, the Gorge, and the Tugela Falls. At the headwaters of the Tugela R., precipitous cliffs and buttresses of the Drakensberg escarpment rise majestically above a high plateau, carved in part by canyons and steep foothills.

The national park is an area of high rainfall.

FLORA Mountainous grassveld dominates, but nine important plant communities may be distinguished.

Between 1,370 and 1,830 meters: a well-developed protea savanna with *Protea rouppelliae* and *P. multibracteata* predominant among trees, and a continuous grass understory of *Tristachia*, red grass (*Themeda*), umhala, (*Miscanthidium*), love grass (*Eragrostis*), *Hyparrhenia*, *Cymbopogon*, and *Digitaria*. These grasslands are associated with many veld flowers including ground orchids and lilies.

At higher altitudes temperate grasses of such genera as *Pentaschistis*, *Bromus*, *Festuca*, *Danthonia* succeed the tropical grasses.

Sheltered valleys have forests with rich undergrowth of shrubs, herbs, and ferns. The dominant tree is the upright yellowwood; others are common yellowwood, wild chestnut, wild peach, *Olinia emarginata*, assegai, and black bark. Common climbers in these forests: *Secamone alpinii*, *Cassina tetragona*, and *Dalbergia obovata*. Epiphytes include old-man's-beard.

Gallery forests decorate banks of streams and rivers with whitewood, wild willow, and *Bowkeria verticellata*. Treeferns are common.

Grasslands up to an elevation of about 2,740 meters may have sagewood and oudebos, and also trees like Cape beech and upright yellowwood.

Another type of scrubland growing on boulders and on cliffs up to about 2,290 meters has berg cypress, cabbage tree, berg cycad, and heath.

A dense small tree or scrub habitat (2,290–2,745 m) has heaths (*Erica abracteata* and *Philippia evansii*), berg cypress, gannabast, and Cape myrrh.

Above 2,745 m: a heathland with several species of *Erica*, dwarf shrubs, short grasses, and everlastings.

And finally a large number of ferns, club mosses, mosses, lichens, and algae grow on bare cliffs and rocks at various altitudes.

MAMMALS The park protects gray rhebok, reedbuck, mountain reedbuck, bushbuck, duiker, klipspringer, white-tailed wildebeest (8 in 1971), dassie (rock hyrax.), and chacma baboon.

BIRDS Commonly observed: familiar chat (*Cercomela familiaris*), malachite sunbird, striped pipit, grass warblers, secretary bird, black eagle, and white-necked raven. Among the most interesting of the 154 recorded species: the bald ibis, lammergeier, and great snipe.

OTHER VERTEBRATES At least 16 species of frogs and toads have been found. Trout have been introduced and angling is permitted.

The upper ridge is part of the magnificent amphitheater of the Drakensberg in the Royal Natal National Park.

Mountain zebra grazing on a high plateau in the Mountain Zebra National Park, which protects the rarest zebra of Africa.

MOUNTAIN ZEBRA NATIONAL PARK (created 1937)

This national park was established to save one of the few remaining herds of the very rare mountain zebra. Apparently never very numerous, the small mountain zebra once occurred in the mountain ranges of southernmost Africa from Namaqualand to the Drakensberg, where it climbed on steep slopes up to about 2,135 meters. Professional hunting increased over several centuries and the animals declined. Three private estates probably saved this zebra from extinction. The national park was established in 1937 on a farm in the eastern Cape Province that gave protection to six zebras. It was only after these had been joined by 11 more in 1950 that the first foal was born. By 1969 the number had increased to 101 animals.

The rugged mountainous area of the park is a transitional and mixed Karoo steppe situated in the middle of the Great Karoo on the northern slopes of the Bankberg at an altitude of about 760–915 meters.

Location: eastern Cape Province, about 27 km west of Cradlock

Area: 5,020 ha

Protection: total; staff of seven; mountain trails; riding horses available; entrance fee

Access: by road from Cradlock

Accommodation: available in two rest camps (33 beds) and youth hostel accommodating 56 children; store and restaurant

GEOLOGY AND CLIMATE The Karoo is a great basin of ancient sedimentary rocks. Rain (some years no more than 150 mm) falls in winter, but there can be long periods of drought. Climate range: from winter frosts to summer hot spells.

FLORA The most important grass cover of this highland veld is the drought resistant *Setaria neglecta*. Buffalo grass, turpentine grass, assegai grass, and stick grass occur.

Typical shrubs are raisinbush, broombush, *Pentzia*, aloes, dgom bush, and bitterkarro. Trees include white stinkwood, wild olive, cabbage tree, acacia, and karree trees. Flowering plants are mesembryanthemums and cotyledons.

MAMMALS The attractive small mountain zebras are the most important animals of the park (in 1971 there were 127). Other protected mammals (some reintroduced) include small numbers of mountain reedbuck (about 250), reedbuck, steenbok, springbok (250), Cape grysbok, gray duiker, white-tailed wildebeest (116), red hartebeest (16), blesbuck (about 150), eland (90), gemsbok (40), klipspringer, chacma baboon, vervet, caracal, aardwolf, black-backed jackal, side-striped jackal, and of course many other small mammals.

BIRDS Some 160 recorded species include the ostrich, highveld waders, bustards, the blue crane, black and martial eagles, and the secretary bird.

A flowering aloe (*Aloe striata*) in Mount Zebra National Park

The famous elephants of the Addo are living in a wide enclosure of the Addo Elephant National Park.

ADDO ELEPHANT NATIONAL PARK (created 1931)

Lying between the Suurberg Mountains and the Sundays River Valley (at an elevation between 60 and 180 m), the undulating area of the national park covers an almost impenetrable bush wilderness. In this mass of dense bush, herbaceous and succulent plants such as *Crassula*, *Aloe*, *Mesembryanthemum* and *Cotyledon* are somehow able to interlace their stems, making the area a kind of flower paradise, quite unique for the bush of southern Africa.

The area was set aside to give refuge to one of the two remnants of once numerous herds of the southern elephant (the other herd of 10 elephants lives in the Knysna forest west of Addo and is seldom seen). Merciless hunting pursued the elephants living there through centuries until understandably the few surviving animals became aggressive toward man and were doomed to extermination. Before the last had been shot, human attitudes changed, and the national park was established in 1931 to protect the survivors. Now numbering 57 individuals, these famous elephants live in about a third of the park's area, which is fenced off with steel cables to contain them. Excellent viewing is possible at an observation camp every afternoon when the elephants are enticed out of the bush with oranges and oat hay.

Location: Cape Province, about 64 km from Port Elizabeth
Area: 6,397 ha
Protection: total, insured by 17 guards; watching towers; entrance fees

Access: by road from Port Elizabeth
Accommodation: self-contained rondavels (24 beds); café and restaurant available to visitors; camping sites

117

The bushbuck has a wide range in Africa, both ecologically and geographically, and varies considerably in coloration.

CLIMATE Subtropical. Weather conditions and rainfall favorable in general, maintaining natural vegetation though short periods of drought may occur. Mild winters.

FLORA Spekboom dominates (height 3—4 m, even higher and more luxuriant in ravines and on slopes); other species of bush: boerboon, with scarlet flowers and usually covered by lichen and moss, melkout, ghwarris, bushman hemp, acacias.

Debushed areas with excellent growths of grass, especially *Themeda triandra*, help the grazers to increase their numbers.

MAMMALS The elephants are, of course, the focal point of interest to visitors. The park has many other mammals, including bushbuck, Cape grysbok, steenbok, mountain reedbuck, eland, red hartebeest, greater kudu, gray rhebok, springbok, duiker, blue duiker, oribi, Cape buffalo (about 300) bushpig, antbear (aardvark), porcupine, caracal, side-striped jackal, black-backed jackal, honey badger (ratel), vervet, and several smaller species.

The hippopotamus and the black rhinoceros, as well as several of the larger antelopes mentioned above, many of which had become locally extinct, have been reintroduced in this national park.

BIRDS The ostrich is quite common, and the secretary bird nests in this park. There are various species of birds of prey, guineafowl, francolins, and passerines.

Male ostrich is the world's largest bird.

BONTEBOK NATIONAL PARK (created 1931)

This national park was established to save the bontebok from extinction.

Originally the bontebok had occurred only in areas around Cape Agulhas where it was intensively hunted by early European settlers; it was then driven to poor grazing lands, and finally became almost extinct in the wild state. Four families saved these animals on their estates in 1864, and it is they and their descendants who deserve credit for protecting them (the largest herds are still on private lands).

Some 17 of these rare antelopes that had survived on nearby plains were first established in a national park near Bredasdorp in 1931; the herd was transferred in 1960 to the present more adequate environment near Swellendam and has increased to 250. The entire bontebok population is believed now to number almost 900 animals.

Until the beginning of the 18th century this area of undulating plains—the park a sandy depression beneath a mountain range—was inhabited by Hottentots.

Location: Cape Province, about 240 km from Cape Town
Area: 1,330 ha
Climate: mild, subtropical
Protection: total; staff of three units; entrance fees
Access: by road (6 km south of Swellendam)
Accommodation: camping permitted, picnic spots

FLORA Plant cover is a Mediterranean type, the so-called maquis (fynbos, macchia, or chaparral are other terms). Vegetation is rather poor, chiefly scrub veld of various proteas and herbaceous plants with scattered sweet thorn acacias and some Breede River yellowwood. Along the banks of the river is a thick bush of acacias; in the southern part, a hillside clad in Cape aloe. Near the river, trees and shrubs (turkey berry, cherry-wood, and dune taaibos) are to be found.

MAMMALS The chief protagonist of the park is, of course, the bontebok. Other antelopes include Cape grysbok, steenbok, gray rhebok, duiker, and bushbuck.

Bontebok (from which park gets its name) with calf

Cape buffalo, eland, springbok, reedbuck, and red (Cape) hartebeest have been reintroduced.

BIRDS Among the total of 104 avian species recorded in the park are hammerkop, secretary bird, fish eagle, Stanley bustard, black korhaan, crowned plover, Namaqua sandgrouse, spotted eagle owl, giant kingfisher, cardinal woodpecker, pearl-breasted swallow, gray-backed cisticola, paradise flycatcher, and yellow bishop.

The ostrich is the only bird to have been reintroduced.

Area: 592,800 km^2 Population density: 11/km^2

The Malagasy Republic has as many as 31 protected areas: two national parks, described below, 11 strict nature reserves (one described below), which have very strict protective provisions—entrance even for scientific researchers is limited—and 18 special reserves, almost all in remote regions. Communications beyond Tananarive are generally very poor.

MONTAGNE D'AMBRE NATIONAL PARK (created 1958)

The Parc National de la Montagne d'Ambre is located on the higher elevations (between 380 and 1,475 meters) of the Ambre massif about 50 km southwest of Diego Suarez. The mountain is an ancient volcano with numerous small craters, some of which have been filled by lakes, and with rugged ridges and valleys; rivers cascade down the mountain flanks.

Location: northern Madagascar
Area: 18,200 ha
Climate: rainy season: Nov.–March.
Protection: general
Access: at present, park practically inaccessible to cars in the rainy season
Accommodation: organization of tourism is under consideration; accommodation in hut available at the ''Roussettes'' station, much used by researchers

FLORA   Moist dense forests have numerous epiphytes, treeferns, orchids, mosses, and lichens. The vegetation is characteristic for low and medium altitudes of eastern Madagascar.

FAUNA   Mammals in this park include the gray gentle lemur, Sanford's lemur, which nowadays does not exist anywhere but on Mount Ambre, the crowned lemur, lesser mouse lemur, bushpig, and several rodents. There are also many birds, reptiles and amphibians. Fishes occur in the crater lakes.

Rain forest in Montagne d'Ambre National Park

MAROJEJY STRICT NATURE RESERVE (created 1952)

The Réserve intégrale Marojejy is located in the northeastern part of Madagascar within the eastern moist forest belt, of which, unfortunately, not much remains today. This reserve presents, however, the only example of an area with unaltered, successive vertical stages of vegetation from 90 to 2,137 meters. The protected zone, only some few kilometers wide, runs like a vertical corridor up the mountain side.

The reserve has more than 2,000 species of plants—several do not occur elsewhere—and an abundance of orchids.

Location: NE province of Diego-Suarez,
Area: 60,150 ha
Protection: no human habitation; severe control of admission even for scientific researchers; staff of three persons
Tourism: prohibited

TOPOGRAPHY AND CLIMATE
These vary with the altitude (90m–2,137m). The terrain is intersected by mountain slopes and valleys. In the eastern and southeastern parts, rainfall is about 3,000 mm.

FLORA Vegetation of the lowland (800–1,450 m) is of the eastern moist type, succeeded at higher elevations by montane evergreen forests. There is an abundance of palms, ferns (over 100 species), and orchids (more than 100 species).

FAUNA Several of Madagascar's peculiar mammals are found in the reserve: gray gentle lemur, weasel lemur, a race of the black lemur, lesser mouse lemur, sifaka, bushpig, Madagascar ring-tailed mongoose, fossa, and Madagascar tenrec.

About 50 birds have been recorded. Several peculiar forms of butterflies specialized to high altitudes can be found.

ISALO NATIONAL PARK (created 1962)

The Parc National de l'Isalo covers the northern part of the Isalo massif in southern Madagascar. It is a mountainous country with steep escarpments, deep canyons, and numerous rivers and waterfalls.

The supervising staff collects samples and conducts ecological investigations.

Location: southern Madagascar
Area: 81,540 ha
Protection: general, some cattle grazing
Accommodation: nothing organized to facilitate tourism

FLORA The varied topography provides a great diversity of habitats. Situated along the road between Antananarivo (Tananarive) and Tulear, the park is surrounded by grass savannas, but its highlands harbor plant elements of both the western dry flora and the eastern moist flora with several endemic species. Very little primitive forest remains, but there are stands of Uapaca. Herds of grazing cattle prevent adequate protection of the plant cover. The lower slopes of the massif, which should have a dense rich forest, are now at least in part degraded to savannas.

FAUNA The vertebrate fauna is still very little known. There are several species of lemurs and birds.

There are few areas in Asia that are holding normal populations of the tiger. Only in the parks has this magnificent cat a refuge.

The world's largest continent extends from the Arctic Ocean to the Indian Ocean, and from the Mediterranean to the Pacific. Its climatic zones range from the Arctic to the tropics. Within this enormous landmass there is a wide variation of vegetation zones from north to south: tundras, coniferous forests, woodlands, Mediterranean chaparral, steppes, deserts, deciduous forests or jungles, rain forests, coastal vegetation, montane rain forests, and alpine vegetation. The altitudinal range, moreover, is enormous: from Lake Baikal, the world's deepest lake, to the Himalayas at the top of our globe.

In many Asian countries, particularly in tropical Asia, destruction of nature has unfortunately gone so far that several of the larger mammals can scarcely be found anywhere outside the national parks that constitute their last stronghold; this is often the case on the numerous islands of northeastern and eastern Asia, where many species or races peculiar to each island live. It is significant that it is in the Asian tropics, only a minor part of the Asian continent, that most animals have become extinct or have come dangerously near the same fate—a consequence of the fact that man has utilized the tropical lands much longer than the more northern regions. Tropical and subtropical areas are also more sensitive to human misuse than are temperate and arctic tracts.

A reaction to this far-reaching destruction of nature in tropical Asia is that numerous national parks—but still not enough—have been set aside by several forward-looking countries in order to save threatened animals and representative habitats. These areas, therefore, are of extreme importance for conservation.

These are some of the reasons for dealing in this book with a proportionately higher number of national parks situated in southern and eastern Asia than in the northern and western parts of the continent. Of the 40 areas in Asia here treated, 28 belong to tropical and subtropical regions while all the others lie on temperate latitudes, five in westernmost Asia, and seven in the easternmost part. This means that northern Asia is not represented at all, a circumstance explained by the relatively few national parks in Siberia that have been opened for tourism, a situation that will no doubt change in the future.

The UN List mentions only 15 countries with some 202 protected areas for the whole of Asia, a continent where the difficulty of setting aside large national parks is due in great part to the population density. Exceptional cases are Japan, of course, and Israel and Turkey, countries making a large effort toward conservation, but the national parks and reserves that can be considered as most representative of Asia are located in India, Ceylon, Thailand, Indonesia, and the Philippines. Actually, these eight countries possess exactly 137 among the 202 areas of the United Nations List for the continent of Asia.

The following countries have no national parks or equivalent reserves answering the criteria of selection of the UN list: Aden, Afghanistan, Brunei, China (Taiwan), Hong Kong, Iran, Iraq, Jordan (one national park is in process of being

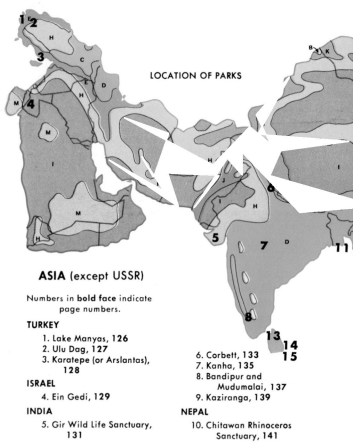

LOCATION OF PARKS

ASIA (except USSR)

Numbers in **bold face** indicate
page numbers.

realized: Azraq Desert, 400,000 ha), Kuwait, Laos, Lebanon, Mongolia, Saudi Arabia, South Korea, Syria, Vietnam, and Yemen.

As to the other areas omitted, it is difficult to obtain information on the situation prevailing in the Peoples Republic of China. In North Korea, there are several excellent reserves (Mt. Chilbo, Kwanmo-Bong, and others). It must be pointed out, too, that several Russian reserves should be added to this list since most of the largest of them are in fact located in Asia, for example, Petchora-Ilych, Sikhote-Alin, and Barguzin. Lake Baikal, harboring over 700 endemic species, became the center of a new national park in 1971.

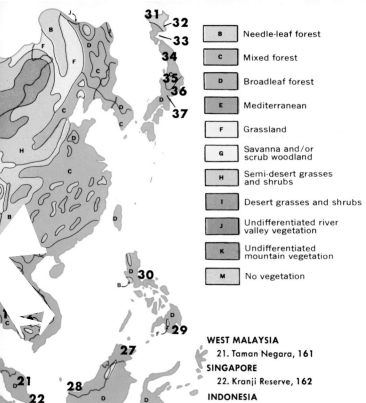

B	Needle-leaf forest
C	Mixed forest
D	Broadleaf forest
E	Mediterranean
F	Grassland
G	Savanna and/or scrub woodland
H	Semi-desert grasses and shrubs
I	Desert grasses and shrubs
J	Undifferentiated river valley vegetation
K	Undifferentiated mountain vegetation
M	No vegetation

Area: 770,900 km²   Population density: 44/km²

Seven national parks have already been created in Turkey (three are described below), and others are planned for the near future. All are administered by the National Park Department of the Ministry of Forestry, Ankara.

LAKE MANYAS NATIONAL PARK (created 1959)

A bird paradise throughout the year, Lake Manyas is located on one of the migratory flyways from Africa to Europe or vice versa, but the lake is also an important breeding and wintering area. The national park lies along the northeastern shores of the lake.

Location: south of the Sea of Marmara, 20 km S of Bandirma
Area: 52 ha
Climate: Mediterranean: temperate and mild
Protection: strict nature reserve; traffic controlled; many visitors
Access: by road
Accommodation: none within park
Of special interest: scientific research station; small museum, Kus Cenneti

TOPOGRAPHY A flat area flooded every winter and spring. The lake (not deeper than 10 m) is rich in suspended inorganic matter and calcium carbonate, and plankton.

FLORA Vegetation dominated by willow bushes and sallow trees. Vast reedbeds fringe the shoreline.

BIRDS The birdlife is spectacular. Willows, sallows, and reeds provide nesting habitats for about 2,000 pairs of cormorants, for pygmy cormorants, egrets, gray and purple herons, night herons, little bitterns, spoonbills, glossy ibises, and Dalmatian pelicans, while white pelicans pass on migration to and from the Danube Delta. Many other species breed there as well. The roosts are sometimes impressive when birds of 25 species gather in the same tree.

Waders, coots, and ducks are numerous, particularly during the winter and the migration periods.

Nesting cormorants in Lake Manyas National Park

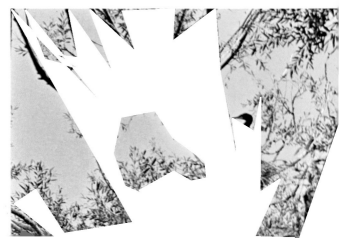

The peak of Ulu Dag in the middle of July—the most prominent feature of northwest Turkey

ULU DAG NATIONAL PARK (created 1961)

This national park offers beautiful views and a vertical series of forests and vegetation zones on Ulu Dag ("Mount Olympus"), rising like a great wall southeast of Bursa.

Location: northwestern Turkey, SE of Sea of Marmara, near Bursa
Area: 27,300 ha
Protection: theoretically total, though half still grazed; staff of 12
Access: by road from Bursa; teleferique
Activities: skiing, camping, picnicking, hiking
Accommodation: many hotels
Best visiting: July and August; winter months offer skiing

GEOLOGY Ulu Dag (2,543 m) is a product of great upheaval and twisting forces over long ages. It consists chiefly of granites and gneisses, overlaid with layers of crystalline schists. There is a wolframite mine near the summit. Once the massif was an island in the prehistoric sea.

TOPOGRAPHY The Ulu Dag massif is the most prominent land feature in NW Turkey, rising abruptly on N side and rolling back into a series of plateaus with several deeply incised river valleys.

CLIMATE Different from the rest of the Marmara region. Snow falls almost 64 days a year and stays 171 days. At 1,540 m above SL, maximum snow depth is 2.03 m, but at an elevation of 1,920 m, it is 7.5 meters. Even in summer the alpine lakes occasionally freeze. Summer climate is always excellent, temperate.

FLORA The forest is an excellent example of vertical zonation. Below 850 m: beech, chestnut, maple, and elm; 850–1,200 m: Austrian pine; upper levels are composed of pure stands of Bornmueller fir; tree line at 1,900 m: low junipers, tree heaths, alpine shrubs and grasses. Scattered oriental spruce, aspen, and hornbeam are found.

FAUNA Larger mammals are represented by jackal, red fox, wolf, brown bear, pine marten, and wild boar. Unfortunately, sheep, goats, and water buffaloes have been grazing the area for many years. The mountain also supports a large variety of birds.

KARATEPE (or ARSLANTAS) NATIONAL PARK (created 1958)

On the slopes of the Taurus Mountains this national park comprises a hilly country with forests and coppices, a rich animal life, and ancient ruins. The Hittites, one of the earliest civilizations, were dominant in Anatolia about 2000 B.C. Bilingual inscriptions found in the area provided the key to hieroglyphic Hittite. The area contains Hittite epitaphs, mosaics, and reliefs, as well as relief sculpture from Phoenician and Roman times.

Location: Taurus Mts. of Anatolia, southern Turkey
Area: 7,715 ha
Protection: theoretically total; about one third still grazed; many tourists
Accommodation: one motel in park; hotels at Adana (123 km SW)
Nearest village: Kadirli

GEOLOGY AND TOPOGRAPHY

Asia Minor is a high plateau, a part of the alpine configurations formed more than 50 million years ago during the Tertiary period. The Taurus range runs along the Mediterranean.

The national park is on a lower plateau (80–630 m), across which the Ceyhan River flows.

FLORA Forests predominate, consisting chiefly of aleppo pine, holly oak, kermes oak, sumac, cyctus, and madrone.

MAMMALS Animals include wild boar, roe deer, wolf, jackal, pine marten, badger, and beaver.

BIRDS Larger birds are eagles, falcons, hawks, buzzards, and partridges.

Archeological treasures from the Hittite period about 2000 B.C. with snow-capped Taurus Mountains in the background

Steep, eroded cliffs rise above the oasis Ein Gedi in the desert.

Area: 20,782 km^2 Population density: 136/km^2

Israel has one national park, Mount Carmel, and 17 other protected areas including 12 nature reserves (nine recently upgraded to N.P.'s), all under the Minister of Agriculture.

EIN GEDI NATURE RESERVE (created 1966)

A remarkable oasis in the desert, its eastern boundary the Dead Sea, is the setting of this reserve. In the south a steep cliff rises at the head of the southern bank of Nahal Arugot. The famous ruin of Masada is just north (18 km) of the reserve. Proposals have been made for a Judean Desert Nature Reserve of 3,000 hectares to include this reserve.

Location: in the desert, W of the Dead Sea
Area: 850 ha
Climate: hot, subtropical
Protection: total; staff of three units; one main road and tracks; 200,000 visitors annually
Accommodation: youth hostel
Of special interest: scientific investigation (field study center)

TOPOGRAPHY The existence of the oasis is chiefly due to a system of springs. Ein Gedi spring, arising on a hill between two rivers, is surrounded by trees and shrubs until it runs dry and disappears in the desert gravels.

The water of two wadis (river beds), Nahal David and Nahal Arugot, have cut deeply across the rock formations of the Judean Desert on their paths to the Dead Sea. Over a period of thousands of years the two rivers have built up a layer of sediments in the two wadis. Most of this land is now cultivated, but there is also natural vegetation.

FLORA The vegetation, providing a great contrast to the poverty of the surrounding deserts, consists of elements with East African or

129

Asiatic hot-dwelling species. Reeds grow along wadi banks, but trees, like common figs, willows, and poplars, are also found, as are maidenhair ferns and flowers. The true oasis region has a rich and varied vegetation including big Christi trees with orange-colored fruits, and Sodom apples. Curiously there is a single tree of *Maerua crassifolia* at Ein Gedi and only two or three species of its kind in all of Israel. Hundreds of various shrubs, flowers, and grasses blossom Feb.–April if there have been any rains. Peculiar to Ein Gedi is *Solanum incanum* with violet flowers. The only orchid is *Helleborine veratrifolia*.

MAMMALS For an area surrounded by deserts the fauna is remarkably rich: red fox, striped hyena, caracal, rock hyrax, Nubian ibex, and gazelle.

BIRDS The area has many birds. Although the most spectacular bird, the lammergeir, is very rare, it may be seen soaring widely over deserts and wadis.

Of special interest: the locally breeding wheatear, white-rumped black chat, the Palestine sunbird, Tristram's grackle, and sand partridge.

Other interesting birds include blackstart, Arabian babbler, desert bullfinch, house bunting, scotocerca, a sand martin, and others.

OTHER VERTEBRATES Of several species of small reptiles, geckos and an agama (*Agama sinaica*) are the most visible during the day.

A system of springs, rising at Ein Gedi, nourishes the oasis before its waters gradually fade out in the desert.

The Asiatic lion has been exterminated everywhere in Asia except in the Gir Wildlife Sanctuary, where a small population survives.

Area: 4,280,152 km^2 Population density: 164/km^2

The great population density of India and the necessity of utilizing as much as possible of the country's natural resources has in general not been favorable to the creation of large national parks or to checking the practice of lumbering in protected areas. India has 15 protected areas (seven described here).

Areas in India not covered in this book are Manas Wild Life Sanctuary (Assam), Hazaribagh N.P. (Bihar), Periyar W.L.S. (Kerala), Taroba N.P. (Mararashtra), Shivpuri N.P. (Madhya Pradesh), Bandhaughar N.P. (Madhya Pradesh), Sariska W.L.S. (Rajasthan), Jaisamand W.L.S. (Rajasthan), and Jalda W.L.S. (West Bengal).

The creation and administration of the national parks and reserves are under the respective states. At the central level is an Indian Board for Wild Life and the Forest Service.

GIR WILD LIFE SANCTUARY (created 1965), Gujarat
The Gir Forest Sanctuary is famous for being the only place where the Asiatic lion now exists. It is a race of the same species as the African lion and was once found in most parts

131

of western, northern, and central India. About 1880 it became extinct in India except for the Kathiawar Peninsula. Since 1884 the range of the Asiatic lion has shrunk to the Gir Forest alone, where the population in 1963 was estimated at 285 lions, but in 1968 it had decreased to 162.

Location: Kathiawar Peninsula of westernmost India, 63 km from Junagadh
Area: 1,295 sq. km.
Protection: protected but includes many villages, cultivations, domestic animals
Access: by rail, Sasan station, by road, Bombay-Sasan road
Nearest airport: Keshod (56 km from Sasan, 1½ hours flying time from Bombay)
Accommodation: two forest rest houses
Best visiting: January—May

CLIMATE Annual rainfall of this lowland area: about 635 mm in monsoon months July—October. Temperatures: April—July (80°—105°F); Dec.—Feb. (55°—85°F).

FLORA A mosaic of teak woodlands and open thorn scrub among light stands of grass. "Flame of the forest" trees are in full scarlet bloom Jan.—Feb.

MAMMALS In addition to the Asiatic lion, the reserve contains three other powerful predators—the striped hyena, leopard, and sloth-bear. Besides the enormous number of domestic livestock (buffaloes, cattle, sheep, and goats) there are several species of wild herbivores, on which the lions prefer to prey: the huge nilgai, four-horned antelope, Indian gazelle (chinkara), sambar, spotted deer, and wild boar (the lion's favorite food in Gir).

BIRDS In addition to the vultures and crows of various species due to the human settlement, there are also tinier birds, such as sunbirds and other nectar-feeders. Peafowl are numerous, as they are in all jungles in India.

The spotted deer, also called axis deer or chital, is one of the commoner larger mammals in southern Asia.

The tiger has decreased enormously in India and elsewhere in Asia during the last decades through persecution and changing habitat.

CORBETT NATIONAL PARK (created 1935), Uttar Pradesh

Probably the best place in India for seeing tigers. This is the first and principal nature reserve of India (formerly named Hailey National Park), now named as a tribute to the famous Jim Corbett whose writings have done so much to promote the preservation of the Indian fauna. For further information, apply to Chief Wild Life Warden, Uttar Pradesh, Wazir Hasan Rd., Lucknow.

Location: lower slopes of Himalayas and plains, 244 km NE of New Delhi
Area: 52,600 ha
Protection: total (in theory); staff of 26; eight watch towers; two riding elephants of Dhikala; guides; roads
Access: by road from New Delhi; by rail to Ramnagar (47 km from park), where Jeep is available
Accommodation: forest rest house and tourist hut at Dhikala; many other rest houses at Sulta, Sarapduli, and Boxar
Best visiting: December—March

TOPOGRAPHY The foothills of the Himalayas and lowlands of the Indo-Gangetic plain give the park varied altitude (460—915 m). Precipitous gorges with great slabs of bare sandstone and vertical rock strata alternate with broad, flat valleys (duns) of old alluvial terraces. There are also cascading rivers, dark unfathomed forest pools, sun-sparkling swamps, open plains.

Main watercourse: the Ramganga River, which winds through the famous Patli Dun, a valley flanked by low hills.

CLIMATE The area is swept by monsoon winds with rains and moisture June—Oct., when no hu-

133

man beings remain in the reserve, at that time completely cut off from the rest of the world. Roads do not usually open until mid-December. Hottest months: April—Sept. (70°–95°F); coldest: Dec.—Jan. (30°–35°F).

FLORA Chief vegetation is deciduous jungle; sal trees are everywhere, in April their new leaves a mass of light green and yellow gold.

Ramganga R. is bordered by shisham trees and bauhinias or orchid trees with pink or mauve flowers in April, by kusum trees with leaves of bright pale mahogany, and by spectacular flame-of-the-forest trees with gorgeous scarlet flowers in bloom from mid-February until the end of March. Tall semal trees display crimson blossoms.

In the moister thickets: draperies of creepers and ferns and flourishing orchids.

MAMMALS Animals abundant, most of them representing the sub-Himalayan fauna. The Indian elephant, sambar, spotted deer (chital), hog deer, muntjac, goral, and wild boar are the grazers and browsers preyed upon by the tiger, the most important species of the park.

Other mammals: leopard, jungle cat, striped hyena, jackal, wild dog (dhole), sloth-bear, Himalayan black bear, otter, honey badger (ratel), yellow-throated marten, mongoose, langur, rhesus monkey, porcupine, flying squirrel, and palm squirrel (two species). Occasionally a serow wanders down from the higher elevations of the Himalayas.

BIRDS A few of the many that can be observed: red junglefowl, black partridge, flycatchers, drongos, babblers, bulbuls, orioles, chloropsis, doves, kingfishers, hornbills, herons, kites, and eagles of various species.

OTHER VERTEBRATES Reptiles include two crocodiles, the gavial and the marsh crocodile, called mugger in India. The Indian python is the largest snake; the mahseer and goonch are best-known fishes.

Sal forest predominates in many parts of Corbett National Park.

The swamp deer in the Kanha National Park belongs to a race that does not occur elsewhere.

KANHA NATIONAL PARK (created 1935), Madhya Pradesh

One of the best national parks in India for easy views of hoofed animals and scenic vistas. Kanha National Park is chiefly a forest, but the many open woodlands and grassy plains provide opportunities to see the larger mammals. This national park covers the Upper Banjar Valley and was formerly called the Banjar Valley Reserve. Information about the park is obtainable from the Divisional Forest Officer, West Mandla Div., Mandla, Madhya Pradesh.

Location: central highlands of India, 55 km SE of Mandla
Area: 31,598 ha
Protection: total; six guards; many roads; watch towers and observation posts; riding elephants available
Access: by road from Jubbulpore, 96 km to the north, or from Nagpur 320 km to the south
Accommodation: rest houses at Kanha and at Kisli
Best visiting: March—May

TOPOGRAPHY The park lies within the undulating hills of the Satpura range, the highlands separating the Deccan plateau and the Indo-Gangetic plain. Elevation varies: 533 m in NW to 840 m in

Scene in the Kanha N.P.

The blackbuck, once one of India's most characteristic mammals, still occurs in the Kanha National Park.

SE. Grassy valleys (maidans) are interspersed with scattered wooded belts or islands. Many rivers and springs and some minor lakes.

CLIMATE Rainy season: July—Oct. (park closed Aug.—Oct.). Annual rainfall: 1,525 millimeters. Hottest months: May—July (75°—105°F); coldest: December—January (30°—70°F).

FLORA Forests mostly of the hardwood sal tree, succeeded at higher altitudes by featherlike leaves of bamboo. The famous flame-of-the-forest tree is seen here and there.

MAMMALS Hoofed animals are abundant: the gaur, spotted deer (chital), swamp deer (barasingha), sambar, muntjac, mouse deer (chevrotain), blackbuck, four-horned antelope, nilgai, and India gazelle.

Carnivores include tiger, leopard, wild dog (dhole), jackal, Bengal fox, striped hyena, and sloth-bear. The tiger is relatively common, but the leopard and the wild dog are rare. The reserve is famous for its swamp deer, a species peculiar to India and Nepal. Though elsewhere living in swampy areas, it frequents the monthly dry maidans of the Kanha National Park, where it can be seen in herds of 20—45 animals.

BIRDS A rich and varied birdlife with more than 90 species recorded includes junglefowl, peafowl, quail, sand grouse, green pigeon, blue rock pigeon, emerald dove, snipe, various ducks such as teal (Anas crecca) and the ruddy sheldrake.

OTHER VERTEBRATES Indian pythons occur in this national park.

BANDIPUR WILD LIFE SANCTUARY (created 1941), Mysore, and **MUDUMALAI WILD LIFE SANCTUARY** (created 1940), Madras

These contiguous reserves on the eastern slopes of the Western Ghats lie in different states, separated by the Moyar River, and form an ecological unit at the foot of the Nilgiri Hills. Both have a fauna typical of southern India. Bandipur is probably the best sanctuary in India for observing the gaur, a wonderful wild ox, largest of all bovines and more magnificent than the European and American bisons. Bandipur is rewarding to visit throughout the year; it is less advantageous to visit Mudumalai during July–September.

Information about the Bandipur reserve obtainable from Divisional Forest Officer, Mysore City, about the Mudumalai reserve from State Wild Life Officer, 136 Peters Road, Madras 14.

Location: southern India
Bandipur Area: 5,698 ha
Protection: "strict" but heavy grazing by livestock; staff of 40; watching towers and elephant rides both areas

Access: by Mysore-Cotacamund rd. (Mysore, 130 km; nearest airport: Bangalore, 160 km)
Accommodation: within park
Best visiting both areas: April–May

Gaurs, largest of all wild cattle, inhabit forests and glades. The species is mainly nocturnal.

The Nilgiri tahr is a mountain animal living at elevations of about 1,300 to 2,000 m in the Western Ghats.

Mudumalai Area: 32,116 ha
Protection: "total" but grazing by cattle; staff of 31
Accommodation: tourist lodge

CLIMATE Semiarid because Western Ghats and adjoining hill ranges too high to allow eastward passage of the southwest monsoon with its rains and moisture. Rainy season: June—Oct.: Bandipur, 890 mm, Mudumalai, 1,422 millimeters. Hottest months: April—June (70°—95°F); coldest: December—January (55°—70°F).

FLORA Deciduous forests, chiefly stunted teak, bamboo, sandalwood, and drought-resisting plants. At beginning of year, Bandipur jungle undergrowth is rather thin, favoring observation of a wealth of animals.

MAMMALS The two sanctuaries contain a wealth of animals. Predators: tiger, leopard, sloth-bear, civet cat, ruddy mongoose, wild dog (dhole), and striped hyena.

Other mammals: muntjac, sambar, spotted deer (chital), mouse deer (chevrotain), gaur, Indian elephant, four-horned antelope, Nilgiri tahr, wild boar, gray langur, bonnet macaque, Malabar squirrel, and porcupine.

BIRDS A great variety of birds includes red spurfowl, several species of quail and partridge, gray junglefowl, peafowl, green pigeon, wood pigeon, Malabar trogon, black-headed oriole, and Malabar gray hornbill, to list just a few.

KAZIRANGA NATIONAL PARK (created 1908), Assam

This park is perhaps India's most interesting game reserve, chiefly as a refuge for the great Indian rhinoceros, but there are also other mammals to be seen in these vast swamp lands. From the park the snows of the eastern Himalayas, 176 km away, can be seen on clear days in October. Information about the park may be obtained from the Divisional Forest Officer, Sibsagar Division, Jorhat P.O., Assam.

Location: Sibsagar District, Assam, S of Brahmaputra River
Area: 42,994 ha
Protection: total; staff of 122 units; watch towers; wildlife observed from elephant back
Access: between two airports: Gauhati (225 km west), Jorhat (88 km east); motor transport available
Accommodation: fully equipped tourist lodge, Kaziranga; also two rest houses (no food) at Baguri and Arimora
Best visiting: December—March

TOPOGRAPHY The Brahmaputra R. has created a wide valley between the Himalayas and the mt. ranges in the S and E. On its southern bank the sanctuary covers an area of swamps in lowland country about 76 m above sea level.

CLIMATE Rainy season coincides with hot weather; temps. between 65° and 95°F. Coolest months Dec.–Jan., have 45°–75°F.

FLORA Vegetation dominated by tall, dense "elephant grass," chiefly *Phragmites karna* but also *Saccharum* spp. This "grass" can attain 6 m, hence the need for elephant-back rides to observe animals over the tops. Many pools are thickly covered with water hyacinths, introduced from S. America 50 years ago as an ornamental plant. Gallery forests of acacias like "koroi" (*Albizzia procera*) and the Indian silk-cotton tree surround the Brahmaputra and patch the swamp and valley slopes.

MAMMALS Elephant-back excursions usually take place in early morning, except in Dec.–Jan. when mornings are misty and Indian rhinos are visited in the afternoon. Rhinos may be seen grazing

A long stretch of marsh with two Indian rhinoceroses in Kaziranga N. P.

Indian rhinoceros

or wallowing in the mud; they are unafraid and quite accustomed to tame elephants.

Still widely distributed in the 19th century, by 1900 there were only about a dozen rhinos left in Kaziranga. By 1971 with protection this number had grown to 400—more than half of the world population. Cattle egrets associated with the Indian rhinos make them visible at a long distance.

Occasionally big herds of wild Indian elephants (349 in 1966) can be seen; the herds of the more sedentary wild water buffalo (about 550) love the tall grass jungle and reed brake where they graze, roll in the mud, or rest deep in the pools.

Swamp deer and hog deer are often seen in herds of ten or 15. Wild boar are common; also sambar and muntjac (keeping to wooded areas). Gaur occurs.

Sloth-bear, Himalayan black bear, tiger, and leopard are rather rare; luck is needed to see them. Other carnivores are jungle cat, large Indian civet, wild dog, jackal, mongoose, otter, pangolin, porcupine, and hog-badger. Kaziranga is the last stronghold of the nearly exterminated pygmy hog (*Sus salvanius*).

Monkeys include rhesus and common langur.

BIRDS occur in great variety. One of the most interesting nesting birds is the Pallas' fishing eagle. Numerous waterfowl, herons, and egrets are dispersed in pools and marshes. Also the adjutant stork and the smaller adjutant stork, the black-necked stork, the Indian darter, and a large breeding colony of the gray pelican. Other birds: the black bittern, the lesser florican and black partridge.

OTHER VERTEBRATES Reptiles include water monitor, Indian python, common cobra, and king cobra.

Indian elephant

Area: 141,341 km²   Population density: 65/km²

Nepal created the Kang Mahandra National Park in 1959 with which the Chitawan Rhinoceros Sanctuary, described below, is contiguous. Another smaller sanctuary in the Kanchanpur District is the Sukla Phanta nature reserve (12,500 ha). These sanctuaries are administered by the Forest Dept.

CHITAWAN NATIONAL PARK (created 1964, upgraded to national park, 1971), Chitawan District

Extensive areas of seasonal swamps, which are the habitats of the great Indian rhinoceros. From these swamps, found along the Rapti and Reu rivers, on clear winter days one can see a magnificent panorama of forested hills with the Himalayan peaks Annapurna and others on the horizon.

Location: at southern base of Himalayan foothills, 80 km SW of Katmandu
Area: about 76,000 ha
Protection: "total" but at least 50,000 people live, cultivate, and graze cattle within the sanctuary; staff of 200
Nearest town: Hitdura

GEOLOGY The reserve is chiefly on moist alluvial land, formed by the sedimentation of rivers spreading out a few miles from the base of the Himalayas.

TOPOGRAPHY The area lies between the Churia Hills and the steep hills of the Mahabharat range, that is, inside the foothills of the Himalayas. A number of transverse valleys (duns) break and dissect the hills. The Rapti Valley is a flat plateau (alt.: 275—300 m). This area and the Reu Valley vary from low-lying river beds to undulating plains below the hills.

The range of the Indian rhinoceros, now existing in nature reserves, has been greatly reduced during the last centuries.

CLIMATE Cold weather months: Nov.–April, but hot weather can start as early as March; rainy season: June–Sept. (1,650–1,780 mm), when riverine tracts are flooded.

FLORA Vegetation consists of tall swamp grass (*Saccharum*), which grows up to 6 meters. Some river banks have dense thickets of shisham, simul, khair, and *Bauhinia*. On smaller hills are extensive forests of sal with a grassy undergrowth. The vegetation of the savanna varies with the flood level—reeds and grasses, such as plume grass, and alang alang.

MAMMALS The protagonist of the sanctuary is the great Indian rhinoceros, numbering some 60 individuals. When the swampy areas are flooded, the rhinos move to the drier scrub jungle.

Four species of deer occur: muntjac, sambar, spotted deer, and hog deer. Other ungulates are nilgai, gaur, and wild boar (very common here). Indian elephants visit the reserve coming from the surrounding dense forests. The largest predators are tiger, leopard, striped hyena, and sloth-bear. In the deeper water of the Marayni River (of which the Rapti and Reu are tributaries) the Gangetic dolphin may be seen swimming.

BIRDS The rich birdlife includes water birds like egrets, herons, black-necked stork, adjutant stork, black ibis, pintail, ruddy sheldrake, and other ducks.

Several species of eagles, hawks, and vultures occur, as well as peafowl, junglefowl, black partridge, and many others.

OTHER VERTEBRATES Both the gavial and the marsh crocodile are to be found in the Rapti River.

Wild boars are numerous in the Chitawan Rhinoceros Sanctuary.

Sundarbans Game Sanctuary in the delta of the Ganges is a labyrinth of rivulets and river arms intersected by forest islands.

(former East Pakistan)

Area: 21,279 km^2

Two national parks in former East Pakistan, now Bangladesh, were fully protected, Chittagong Hill Tracts, described below, and Madhupur, also called Mymensingh N.P. (10,360 ha). Sundarbans Game Sanctuary in former East Pakistan was omitted from the UN List but is briefly described here.

The UN List omits three other areas in Pakistan (former West Pakistan) because they are all actively exploited: Changa-Manga N.P. (lumbering), Shogran N.P. (cultivation), and Ayub N.P. (too small, 230 ha).

SUNDARBANS GAME SANCTUARY, Bangladesh

This sanctuary is included here because of its famous tiger inhabitant. It is not included in the UN List because the area is intensively exploited, with large numbers of people engaging in lumbering, hunting, fishing, and honey collection throughout the year. It was planned to permit all activities except for hunting and shooting. Guided tours and other facilities were projected for the near future.

143

The marsh crocodile is one of the many animals continuously depleted in Asia because its skin is commercially valuable.

Location: in the Ganges Delta, at the Bay of Bengal
Area: about 27,000 ha
Tourism: not yet organized

GEOLOGY, TOPOGRAPHY, AND CLIMATE A level tidal plain in the enormous delta, the entire area is a network of rivers and rivulets but with dense forests. The plain was formed by sediments from the Ganges though it is located west of the main arms of the river. The area is without even a single hill. The climate is tropical.

FLORA This mosaic of land and waterways is covered by a thick natural forest that includes such species as keora, cawa, golpatta, sundri, and ferns.

MAMMALS The abundance of animals includes numerous spotted deer (chital). But the area is most notable because it is the home of the famous Royal Bengal tiger, which, however is not subspecifically distinct from the race occurring elsewhere in India, Pakistan, and the surrounding regions. It is called "Bengal tiger" simply because the scientific description of the tiger was based on a specimen from Bengal.

Brown kingfisher

Brahminy kite

CHITTAGONG HILL TRACTS NATIONAL PARK (created 1927), Bangladesh

This national park is a portion of a vast forest reserve. The most prominent member of its fauna is the tiger, who preys on deer; jungle fowl the most conspicuous of many birds. The Karnfuli River runs from east to west, cutting deep gorges across the north–south strike of minor hills. Plains between hills contain many crescent-shaped depressions with marshes (*dhepas*). The tropical climate of this low-lying area favors dense tree bush and creeper jungles, with such trees as gamar, tun, rain tree, teak, and bamboo.

Location: southeastern Bangladesh, on Assam and Burma borders
Area: 25,900 ha
Visiting: tourism not yet organized but camping grounds, tourist homes, guided tours have all been projected; it is difficult to find out if projects have been carried into effect.

Marshes and lakes fill the lower valleys of the Chittagong Hill Tracts N. P.

Area: 65,863 km^2 Population density: 187/km^2

Ceylon effectively protects seven areas including the three national parks described below and four strict nature reserves where tourism is forbidden: Wasgomuwa, 28,000 ha, Yala, 27,500 ha, Ritigala, 1,450 ha, and Hakgala, 1,100 ha. All of these areas are administered by the Department of Wildlife, Colombo.

WILPATTU NATIONAL PARK (created 1937)
Ceylon's largest national park, a vast area entirely encircled by sanctuaries. Wild animals and abundant birdlife are the chief attractions for naturalists; for archaeologists: the ancient cave temples, ruined dagobas, and stone columns of the Buddhist civilizations of the Sinhalese, from pre-Christian to medieval times. A royal edict of the 12th century declared that no animal should be killed "within a radius of seven gavu from the City of Anuradhapura," a decree including not only mammals but also birds and fish.

The spotted deer often occur in herds that are larger than those of any other deer in Asia.

Wild water buffaloes are impressive animals, much larger and with wider horns than their domestic relatives.

Location: western Ceylon, on Indian Ocean
Area: 108,780 ha
Protection: total; staff of 30; movement on foot forbidden; Jeeps for hire; 320 km of roads
Access: by Puttalam-Anuradhapura road (182 km from Colombo)
Best visiting: July, August, September

TOPOGRAPHY A flat and sandy area with some 42 shallow lakes (*villu* in Tamil and *wila* in Sinhalese), holding the monsoon rains. The eastern section has many streams and richer vegetation, with woods, forests, and meadows.

CLIMATE Both wet and dry season visits have their own advantages and disadvantages and give much to the visitor. Wilpattu climate dry, much like that of Gal Oya and Ruhunu (see below).

FLORA Forests are in no way primeval, due to the area's ancient human history. Secondary growths, constantly exploited, should be more precisely termed "tertiary" or "quaternary" growths. Richness of wild flowers in this parkland turns the national park into a great flower garden January—March.

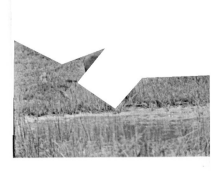

Wild boar

147

Common crow

MAMMALS Spotted deer (chital) in herds up to 200 are the most common larger mammals. Wild boars frequently seen, also water buffaloes bathing in the mud. Sambar and Indian elephants are other impressive mammals. Woodlands contain porcupine and monkeys of various species. Among the carnivores: sloth-bear, jackal, leopard, and jungle cat.

BIRDS Kingfishers (three species), bee-eaters, white ibis, spoonbill, storks (four species), herons and egrets (seven species), waders and ducks, parrots, sunbirds, birds of prey, owls, junglefowl, peafowl, and hornbills.

OTHER VERTEBRATES The marsh crocodile can be observed; some pools are teeming with baby crocodiles.

Painted storks are to be found mainly in the dry lowlands of Ceylon.

Wild Indian peafowl running over a glade in Ceylon, where the species is common

GAL OYA NATIONAL PARK (created 1954)

Gal Oya is situated in a lake region partly serving as a water storage reservoir and surrounded by jungle forests. Birdlife is rich and diversified. Excursions can be made by launch on the large expanses of water.

Location: eastern Ceylon
Area: 25,000 ha
Protection: total; three sanctuaries form a buffer zone; guides available; tracks for Jeeps
Accommodation: one bungalow
Best visiting: May–September

TOPOGRAPHY The Gal Oya River drains the lakes, of which Senanayake Samudra is the largest in Ceylon. Some gneissy hills occur and a low mountain range.

CLIMATE Dry. Little or no rain during southwest monsoon period (May–Sept.) when the great mt. massif in south central Ceylon catches the moisture and precipitation of the oceanic winds. Most rainfall is Nov.–February.

FLORA The terrestrial habitats around the lakes are wooded savannas with grass and scattered trees. There is also a dry evergreen forest of the jungle type.

MAMMALS Among the mammals of this national park are Indian elephant, leopard, jackal, small civet, mongoose, otter, purple-faced langur, slender loris, Indian pangolin, Indian porcupine, water buffalo, sambar, spotted deer (chital), mouse deer (chevrotain), and muntjac.

BIRDS The rich avian fauna includes paradise flycatcher, black-headed oriole, green bee-eater, and stork-billed kingfisher.

Others are Ceylon gray hornbill, Malabar pied hornbill, rose-winged parakeet, serpent eagle, Ceylon hawk eagle, gray-headed fishing eagle, brahminy kite, Indian peafowl, and Ceylon junglefowl.

OTHER VERTEBRATES Reptiles include python, rat snake, cobra, swamp crocodile, and monitor lizard.

RUHUNU NATIONAL PARK (created 1937, enlarged 1950)

The national park, known everywhere as "Yala" because of the contiguous Yala protective zones, offers exciting scenes of wildlife with typical jungle setting where almost all the larger mammals of Ceylon may be seen. (The nucleus of this nature reserve has been protected since 1899, one of the oldest conservation areas in the world.) The park contains ruins from the 2nd century B.C. when 10,000 monks lived in the numerous caves of the area. On a stupendous rock at Situlpahuwa is a restored ancient dagoba.

Location: SE corner of Ceylon, facing the sea
Area: 23,000 ha
Protection: total; 30 guards; travel in park authorized only if by Jeep with Wild Life Dept. guide
Access: by car from Colombo (290 km); proposed airfield at Wirawila (22 km from park)
Accommodation: three bungalows; visitors provide own food and linen
Best visiting: December—May

GEOLOGY The island of Ceylon, a detached portion of the peninsula of southern India, consists chiefly of Cambrian gneisses, granites, and quartzites.

TOPOGRAPHY The few rocky hills arising at seashore and in the interior are surrounded by plains, scrub jungle, and high forest. Shores are rocky, pebbly, and sandy. There are numerous seascapes and brackish lagoons, rivers and their deltas, freshwater pools, and water holes.

Two rivers, the Menikganga and the Kumbkkan oya, still carry water during the dry season (by August most lakes and water holes are dry) and attract high numbers of mammals and birds from the rest of the reserve. Elephants migrate out of the park area during the dry season.

CLIMATE The park is in the dry zone of Ceylon and exposed annually to drought. No rain: July—

Sandy and rocky shores, grassy meadows and bushes form the coast of the Ruhunu National Park on the Indian Ocean.

The Ceylon elephant is considered to be a subspecies of the Indian elephant, but in Ceylon many males do not have tusks.

Sept. The rainy season (Oct.–April) revives area, and this is therefore most beautiful period: local birds breed and avian migrants arrive from northern Asia and Europe.

FLORA Sandy scrub and thorn; jungle intersected with grassland, acacia woods; some local high forests along the Menikganga River. Many swampy waterholes carry aquatic grasses and wild rice.

MAMMALS Animals are the main attraction: the rare and endemic race of Ceylon elephant still has a refuge here; large herds of graceful spotted deer move over plains and jungles; sambar fairly numerous, also wild boar; impressive water buffaloes occur but are shy and mostly found in interior jungle marshes. Most buffaloes in the national park are feral animals, not so heavy as the pure wild ones; the sloth-bear and leopard are the largest predators, the langur the most often observed monkey. Hares are common.

The leopard has strongholds in the jungles of Ceylon's national parks.

BIRDS A very rich and varied bird fauna here: the author's list of birds observed at Ruhunu comprises 119 species. Peafowl plentiful and their display wonderful to watch in mating season; another ornithological highlight: junglefowl with their intensive colors.

Near the Buttuwa bungalow, gray pelicans, Indian darters, and

Black-winged stilt

other waterfowl frequent the pools. In late October newly arrived Malay bitterns visit these pools in early mornings. Other examples of Ruhunu birds: tiny flowerpeckers, the Ceylon finch lark, black-winged stilt, Ceylon brown baza, Ceylon hawk eagle, and pygmy woodpecker.

Also: hornbills, flycatchers, orioles, babblers, sunbirds, barbets, bee-eaters, kingfishers, terns, storks, and herons.

OTHER VERTEBRATES The saltwater crocodile and the mugger or marsh crocodile occur, and the monitor lizard is extremely common.

The saltwater crocodile, now rare in south Asia, in Ruhunu N.P.

Area: 680,651 km^2 Population density: 30/km^2

Of Burma's 12 reserves, Pidaung Game Sanctuary deserves mention as the largest and most interesting; the others, also based on the country's game rules of 1927, seem to have insufficient supervisory staff, and many of them probably deteriorated under war conditions and later suffered from illicit hunting and lumbering.

PIDAUNG GAME SANCTUARY (created 1927)

Situated in the lowlands of northern Burma, this game reserve is still relatively rich in animals though many of the large mammals were slaughtered during World War II. The area covers several ranges of low rounded hills.

Myitkyina, capital of the Kachin state, is only a few miles to the east and accessible by air, rail, and road from Mandalay and Rangoon (965 km). Tea cultivation prevails in the south of the reserve.

Several platforms (*machans*) are placed in big trees on the edge of the forest giving good views of waterholes, salt licks, and clearings, where animals frequently come into the open.

Location: northern Burma, W of Irrawaddy R.
Area: 72,500 ha
Protection: staff of 12; observation towers
Accommodation: at Myitkyina, and at Kasung Hka near the park; forest house at Pidaung
Best visiting: February–April

TOPOGRAPHY Mosaic pattern of grassy plains *(Iwins)* surrounded by forests and scrub jungle *(indaing)*. Some plains contain saline earth, and these salt licks are constantly frequented by mammals, as are waterholes and swamps around the Pidaung River.

CLIMATE Visits by car are out of the question in rainy season (May–Oct.), all roads becoming rivers of mud. Visitors may reach the rest house in rainy season by rail but will be cut off from the northern section by an unfordable Pidaung River. Impractical to drive into reserve before late January.

FLORA Scrub forests, chiefly gurjun oil trees. The evergreen forests of the hills are not of a pure rain forest type but do display examples of primeval beauty in giant figs and teaks.

Orchids grow on trunks and branches overhanging the Pidaung River.

MAMMALS The sanctuary was primarily constituted for the following species: sambar, hog deer, muntjac, gaur, banteng, wild boar, Indian elephant, tiger, leopard, Asiatic black bear, and the Asiatic wild dog, and these are all still present.

Animals most numerous and most readily observed in forests and open plains and meadows are the

153

Alexander's ring-necked parakeet

gaur, elephant, and the sambar, but none of these species exceeds 100 individuals.

In the forest are found the Phayre leaf monkey, the Chindwin langur, the Burmese pig-tailed macaque, rhesus monkey, and hoolock gibbons with their melodious chorus, a characteristic sound of these jungles.

Other forest dwellers are the Oriental civet and the yellow-throated marten.

BIRDS Of great interest are Kilij pheasant, Chinese francolin, partridges of several species, painted quail, junglefowl, green peafowl, green pigeons of at least four species, pied hornbill, black-necked stork, white-winged wood duck, and many waders and passerines.

The swamp at Nanaw Maung is particularly favorable to waterfowl.

The sambar is Ceylon's largest deer. Its lack of spots easily distinguishes it from the spotted deer.

Deciduous forests with bamboos in flower in the Khao Yai N.P.

THAILAND

Area: 520,385 km^2 Population density: 65/km^2

There are nine protected areas in Thailand including four national parks (of which three are described below). These areas are administered by the Royal Forest Department, Bangkok, where further information may be obtained.

KHAO YAI NATIONAL PARK (created 1962)

A mountainous region with vast forests, many species of large mammals, and a very rich birdlife. Originally uninhabited, this area was settled by farmers who abandoned it about half a century ago; later, outlaws made it their hideout, hunting game and burning parts of the forest. Fortunately this beautiful territory is now protected, and there is still a wealth of animals.

Location: about 200 km NE of Bangkok
Area: 216,875 ha
Protection: total; staff of 60 units; 40 km of trails; watch tower
Access: by asphalt road branching off "Friendship Highway"
Accommodation: bungalows, motels, tourist cottages; camping; golf course
Best visiting: November to May

GEOLOGY AND TOPOGRAPHY
Khao Yai is a rolling plateau with several sandstone ranges of which the massifs of Khao Laem (1,328 m) and Khao Khieo are the most important and form a watershed, headwaters of many rivers. There

155

Rain forest in Khao Yai N.P.

are waterfalls, caves, and a network of forest-clothed valleys.

CLIMATE The heat of the tropical climate is reduced by the area's elevation. Hottest months: April—May. Monsoon rains: July—October.

FLORA The rain forest of Khao Yai is a drier type than those in southern Malaysia and in Indonesia. Lower levels are chiefly mixed deciduous forest with many bamboos; at 600—1,200 m is a dense forest of gurjun oil, and many other trees, the branches ornamented by orchids. Above this zone on the mountain ridge is a low dense forest of oak and coniferous trees.

The previously cleared lands are colonized by alang alang grass.

MAMMALS Many species of large mammals are to be found in abundance. Their tracks are observed almost everywhere along streams and in muddy soil: muntjac, mouse deer, sambar, hog deer, banteng, gaur, wild boar, Indian elephant, tiger, and leopard. Strangely enough the tiger is more numerous than the leopard in Khao Yai. Civet cat, mongoose, porcupine, white-banded gibbon, and langur, among others, also occur in the N.P.

BIRDS The birdlife is very rich (175 species lately reported by ornithologists). Many species of hornbill can be found in the national park throughout the year, including pied hornbill and great hornbill. Some other common species are silver pheasant, Indian lorikeet, red-billed blue magpie, emerald dove, numerous woodpeckers, sunbirds, crested serpent eagle, green-legged hill partridge, red junglefowl; at higher altitudes: scarlet minivet and nuthatches. Song thrushes and shama are very common but more heard than seen.

OTHER VERTEBRATES The common cobra, king cobra, and tree snakes are common but usually overlooked.

Crested serpent eagle

A mountain landscape in Tung Slang Luang National Park

TUNG SLANG LUANG NATIONAL PARK (created 1963)

This national park extends over a plateau, mountains, and valleys with partly virgin vegetation and rich animal life.

Location: northern Thailand, 400 km from Bangkok
Area: 128,000 ha
Climate: tropical; monsoon rains: July–October
Protection: total; staff of 65
Access: by rail and by road (Friendship Highway between Phitsanulok and Lomsak)
Accommodation: guest house, cabins; hotels: available at Phitsanulok (64 km)

GEOLOGY AND TOPOGRAPHY

The park lies on an extension of the Khorat Plateau, consisting chiefly of sandstone in flat or gently rolling tables of mesas (highest is 1,200 m), separated from each other vertically by steep cliff walls. There are extensive savannas and forests, rivers and waterfalls.

FLORA Forests present a series of zones. Tracts of virgin high forest include large trees: gurjun, *Vatica*, merawan, shorea, evergreen chinkapin, pharsa, and mango. Other expanses have been occupied by pines and oaks. In cleared areas a jungle of *Eupatorium odoratum* and other species have replaced the high forest.

Many of the rocks have been colonized by orchids, rhododendrons, and *Agapetes saxicola*.

MAMMALS The higher mammals are represented by tiger, leopard, sambar, gaur, wild boar, gibbon, and many rodents.

BIRDS A large number of species occur in the park area. At a higher altitude of about 1,000 m silver pheasant and the beautiful Burmese gray peacock pheasant are very common; the Siamese fireback is confined to a lower level around 680 meters.

Other species that may be commonly observed by visitors: brown-breasted partridge, red junglefowl, doves, hanging parrot, owls, trogons, and barbets.

The rare red-billed ground cuckoo has been reported from this park.

157

PU KRADEUNG NATIONAL PARK (created 1962)

A unique mountainous landscape of subtropical pine forest and extensive meadows, harboring interesting mammals and birds.

Location: Loey Province, NE Thailand, 600 km from Bangkok
Area: 34,813 ha
Climate: for the tropics, very cool
Protection: total; staff of 20
Access: by road
Accommodation: guest house, cabins

GEOLOGY AND TOPOGRAPHY

The park is part of a peneplain, including a flat-topped sandstone plateau (elevation: 1,350 m) with precipitous walls. Topography very variable: there are rolling plains, rock outcrops, caves, streams, waterfalls, and creeks. Open grasslands are interspersed with forests.

FLORA Pines predominate: merkus pine at lower levels and khasia pine higher up. Others are birch, maple, oak, *Phyllotaxus*, horn-beams, chinkapins, and others. Rhododendrons in large numbers cover the meadows; orchids and other flowers abound.

FAUNA Inhabitants of the park include leopard, tiger, muntjac, sambar, and wild boar.

BIRDS More than 150 species have been observed. Large birds are rare. The common species that can be found on the plateau are francolin, brown-breasted hill partridge, mountain imperial eagle, trogons, and long-tailed broadbill. Silver pheasant is a rare resident of the park.

OTHER VERTEBRATES Among the reptiles the rare big-headed turtle must be mentioned.

Subtropical pines and other trees border a grassy meadow in Pu Kradeung National Park.

Angkor Wat (12th century), Angkor National Park

CAMBODIA

Area: 181,739 km^2 Population density: 38/km^2

Angkor National Park is the only effectively protected area in Cambodia, but several projects have been in the process of creation. Some game reserves, the largest being Koulen Promtep (1,460,000 ha), may be upgraded to the status of national parks or equivalent reserves.

ANGKOR NATIONAL PARK (created 1925)

Visitors are chiefly attracted by the world-famous archaeological environment and the magnificent ruins of Angkor, the capital of the Khmer civilization that flourished for 600 years before 1431, when the city was sacked by invading Thais. Abandoned and forgotten, it was reconquered by the dense forest until a French naturalist discovered the sleeping ruins in 1860. The national park protects the ruins and the living nature around them. A great effort was started to retimber and to reintroduce game, destroyed by the inhabitants over many years.

The Ministry of Tourism, Phnom Penh, directs the SOKHAR (Societé Khmère des Auberges Royales). Siem Reap, provincial capital near Angkor, is an hour's flight from Phnom Penh and usually linked by air from Bangkok and Saigon.

Location: 320 km NW of Phnom Penh
Area: 10,717 ha
Protection: 45 guards, who chiefly supervise the monuments
Accommodation: Auberge Royale des Temples, near Angkor Wat; also hotels in Siem Reap

HISTORY

At its peak the Khmer civilization included not only Cambodia but also much of present-day Thailand, Laos, Vietnam, and even part of the Malay Peninsula.

The ruins at Angkor are spread over an immense area, set in a network of ancient canals. The main tourist attractions are the Angkor Wat (dating from the 12th century) with its enormous moat-surrounded square and half-mile-long frieze depicting scenes from the Hindu epics *Ramayana* and *Mahabharata*; the Bayon; the enclosure of Angkor Thom; and the temple of Ta Prohm. The latter is particularly interesting because it has been deliberately left as it was found and gives impressive scenes of how an invading tropical forest conquers a deserted city.

CLIMATE

Rainy season: May to October, when the Mekong River rises as much as 15 m and reverses the flow of the Tonle Sap River back to the lake at Angkor.

FLORA

At Ta Prohm, vines and roots have prized stones apart and now entirely cover massive stone sculptures. Giant trees occupy buildings and grow out of the roofs; vegetation fills moats and canals. The lush forest sweeps everything in its green embrace.

The original forest around the temples was destroyed at least five or six centuries ago. Though the actual forest around Angkor resembles the virgin forest still existing in this part of Cambodia, it shows differences and has not reestablished its climax.

FAUNA

Unfortunately much of the forest and its animals were destroyed by the villagers living within the area of the Angkor National Park over a long period. The authorities are trying to relocate this population and plan to reintroduce some of the mammals that formerly existed in the forest. Sambar deer at present browse among the temple ruins, and there are tigers, leopards, and monkeys around.

The birdlife is rich, colorful, and interesting and so are the fishes living in the nearby Tonle Sap, an artificial lake and irrigation system built by the Khmer civilization and still functioning.

Sambar deer among Angkor ruins; vegetation and animals reconquer the old temples.

Muntjac (*Muntiacus muntjak*), the barking deer

Area: 333,918 km² Population density: 69/km²

There is one national park in the 11 states of West Malaysia: Taman Negara National Park, described below. Within the Federation of Malaysia two member states, which together are known as East Malaysia, have each one national park (see Sarawak, p. 169, and Sabah, p. 171).

TAMAN NEGARA NATIONAL PARK (created 1938)
A mountainous area covered by dense tropical forests that protect interesting fauna, including the extremely rare Sumatran rhinoceros. This reserve, formerly known as the King George V National Park, is located in the states of Pahang, Kelantan, and Trengganu; headquarters are at Kuala-Tahan, which has an airstrip. A large part of the park is inaccessible, but there are paths and loop trails; up-river lodges are reached by boat.

Four-horned antelopes (young)

Location: northeastern Malay Peninsula
Area: 440,000 ha
Climate: tropical, with high rainfall
Protection: total; no occupation or exploitation; staff of 62
Accommodation: modern rest house and chalets (total of 24 beds available); one hotel (40 beds)

TOPOGRAPHY The area includes Gunong Tahan, Malaya's highest mt. (2,190 m), wide plateaus, and limestone outcrops. Almost the whole area is clad in lowland and mountain rain forest. Other mts. are Gunong Gedong (2,033 m) and Gunong Ulu Kechau (1,914 m).

MAMMALS Most of Malaya's larger mammals can be found: Malayan tapir, Sumatran rhinoceros, muntjac (barking deer), sambar, gaur, wild boar, Asiatic elephant, tiger, leopard, binturong, and the sloth-bear.

SINGAPORE

Area: 585 km²   Population density: 3,530/km²

There are four reserves in Singapore: Water Catchment Area (the largest, 1,602 ha), Pandan Reserve, Bukit Timah Reserve, and Kranji Reserve (the smallest, described below). Information may be obtained from the Botanical Garden, Singapore.

KRANJI RESERVE (created 1883)

In spite of its small size, Kranji Reserve was included in the United Nations List because of the interest of its vegetation; it protects a climax salt-loving mangrove vegetation, where the pioneering and land-building characteristics of the marine and brackish vegetation is in the process of changing to an association of dry-land plants.

Situated just north of the Equator, the reserve has a climate that is, of course, tropically hot and moist. There are no well-marked wet and dry seasons.

Location: Straits of Johore, N side of Singapore Island
Area: 20 ha; used for scientific research
Climate: tropical
Access: by Bukit Timah road
Accommodation: in Singapore City (24 km away)

FLORA The vegetation is dominated by mangrove; progress of land building is greater than at Singapore Strait, resulting in a pronounced invasion of foreshore and dry-land plants. Presumably this is due to Kranji's distance from the open sea, as well as to differences of water, current, mud accumulation, and elevation.

Area: 1,913,249 km²   Population density: 62/km²

Indonesia has altogether some 43 protected areas: 12 in Sumatra, 21 in Java, two in Kalimantan (Borneo), six in Sulawesi (Celebes), one in Lesser Sunda, and one in Maluku (Moluccas). In addition there are many smaller or insufficiently protected areas. The UN List omitted a larger area (320,000 ha) in West Irian (formerly New Guinea) called Lorentz Natuurmonument because it lacked any management or supervision. Information on these sanctuaries can be obtained from the Department of Forestry, Bogor, Java.

LÖSER MOUNTAINS NATURE PARK (created 1934), Sumatra

Though this is the largest nature reserve in Indonesia it is not included in the UN List since it seems that only fauna are protected there. It is an important area, however, for several rare animals. Scenically it is also very attractive, covering the foothills and slopes of Mt. Löser, (3,465 m).

Location: northern Sumatra
Area: 416,000 ha
Visits: on foot or on horseback
Access: 10 hrs. by Jeep from Medan (nearest tourist city, airport)

TOPOGRAPHY The reserve is a country of grass plains consisting of cogonates (1–3 m high) interspersed with groves of merkus pines, dense jungles, and swamps.

MAMMALS The most precious mammal is the Sumatran rhinoceros, once distributed over almost the whole of southeastern Asia but today limited to a few localities in Burma, Malaya, Sumatra, and Sabah on Borneo. In 1970 there were 58 Sumatran rhinos on Mt. Löser.

The reserve's second most valuable mammal is the orangutan, numbering about 930 (1972).

Third in rarity comes the Sumatran serow, a relative of the chamois, exterminated in most parts of its former range and now confined to the mts.

Other mammals include Indian elephant, mouse-deer, Malayan sambar, muntjac, wild boar, tiger, clouded leopard, Malayan bear, wild dog, otter, white-handed gibbon, siamang, pig-tailed macaque, crab-eating macaque, and leaf-monkey (two species).

BIRDS The argus pheasant and hornbills are the most conspicuous.

Green magpie

Shore in Udjung Kulon, westernmost Java

UDJUNG KULON STRICT NATURE RESERVE (created 1937), West Java

One of the most important reserves in tropical Asia, 41 km from Krakatau Volcano Island in the Sunda Strait. It is the home of spectacular and very rare mammals, the most famous of which is the Javan rhinoceros.

Location: Udjung Kulon Peninsula, southwestern point of Java

Area: 61,000 ha

Protection: total; staff of 40; guides available; open only from April 1 to October 31; visitors scarce

Access: by motorboat: Labuhan to Handeuleum Is. (6 hrs.); by car: Djakarta to Labuhan (5 hrs.)

Accommodation: on Handeuleum Is. and Peutjang Is.

GEOLOGY The Udjung Kulon Peninsula is of volcanic origin; the western part has volcanic rocks with bare vertical cliffs (some are 50—70 m high). Most of mts. consist of layered rock formations: marl, tuff, breccia sandstone, conglomerates.

TOPOGRAPHY Jungles and varied seascapes: rocky and sandy shores, lagoons, dune formations, mt. ridges radiating from the top; cliffs and hills and in the southeast a marshy shore girdle. Streams and rivers originating in mt. ridges have rapids and sharp falls.

CLIMATE Tropical, with a wet western monsoon Dec.—March, and a more dry eastern monsoon during the rest of the year. Temperature ranges: 18°—22°C.

FLORA The actual forests of the peninsula and islands are regrowth vegetation because of the tidal

Green bee-eaters

wave accompanying the violent 1883 eruption of Krakatau which swept over and flooded the area.

In the interior, vegetation includes spectacular virgin rain forests with several canopy stories of giant figs, tjerlang, white-flowered *Gossampinus veletonii*, and coral tree; a remarkably high number of different palm species; bamboos, giant ferns, vines, and lianas. Open pastures have alang alang grass.

MAMMALS The reserve is of special importance because it harbors the Javan rhinoceros, the rarest of the world's five species of rhinos. About 28 animals live in the reserve; it is uncertain whether any survive elsewhere in Asia. In the 1850's this rhino ranged over most of Asia southward to Sumatra (exterminated there in the 1940's) and Java.

The reserve is also a stronghold for the banteng, the wild ox that once was common in southeastern Asia. It is not known whether the mainland race survives. In Udjung Kulon there are about 200 purebred bantengs.

The sanctuary is also the last refuge of the Java tiger, once numerous in many parts of Java. About a dozen were estimated to exist in Udjung Kulon at the beginning of the 1960's, but it is uncertain whether the tiger now exists there.

Other mammals on the peninsula: Javan deer, lesser mouse deer, muntjac, wild water buffalo, Javan pig, wild boar, Malayan giant squirrel, a small Indian civet, Javan mongoose, leopard (of which many are black), wild dog (dhole), flying fox, monkeys like the crab-eating macaque, silvered leaf-monkey, Sunda Island leaf-monkey, and gray gibbon.

BIRDS Over 100 species have been recorded; probably there are many

Banteng in Udjung Kulon

more. The green peafowl, two species of junglefowl, and bee-eaters may be mentioned.

OTHER VERTEBRATES Reptiles include many species of lizards such as geckos, skinks, and monitors as well as snakes, among which the python is the most conspicuous. Salt-water crocodiles occur.

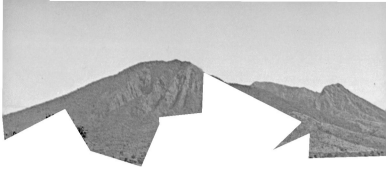

Woodland savanna at the foot of Mount Baluran

BALURAN ANIMAL SANCTUARY (created 1937), Java

This park is probably the best place in Indonesia to see large bovines like the banteng and wild water buffalo and provides a good spot for exciting photographic safari. The area ranges from the shores of Madura and Bali Straits in a gradual rise to the peak of Mount Baluran, 1,103 meters above sea level.

Location: northeastern Java
Area: 25,000 ha
Protection: total, except that cropping of ungulates still tolerated; paths; tracks for Jeeps; boats available
Access: by road from Surabaja or Banjuwangi (port for Bali)
Accommodation: guest house complex at Pondok Bekol for 24 persons
Nearest city: Surabaja (by air from Djakarta)

GEOLOGY AND TOPOGRAPHY

Mt. Baluran is an ancient volcano with several satellites consisting of volcanic soils. Most of the reserve is a lowland covered by swamps, savannas, and open forests.

CLIMATE Mt. Baluran and Mt. Klosot form a barrier preventing wet western monsoon winds from discharging moisture. The result is an unusually short rainy season: from December through February. Dry season is from March to October.

FLORA Due to dry climate, tropical vegetation less luxuriant here than elsewhere in Java. Mangrove forests and marshy nipa palm are along the littoral; grassy savannas form excellent pastures for grazing mammals; parklike open woodlands have acacias, palms; dense teak forests cover lower slopes of the Baluran massif, gradually replaced by Albizzia, Ficus, Podocarpus.

Sambar herd (also called Java deer)

MAMMALS The tiger and the leopard are rarely seen though the black phase of the latter is rather common; the observer is more than satisfied, however, by the extraordinary possibilities of seeing all the Javan ungulates except the Javan rhinoceros.

Large herds of Javan deer, banteng, and wild water buffalo are plentiful; the muntjac is seen singly or in pairs. The lesser Malay chevrotain, no larger than a hare, is chiefly nocturnal. Other mammals: wild boar, Javan pig, wild dog (dhole), palm civet, small Indian civet, Javan mongoose, leopard cat (Felis bengalensis), Sunda Island leaf-monkey, and the crab-eating macaque.

BIRDS A few examples of the abundant birdlife: green junglefowl, red junglefowl, green peafowl, at least three species of hornbill, five species of birds of prey, and five species of pigeons and of doves.

OTHER VERTEBRATES Reptiles are common but only lizards are usually observed. There are, however, two species of pythons—the Indian and the reticulated—plus cobras, banded crait, Russell's viper, whip snakes, and others.

Horns of some males of wild water buffalo span two meters.

The giant monitor, world's largest lizard, occurs only on three small islands of the Indonesian Archipelago.

KOMODO ISLAND and PADAR RINTJAK ANIMAL SANCTUARIES

The two reserves, soon to be open to tourists, protect the giant monitor, largest lizard of the world in modern times, with a length of 3 m and weight of 136 kg.

Location: W of Flores, lesser Sunda Is.
Area: Komodo, 30,000 ha; Padar-Rintjak, 16,000 ha
Visits: made on foot or by boat

Accommodation: Camping on Komodo for maximum of 6 persons
Nearest tourist city: Denpasar, Bali (8 hrs. by plane from Komodo)

WEST BALI NATURE RESERVE (created 1941), Bali

Not on the UN List this reserve is mentioned because it is said to protect a race of tiger that does not exist elsewhere in the world and has had its last refuge here. In 1963 there were no more than three or four left. When one of the authors (K.C-L) visited Bali in 1965 no signs of tigers could be found, but local people gave assurance that they still occurred in the reserve. Since then no records have been made and the subspecies is now probably extinct. The Java deer was the main prey of the Balinese tiger. Wild bantengs were also said to occur in the reserve. The sanctuary is the haunt of the rare Rothschild's starling, a species restricted to Bali—remarkably beautiful, entirely white except for the black tips of the wings and tail, and steel-blue bill, chin, and legs.

Location: westernmost Bali
Area: 20,000 ha

Visits: by car or on foot
Access: from Denpasar (big hotel)

Area: 125,450 km^2 Population density: 6/km^2

Sarawak, a former British colony in NW Borneo and now with Sabah a part of the Federation of Malaysia, has only one fully protected area, Bako National Park, described below, but many projects are under consideration. Provisions are being made to set aside at least 10 more national parks of which the largest, Gunong Mulu, will be 61,900 ha.

BAKO NATIONAL PARK (created 1954)

A sandy peninsula lying just above the Equator between Tanjong Po and Buntul Bay, Bako N.P. is the first land passed by ships entering the Sarawak River from Singapore. The greater part of the reserve is covered by primary forests, mainly tropical heath forests; the area is of special interest to ornithologists and botanists.

The park is administered by a Board of Management of whom the Warden is the ex-officio chairman. Two park rangers are stationed at Telok Asam. Information about renting bungalows or hiring transport may be obtained from the Warden, Bako National Park, c/o Section Forest Officer, Kuching, Sarawak, East Malaysia.

Location: Maura Tebas Peninsula, western Sarawak
Area: 2,550 ha
Climate: equatorial: hot and moist
Protection: total, except for removal of small quantities of poles from coastal areas; 24 km of paths
Access: from Kuching by launch or by speedboat (a journey of about an hour); landing is at Telok Asam
Accommodation: two rest houses (furnished and equipped with refrigerators and cookers) and two hostels at Telok Asam; electricity for lighting installed in all buildings

---

GEOLOGY AND TOPOGRAPHY
The underlying rock, a coarse-grained sandstone, is covered by frequently infertile and podsolized soils. The reserve is bounded on three sides by the coastline of sandy bays, small coves, and cliffs.

FLORA Mixed lowland vegetation: mangrove and littoral forests, exposed coastal cliff vegetation, lowland dipterocarp (gurjun) forests, heath forests (kerangas), padang vegetation, and peat swamp forest.

Above the high tide mark grow a number of beach trees typical for the Malay Archipelago like biansu, ketapang, ru laut, putat laut, and baru laut.

Tropical heath forests cover most of the plateau sandstones. The principal dominants are Dacrydium beccarii and Casuarina nobile. Dipterocarpus borneensis, Whiteodendron moultonianum, and Tristania species are also common. Myrmecophytes, including Myremecodia tuberosa, Hydnophytum, and Phymatodes simnosa, are particularly abundant on padang areas, while on acid soils bladderwort species, pitcher plants, and the interesting small sundew Dresera spatula are to be found.

White-collared kingfisher

Red-wattled lapwing plover

MAMMALS The white dolphin, known only from Borneo, and the rare plumbous dolphin are found in Bantul Bay. Quite common by the shore are the larger Malay chevrotain and the Bornean pig.

Within and near the mangrove forest is the interesting long-nosed monkey *(Nasalis larvatus)*, fully protected in Sarawak. The crab-eating macaque and the silver leaf-monkey are not uncommon.

BIRDS Abundant birdlife includes many migratory species along the shore. Sept.—Oct.: large flocks of whimbrel, redshank, greater and lesser sand plovers, and little stints. Among the mangroves: wood swallows, dyal, black-winged iora, Malaysian fantail flycatcher, and white-collared kingfisher. Around the rest house at Telok Asam: yellow-vented bulbul, dusky mannikin, pied triller, and chestnut-headed bee-eater; foliage birds: brown barbet, fairy blue-bird, straw-headed bulbul, a wonderful singer, and the silent lesser green broadbill, flowerpeckers and sunbirds. Birds of prey: the white-breasted sea eagle, gray-faced buzzard, crested goshawk, brahminy kite, and the rare black eagle.

White-breasted sea eagle

Area: 76,409 km^2 Population density: 6/km^2

Sabah (North Borneo), with Sarawak, is part of the Federation of Malaysia. There is only one protected area, Kinabalu, administered by a Board of Trustees.

KINABALU NATIONAL PARK (created 1964)

The national park includes the whole of Mt. Kinabalu from 600 m to the summit (4,101 m), the highest mountain in southeastern Asia. One can drive up to about 1,830 meters; walking time to summit thereafter without rest stops is between six and seven hours. The incredibly rich flora includes 140 families of flowering plants of the 200 to 250 families that occur in the whole world; it is probable that birds number at least 500 species.

Location: northern Borneo, about 48 km E of Kota Kinabalu

Area: 69,000 ha

Climate: ranges from hot tropical to temperate; night temperatures at upper levels near or just below freezing

Access: by air (airstrip at Ranau, 24 km from entrance); by road, 93 km from Kota Kinabalu on Ranau Road to Mile 35 (park headquarters with visitor accommodation and main road leading toward summit)

GEOLOGY Mt. Kinabalu is part of the Crocker Range, but its granite block rises to more than twice the height of the range. The mountain, a granite intrusion into Eocene shale and older ultrabasic rock, is formed of granodiorite, an igneous rock of early Pliocene that solidified below the surface but is now exposed through the erosion of overlying shale and sandstone rocks.

TOPOGRAPHY Dense forests cover the mountain slopes to about 3,360 meters. Above, bare rocks form a ridge tipped with numerous peaks. The north face of the dome is cleft by a gully that plunges precipitously some thousand meters. The eastern ridge leads through spectacular pinnacles. Pinosuk Plateau (1,500–

1,830 m) was probably formed by the accumulation of rock debris from the mountain above.

FLORA Very varied: no other mountain in the world has so many species of oaks (60) and figs (80). Dense primary rain forest prevails at 1,190–1,830 m on N and E sides, but much of this has been felled on S and W flanks by the local Dusuns. In addition to the oaks and figs there are many other families like chestnuts, wild mangosteens, tulip trees, and a number of species in the myrtle family. Species of conifers: Borneo kauri, celery pine, podocarpa, and dacrydiums abound at 1,220–3,050 meters; at 2,440–3,050 m a moss forest, surmounted still higher by bushes, shrubs, and alpine plants, and, finally, bare rock with tiny cinquefoils seeking shelter in the crevices.

There are 72 genera of orchids besides hundreds of ferns, mosses, and fungi and tree ferns. Huge pitcher plants (four species) are conspicuous; the bowl of *Nepenthes rajah* can hold up to four pints of water.

Shrubs and plants above 900 m

From the summit of Mt. Kinabalu looking south

including photinias, *Pygaeum*, berries of the genera *Rubus* and *Vaccinium*, *Euphrasia borneensis*, several species of gentians, and Low's buttercup.

MAMMALS Since the park covers part of the forest-clad hills below 900 m, virtually all rain-forest forms of Borneo fauna occur, including the rare Sumatran rhinoceros and orangutan.

Other larger mammals: gibbon, proboscis monkey, sambar deer (these occasionally climb to summit), muntjac (up to 3,350 m), banteng, bearded pig, and civet cat. The tufted pygmy squirrel is seen in the trees; the Borneo ferret-badger is today found only on Mt. Kinabalu, at 1,060–2,500 m.

BIRDS The ecological range of this park makes it most probable that more than 500 species occur here. Among the most common (to be seen while walking from 1,400 m up to the summit) are white-bellied swiftlet, golden-naped barbet, gray drongo, little cuckoo dove, Malaysian tree pie, Whitehead's spider hunter, mountain minivet, mountain blackeye, and mountain blackbird. Noisest birds are the babblers, bushy-crested hornbill, and rhinoceros hornbill.

BUTTERFLIES These should be mentioned for their remarkable variety of species and their numbers. Most prominent as they fly through the forest: the kite swallowtails.

Insect-catching plants, Kinabalu

Area: 300,838 km²   Population density: 124/km²

Two thirds of some 23 protected areas in the Philippines are on the island of Luzon. (Some 20 more could have been added but were ruled out from the UN List because their protective status is less strict than those listed and lumbering is permitted in them.) In addition ten national parks have recently been created. All areas are administered by the Park and Wildlife Office. Department of Agriculture and Natural Resources, Quezon City, which provides information.

MOUNT APO NATIONAL PARK (created 1936, reduced in size 1957), Mindanao

An area of extensive forests, unique in the Philippines where most forests have been destroyed, with a rich fauna including birds that are very rare.

Location: southeastern Island of Mindanao
Area: 72,936 ha
Protection: part of area under timber license; most land above 500 m altitude untouched and unexploited; many paths and car tracks

Access: via Digos-Cotabato Road from the Kidapawan side, west of Mt. Apo
Accommodation: hotels at Davao City (30 km from the park); accommodation for tourists within the park is projected

The piedmont of Mount Apo in Mindanao

The monkey-eating eagle occurs only in the Philippines.

GEOLOGY AND TOPOGRAPHY

The Philippines including Mindanao consist of two tectonic areas, related structures, and volcanic uplands. Mt. Apo is a volcano that reaches 2,453 m with numerous waterfalls on its precipitous slopes, hot mineral springs, and a lake.

CLIMATE Tropical at lower levels with generally high temperature and rainfall throughout the year; temperate at higher elevations. Prevailing winds from SW, June to October, and from NE during the remainder of the year.

FLORA Most parts of the slopes are clad in a luxuriant montane rain forest where dipterocarp (gurjun) trees dominate. This area is succeeded above by a montane mossy forest rich in epiphytes. Higher up are stunted, wind-marked trees, their branches covered by mosses, lichens, ferns, and orchids.

On the upper plateaus of Mt. Apo is a tropical—alpine vegetation almost entirely composed of species peculiar to the Philippine mountains above timberline. Unfortunately native populations use fire as a hunting method, with a devastating effect on the upper plant communities where there is less moisture than in the rain forest.

MAMMALS Among the rich variety of species, the larger mammals include Bornean pig, Philippine deer, slow loris, Philippine tarsier, crab-eating monkey, the extremely interesting Philippine flying lemur, Malay civet, and palm civet. (Leopard cats are found in two Philippine islands: Negros and Palavan.) There are also large numbers of insectivores, bats, and rodents.

BIRDS The rare monkey-eating eagle, a spectacular bird, is the pride of the national park. Endemic to the Philippines, it formerly occurred on Samar and Leyte as well but is now confined to the island of Mindanao, where only some 40 pairs remain.

Other birds more or less peculiar to Mt. Apo are the Apo lorikeet and the Apo sunbird.

174

QUEZON NATIONAL PARK (created 1934, enlarged 1940), Luzon

Though practically all natural forests on Luzon have been destroyed, the area of this park still preserves outstanding examples of the originally magnificent flora and fauna of the Philippines.

Location: southern Luzon, 290 km S of Manila

Area: 983 ha

Climate: tropical, but gradually becoming milder at higher elevations; high rainfall

Protection: total; three guards; network of tourist trails; watch towers; scientific research

Access: by rail from Manila, or by road (autobuses)

Nearest large towns: Atimonan and Lucena

TOPOGRAPHY The peak and slopes of Mt. Pinagbanderahan (490 m), situated on an isthmus between Lamon Bay and Tayabas Bay, are included in this park with beautiful views of rivers, waterfalls, and gorges in a setting of intact vegetation.

FLORA An exceedingly misty virgin lowland rain forest is quite dominated by large trees of dipterocarps (gurjuns), the crowns of the trees forming a thick canopy letting in little sunlight.

MAMMALS Abundant wildlife includes the crab-eating macaque, Philippine deer, Javan pig, numerous rodents, and bats.

BIRDS Extraordinary abundance. To list only a fraction: Pompadour green pigeon, white-eared brown fruit dove, Philippine cockatoo, gray-breasted brush cuckoo, Philippine coucal, junglefowl, spotted button quail, megapode, Philippine falconet, tarictic hornbill, rufous hornbill, barred graybird, white-breasted wood swallow, and the Philippine fairy bluebird as well as parrots and others.

OTHER VERTEBRATES Many lizards can be observed of which the most impressive is the monitor lizard (Varanus grayi).

Monitor lizard, which feeds largely on carrion and eggs

Mountains and volcanoes in Daisetsuzan National Park

JAPAN

Area: 371,087 km²   Population density: 266/km²

In front of a real human tide, Japan has set aside areas for recreation, public health, and, wherever possible, the safe-guarding of some habitats considered important for science. Since the Japanese archipelago is located in the volcanic zone encircling the Pacific Ocean, all these areas have frequently been shaped and reshaped by volcanic activities.

There are 23 national parks (seven described here), and some 40 other areas with less severe protective status; such activities as cattle grazing, lumbering, plant picking, or capture of animals are forbidden. In many national parks there is a system of zoning with various degrees of protection and control of human activities. Villages and even towns may be located in these zones because they were there prior to the establishment of the national parks.

Further information may be obtained from the National Parks Bureau, Ministry of Health and Welfare, 1-2-2, Kasu-migaseki, Chiyodaku, Tokyo.

DAISETSUZAN NATIONAL PARK (created 1934), Hokkaido
One of the wildest of the Japanese national parks, as well

as the largest, embracing mountain ranges and volcano groups. The northern latitude (about 43° 30′ N), the alpine character, and volcanic activity with hot springs provide striking contrasts.

Location: central part of Hokkaido, northern Japan
Area: 231,929 ha; no special protection areas (five zones, 34,340 ha, projected); many villages
Activities: mountaineering; skiing; hot springs; tours
Accommodation: available in and near park

TOPOGRAPHY The tectonic Ishikari Mountain range (1,980 m) is surrounded by other volcano groups: the Tokachi (SW) and Shikaribetsu (SE).

The Daisetzu Mts. are formed by nine volcanic ranges surrounding Ohachidaira, a large crater with swamps, poison gas, and hot springs. Highest Daisetsuzan peak and Hokkaido's highest mt. is Asahi-dake (2,290 m). Smoke issues from several fissures caused by past eruptions.

Two gorges in Daisetsuzan are particularly beautiful: Soun-Kyo, the most famous, through which the

Ishikari River flows northward under steep walls, and Tennin-Kyo through which the river Chubetsu flows westward.

CLIMATE Temperate and subarctic, depending on altitude, but always with pronounced humidity.

FLORA Slopes of mts. and volcanoes are covered with virgin conifer forests. Plants in marshes, bogs, valleys, and forests are of a northern character; those on mt. slopes are representatives of an alpine flora.

MAMMALS Animals also are typical for northern haunts. Among the most interesting mammals: the northern pika, which here has its only occurrence in Japan, Siebold's chipmunk, and the brown bear. Sika deer, badger, and sable are common.

BIRDS Many species of the Asian taiga.

AKAN NATIONAL PARK (created 1934), Hokkaido

Located in Japan's northernmost island, this national park has an almost subarctic character despite its smoking volcanoes and hot springs. A mountainous landscape with forests, lakes, and snow-capped peaks offering magnificent scenery.

The only remaining population of the predecessor and perhaps original inhabitants of Japan, the Ainu people now numbering about 15,000 live in Hokkaido and many of them around Lake Akan.

Location: northeastern Hokkaido
Area: 87,498 ha
Protection: special protection area (four zones, 8,445 ha)
Access: by road or rail from Kushiro in the south, or Abashiri and Shari in the north
Activities: mountaineering, skiing, hot springs (baths), fishing, water sports, tours

Accommodation: available in and near park

GEOLOGY Volcanoes and the caldera lakes Akan, Kutcharo, and Mashu occupy the whole N.P., but only the volcanoes Me-Akan and Atosanupuri show volcanic activity

Akan Lake and Volcano Me-Akan, Akan National Park

at present. The summits of these two have a number of craters, and white smoke constantly pours forth (there have been several major eruptions in recent years). Particularly beautiful is the fantastically crystal clear Lake Mashu, whose transparency is 41.6 m, the deepest water visibility in the world.

TOPOGRAPHY Altitude range: 100—1,503 m. The Kutcharo caldera is one of the largest in the world and is filled with the huge lake of that name, 125 m deep. Other types of lakes are those formed by dammed lava flows or crater lakes.

CLIMATE Typical for northernmost Japan: cold and rather humid. Summers are warm, but winters have a subarctic climate with much snow.

FLORA Vast virgin conifer forests, largely Sachalin firs and yezo spruce, are interspersed with stands of white birch, which at higher levels forms a uniform forest belt. Mountain tops are partial-ly covered with rhododendrons and creeping pine.

At the foot of the active volcano Atosanupuri the meadows are cov-ered by dense yezo-azaleas lavish-ly beautiful in flower, June—July.

Lake Akan harbors a unique freshwater plant, the marino or ball weed, a deep-green algae that forms soft velvety spherical struc-tures about 2 to 3.2 inches in di-ameter. These algae grow at the bottom of the lake.

MAMMALS This park harbors the brown bear, badger, ermine, sable, red squirrel, and varying hare—all representatives of the Eurasian fauna—also typical East Asian elements like the Sika deer.

BIRDS Palearctic species include raven, nutcracker, willow tit, nut-hatch, yellow-breasted bunting, bullfinch, pied wagtail, and great black woodpecker, also Gray's grasshopper warbler and Japanese green pigeon.

SHIKOTSU-TOYA NATIONAL PARK (created 1949), western Hokkaido

This park with a remarkable spectrum of various types of volcanoes and caldera lakes of different ages has been called a museum of volcanoes. In addition, virgin forests and broad valleys make the mountain country very attractive. The park is divided into three unconnected sectors: (1) embracing Lake Shikotsu, (2) Lake Toya, and (3) Mt. Yotei.

Area: 98,660 ha; five zones of special protection (1,408 ha); other areas contain many villages and spa towns
Climate: cool, temperate
Access: by road or rail
Activities: climbing, skiing, boating,
Accommodation: in and near the park

GEOLOGY The area around Lake Shikotsu is a large caldera. Of the surrounding volcanoes, Mt. Tarumae is particularly noteworthy: It looks like an aspite but is actually a conide whose summit was broken off in an eruption of 1909 and was replaced by a dome of dark lava, 100 m in height and 460 m in diameter, rising out of the low and leveled crater: a so-called double conitholoide. From a crevice in the lava dome, columns of white smoke are constantly rising.

South of the Lake Toya caldera area the most interesting volcano is Mt. Showa Shinzan. In the winter of 1943 a part of the farmland suddenly started to rise (about 250 m); in June 1944 several eruptions occurred, vigorously ejecting ashes, sand, mud, and later red-hot lava.

In 1945 the lava pouring over the surrounding ground grew to a height of 100 m, forming a rock pyramid. Consequently, all in all, a 300-meter-high mountain was created in two years. Still active, for the moment only sulfurous clouds and vapors indicate that there is life in the young volcano.

Mt. Yotei (or Shiribeshi), with an altitude of 1,893 m, is a typical conide volcano, and therefore is often called the Fuji of Hokkaido.

FLORA Most prominent feature is the virgin forest of yezo spruce covering the slopes of the Hoheikyo Valley. Cherries blossom in early May. Lower mt. elevations have deciduous forest cover: Japanese beech, maple, and oak; white birch and aspen grow at higher elevations. Many meadows and swamps have alpine flora.

MAMMALS An impressive population of brown bear inhabits the park. Others: Sika deer, yezo squirrel, sable, weasels, badger.

A forest has grown up, colonizing lava, at base of Mt. Showa Shinzan.

Lake Hachiman in the Towada-Hachimantai National Park

TOWADA-HACHIMANTAI NATIONAL PARK (created 1936, 1956), Honshu

Two unconnected sectors make up this national park. The northern section contains the gemlike Lake Towada, headwater of the Oirase River, bordered by magnificent primeval deciduous forests, and the Hakkoda volcanoes. The southern section embraces the Hachimantai region, a range of volcanoes and high plateaus.

Location: northern Honshu
Area: 83,351 ha includes a special protection area (9,422 ha)
Activities: skiing, camping, hiking, boating; hot springs; tours
Accommodation: available in and near the park

GEOLOGY Lake Towada is a rare phenomenon because it is a double-structured caldera due to the past three eruptions. About 1,00,000 years ago the area was an active volcano; the central part subsided after lava gushed out; the next eruption created a new mountain, which in turn caved in. A central cone emerging in the third eruption rises over the eastern headland.

TOPOGRAPHY The eight peaks of the Hakkoda volcanoes are separated by plateaus. The Oirase River drains Lake Towada, then courses through mt. gorges and open valleys. The Hachimantai area includes a mt. range with volcanic peaks; Mt. Iwate, 2,041 m, Mt. Komagtake, and Mt. Hachimantai, 1,613 m, are the most important. Remnants of volcanic activity appear in the form of steam and smoke as well as of boiling mud and hot springs.

CLIMATE Temperate; highland weather almost always refreshingly cool in summer, winters rich in snow.

FLORA Magnicent forests of Japanese beech, birch, maple, and oak with coniferous forests of false arborvitae on upper volcanic slopes.

The many interesting alpine plants include a bleeding heart, *Dicentra peregrina*.

BANDAI-ASAHI NATIONAL PARK (created 1950, 1957), Honshu

Outstanding volcanic and tectonic mt. landscapes have an interesting and vast stretch of virgin deciduous forest, one of the largest and most beautiful in Japan. This national park is noted as one of Japan's three best areas for birds. Four unconnected sections make up the park: (1) the district around Lake Inawashiro, (2) Mt. Bandai, a volcano that blew up in 1888 in a tremendous eruption, (3) Mt. Yide, a granite peak, and (4) the Asahi Range (2,000 m) and the shield-shaped volcanic Mt. Gassan.

Location: northern Honshu
Area: 189,661 ha; special protection: ten zones (17,139 ha); many villages, lumbering, cultivation
Activities: spas; mountaineering, skiing, fishing trips, camping
Nearest large cities: Fukushima and Yamagata

GEOLOGY A volcanic area. The titanic eruption of 1888, blasting away one third of Mt. Bandai, created many lakes, marshes, swamps, and ponds. The Adatara Mts. to the east form another volcanic chain. The Azuma volcanoes, a third volcanic range, contain Mt. Issaikyo (1,949 m), which had a large eruption in 1893 and a lesser upheaval in 1950. The primitive tectonic mt. massif of Yide has an altitude of 2,000 m.

FLORA Mt. Yide and Mt. Asahi are clad in virgin beech forests. In general, all mts. have deciduous forests on their lower slopes while conifers cover the upper parts.

MAMMALS The mts. shelter the Japanese serow, the Japanese black bear, and the Japanese macaque.

Katuji, one of the craters in the Azuma volcanoes, Bandai-Asahi N.P.

NIKKO NATIONAL PARK (created 1934, 1950, 1957), Honshu

A vast area of lakes, waterfalls, plateaus, and mountains, with architectural features of great interest notably the gorgeous Toshugu Shrine, dating from 1634–1636. The national park, combining a harmonious blending of natural and artificial beauties, is most typical of Japanese landscape.

Location: about 160 km N of Tokyo
Area: 140,698 ha, in three sectors; 14 zones have special protection; wilderness area at Oze (9,799 ha)
Climate: mild, with abundant rainfall reflected by a luxuriant vegetation
Access: by road or rail from Tokyo
Activities: skiing, skating, fishing
Accommodation: in park and nearby

GEOLOGY This region is an outstanding example of the result of volcanic activity which, beside eruptions and lava flows, has brought about land upheavals and movements of land blocks. Volcanoes with many hot springs dominate the area: Mt. Nantai (2,484 m), Mt. Shirane (2,577 m), Mt. Hiuchi (2,360 m), Mt. Shibutsu (2,288 m), and Mt. Nasu (1,917 m), still active.

TOPOGRAPHY A mountainous region with large open expanses in various stages of evolution, some still water-filled and forming large lava-dammed lakes like the Chuzenji (1,271 m above SL) and the Yunoko (1,478 m), and others which have gradually dried up and are today big swamps or grassy plains.

Many rivers run through the area, some forming spectacular waterfalls, especially the Kegon River (with a freeleaping fall of 97 m).

FLORA The 300-year-old cedars, artificially planted but remarkable, form a superb avenue leading to the historical shrines and temples at Toshugu.

In the mts. at lower elevations are found white birch, maple, Japanese beech, several species of oaks; at higher elevations: Japanese larch, momi fir, southern and northern Japanese hemlocks, and the distinctive Japanese false arborvitae (Thujopsis dolobrata).

Meadows with alpine plants have colorful carpets in white, yellow, and red, formed by myriads of lilies and other plants, matched only by the kaleidoscopic autumn colors of the deciduous forests.

MAMMALS In these montane forest of Nikko lives the Japanese serow, one of the rarest ungulates in the world (about 1,500 animals still exist in some protected areas on Honshu and Kyushu). Other interesting species: the Japanese black bear and Japanese macaque.

BIRDS The most interesting bird is the azure-winged magpie, a beautiful species with an extraordinary distribution: it occurs only in easternmost Asia and in southwesternmost Europe.

Kegon Falls (97 m), Nikko N.P.

Shrubs, grasses and naked lava soil below Fujiyama summit (3,776 m)

FUJI-HAKONE-IZU NATIONAL PARK (created 1936, 1955, 1964)

The dominant feature of this complex of four areas is well known all over the world: Fujiyama, which plays an important part in the religious, social, and artistic life of Japan. The volcano rises from the so-called "Sea of Trees," luxuriant conifers and deciduous trees growing on the lava flow of its foothills. On the northern and eastern bases of Mt. Fuji are the beautiful Fuji-Goko, Fuji Five Lakes. Hakone is another volcanic and lake area with magnificent scenic beauty. The Izu Peninsula and the Seven Isles of Izu in the Pacific form the other sectors of this national park.

Location: southeastern Honshu
Area: 122,309 ha
Access: by rail and by highway from Tokyo
Activities: most visited of Japan's parks, many tourist facilities; boat excursions on lakes; swimming, camping, fishing, boating, skating; mountain climbing on Mt. Fuji; skiing; leaflet from Japan Tourist Assn., 1 Marunouchi, Tokyo.

Mount Fuji viewed from the Izu Peninsula, Fuji-Hakone-Izu N.P.

GEOLOGY All of these areas are of volcanic origin. Fuji probably first erupted over 100,000 years ago; the Hakone Mts. developed from a triple volcano resulting from volcanic activities over a million years ago. Fuji last exploded in 1707, but a large number of hot springs show that volcanism is still at work. There are 18 different eruptions on record, the worst occurring in the years 800, 864 and 1707. All produced extensive lava flows.

TOPOGRAPHY Fuji is surrounded at its northern base by five lakes, all serving to contrast or mirror the model conide volcano towering to a height of 3,776 m, the highest mountain in Japan.

The area of Mt. Hakone, a typical composite volcano, is dotted with peaks, cones, craters, hot springs, plains, rivers, and contains Lake Ashi (800 meters above sea level).

From Hakone, a U-shaped mt. range runs S to Mt. Daruma Pass and the Izu Peninsula, with its many active hot springs, where Mt. Amagi and its coastal belt fringe the entire range.

A chain of volcanic islands, the Seven Isles of Izu, extends south of the peninsula for a distance of some 185 kilometers.

CLIMATE Temperate, permitting visits year around, but the mt. area is snow covered in winter and the lakes frozen. Mt. Fuji is officially open to climbers July 1—Aug. 31, but not closed even in snow-capped winter. (There is a driveway up to the so-called Fifth Stage at

Sika deer

2,298 meters; from there the summit and the crater can be reached on foot in 4—5 hours.)

The Izu Peninsula and the Seven Isles of Izu have a mild climate, with winter temperatures averaging 5.5°C higher than Tokyo's.

FLORA Botanically, it is Mt. Fuji with its altitudinal zones of vegetation that is the most interesting area of this national park. Below the Sea of Trees, Fuji cherry trees and azaleas, in full bloom in early summer, are outstanding.

Seven vegetational belts may be observed below timber line. Progressing upward: several species of oaks, the false camellia, Japanese beech, Japanese red pine and black pine; at high levels: Japanese larch, firs, southern and northern Japanese hemlocks..

In the Hakone Mountains are thick woods with various oaks, magnolia, wild cherry, beech, Japanese cypress, and bamboo. Among other plants the insectivorous round-leaved sundew *(Drosera)* should be mentioned.

The Izu Archipelago has luxuriant growths of subtropical plants.

MAMMALS There are some 39 species represented in the Hakone Mountains; most noteworthy: Japanese macaque, raccoon dog, red fox, Japanese marten, Siberian weasel, badger, Japanese hare, Oriental squirrel, giant flying squirrel, wild boar and Sika (Japanese) deer. The most numerous group: bats, with 11 species.

BIRDS On Mt. Fuji, Lake Yamanaka is a particularly fine area for birds.

Lake Ashi has mute swans introduced from Switzerland in 1957. Other birds in the Hakone Mountains include Japanese pied kingfisher, Japanese ruddy kingfisher, Japanese blue flycatcher, narcissus

The mute swan is an introduced species.

flycatcher, and Himalayan cuckoo.

Shearwaters are among the many birds to be found along the Izu Peninsula.

OTHER VERTEBRATES Lake Ashi has eel, introduced rainbow trout, carp, and catfish.

185

Australia and New Zealand are parts of Australasia, which also includes New Guinea. These large islands, ranging from tropical to temperate regions, represent a wide span of habitats, from deserts and coral reefs to rain forests and high mountains with glaciers and snow-capped peaks.

Oceania is the name for the Pacific island world of the South Seas. These islands have different origins: some are volcanic, others are coral atolls.

To most people the South Sea Islands connote a kind of paradise with palm-ringed beaches, lush island vegetation, rich birdlife, and interesting inhabitants of Micronesians, Melanesians, or Polynesians. In many cases this is true, but it is not always so. East of the 80th Meridian, for example, a broad strip on both sides of the equator comprises archipelagoes consisting of true desert islands, on which the Polynesians and other forms of life could not retain a foothold. Such a negation of the customary image of the tropical Pacific islands as spots of paradise emphasizes again the wide range of habitats in this oceanic area.

Hawaii is also included in Oceania. The Hawaiian Islands are entirely volcanic, rising from the depths of the Pacific

Yellow-eyed penguin (*Megadyptes antipodes*), New Zealand

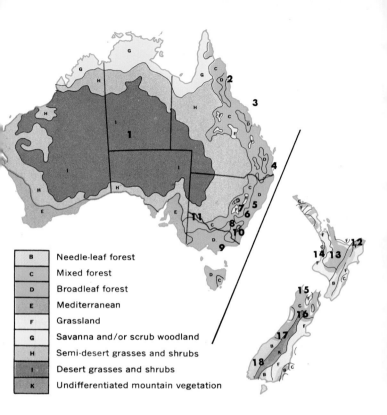

B	Needle-leaf forest
C	Mixed forest
D	Broadleaf forest
E	Mediterranean
F	Grassland
G	Savanna and/or scrub woodland
H	Semi-desert grasses and shrubs
I	Desert grasses and shrubs
K	Undifferentiated mountain vegetation

LOCATION OF PARKS

Numbers in **bold face** indicate
page numbers.

Ocean about 5,500 meters below sea level to a height of 4,207 meters above sea level.

As the climatic and topographical features of Australasia and Oceania are very different from other areas, so are the plant and animal worlds. Oceanic islands that have been isolated from the continental areas for long periods are natural laboratories where evolutionary changes often follow patterns other than those on the continents. On islands the adaption to the environment is, as everywhere in nature, governed by the physical and biological surroundings but with a minimum of environmental interactions compared to the complex ecology in most continental situations.

Australia is an island continent, with the result that it has a remarkable flora and fauna quite apart from the rest of the world, even from nearby southeastern Asia.

It is the same with New Zealand, Hawaii, and many of the Oceanic islands, but during the last centuries man has upset and destroyed in frightful ways much of the ecosystems that characterized these areas. A large number of animal species have been exterminated. Yet much still remains of habitats, plants, and animals, particularly in the national parks, which in this way have become real treasures, storing precious natural areas with their living vegetation and fauna for the benefit of mankind of today and tomorrow.

New Zealand particularly has a very fine network of national parks. Hawaii has two such reserves but needs more. Australia has many nature reserves, but many vulnerable and scientifically important habitats in various parts of the continent are still unprotected. With many valuable habitats rapidly disappearing, it is to be hoped that many more Australian national parks will be established. Unfortunately very few national parks have hitherto been set aside on the islands of the South Seas. Fiji has two reserves. Among the other territories of Oceania, only the Solomon Islands, a British Protectorate, have a reserve area: Queen Elizabeth Park, 6,080 ha, created in 1954 and located near the capital, Honiara.

Four areas are mentioned here: Australia, New Zealand, Fiji, (a former British colony), and Hawaii (one of the 50 states of the U.S.A.).

188

Gray kangaroo (*Macropus major*), Australia

Area: 7,716,545 km^2 Population density: 2/km^2

The UN List of National Parks and Equivalent Reserves lists altogether a total of 72 protected areas for the Commonwealth of Australia, divided among the states as follows: New South Wales, 11 areas, of which we describe four here; Northern Territory, four, (one is described); Queensland, 25 (14 mentioned here); South Australia: ten; Tasmania, three; Victoria, 14 (three described); Western Australia, five. The territory of New Guinea has no protected area.

A few further particulars about the conservation efforts being made in these various states of the huge continent-country are of interest:

New South Wales (capital: Sydney). In addition to the 11 reserves on the UN List, this state has a dozen more, generally very small or poorly protected. Information is obtainable from the Department of Lands, Box 39, G.P.O., Bridge St., Sydney.

Northern Territory (capital: Darwin). In addition to the national park we describe, the other three fully protected areas in this state on the UN List are Katherine Gorge N.P. (22,424 ha) and Howard Spring Recreation Reserve (280 ha), both of which are under the Northern Territory Reserve Board, Darwin, and the Cobourg Peninsula Sanctuary (196,-660 ha), under the Director of Animal Husbandry, Darwin.

Forests of gum trees dominate Kosciusko National Park. Mount Townsend in the background.

Queensland (capital: Brisbane). The UN List of 25 reserves in Queensland is only part of the 74 created in this state. (An additional 179 scenic areas under 400 ha, which have been set aside and protected, should be mentioned.) Information on all of these areas may be obtained from the Dept. of Forestry, 108 George Street, Brisbane.

South Australia (capital: Adelaide). The ten areas listed by the UN comprise one national park, Belair (897 ha), near Adelaide, and nine strictly protected reserves.

Tasmania (capital: Hobart). The three protected areas of this island Australian state which the UN lists are Cradle Mt., Lake St. Clair N.P. (133,250 ha, fully equipped), Mount Field N.P. (16,808 ha, 80 km from Hobart, many visitors), and Freycinet N.P. (6,420 ha, tourism being organized). Information on these parks available from Lands and Surveys Dept., Scenery Preservation Board, Hobart.

Victoria (capital: Melbourne). The 14 parks of this state are administered by the National Parks Authority, 276 Collins Street, Melbourne. The Victorian Government Tourist Bureau (same address) is planning itineraries for visits to Victoria's national parks.

Western Australia (capital: Perth). The five national parks listed by the UN are Stirling Ranges (108,000 ha), Nornalup (13,200 ha), Yanchep (2,664 ha), Porongorup (2,154 ha), and John Forrest (1,459 ha). Information obtainable from the National Parks Board, Ministry of Agriculture, Perth.

AYRES ROCK–MOUNT OLGA NATIONAL PARK (created 1958), Northern Territory

An immense uninhabited area with two impressive tawny-colored stone domes rising 40 km apart in isolation and above the huge sandy plain. The area has given rise to many aboriginal legends.

Location: southwestern part of Northern Territory
Area: 124,672 ha
Protection: total; two curators; car tracks only; visitors (over 12,000 in 1966) do not visit the reserve but go only to the two points named above
Access: by road from Alice Springs (airport, 445 km)
Accommodation: fully equipped camping area at Ayers Rock

GEOLOGY Ayres Rock and Mt. Olga are large monoliths of sedimentary quartzite of granite origin.

TOPOGRAPHY Ayres Rock springs 348 km above the surrounding scrub plain, which is 860 m above SL. The huge boulder, over 3 km long by 2.4 km wide, is famous for its colors that change with the light (tawny to cinnamon or orange, but almost black under clouds, and burning red in the setting sun). Erosion is constantly at work on the steep and precipitous slopes. Winds whining and whistling around fissures produce strange sounds, which have created many of the aboriginal legends. Some caves have aboriginal rock paintings with hunt scenes of ancient times.

Ayers Rock at sunset. Depending on the light, the giant boulder changes color in a wide range from black to blood red.

Hairy-nosed wombat

Mount Olga, from five miles across, looks like a land of fantasy: a dome of gigantic pebbles rising 1,068 m above SL and crowned by a diadem of glowing stones. Actually Mt. Olga is a series of 30 enormous monoliths each with a rounded summit and almost vertical wind- and water-polished smooth sides. It too turns orange-red at sunset but not so blood-red as Ayers Rock.

CLIMATE Hot and dry climate of the desert. Rains are irregular, but fall heavily when they come, cascading off the slopes of Ayers Rock with the roar of ocean waves.

FLORA Vegetation of the plain and foothills is dominated by saltbush, mulga, mallee, desert oak, and porcupine grass.

MAMMALS Wildlife around and partly in the mountains includes kangaroos and other smaller mammals like the marsupial mouse and also the introduced house mouse.

BIRDS There are emu, Keartland's honey eater, white-plumed honey eater, and black-faced cuckoo shrike.

Wedge-tailed eagles soar on the upwinds produced by the vertical rock walls.

OTHER VERTEBRATES The most conspicuous of the reptiles is the large goanna lizard that frequents the base of the rocks.

Red kangaroos inhabit plains and shrublands of inland Australia.

BELLENDEN KER NATIONAL PARK (created 1921, modified 1962), Queensland

Bellender Ker Plateau lies within Australia's greatest belt of dense tropical rain forest. Much of this park is not yet fully explored. It affords some of the most magnificent mountain scenery of the continent with vistas of distant white sandy beaches, the deep blue Pacific and coral reefs, as well as nearby overlooks of verdant slopes, steep cliffs, and waterfalls. One sheer cataract on the eastern face of Bartle Frere has a waterfall of more than 600 meters, its whole length visible from the south peak of Bellenden Ker.

Location: northeastern Queensland, W of Innisfail-Gordonvale Highway
Area: 32,431 ha
Protection: total; climbing route
Access: from Innisfail or Cairns
Accommodation: none in park but campsite with water available

GEOLOGY Bellenden Ker and Bartle Frere consist of granite, interspersed here and there by quartz reefs and slate. Some of the creeks are reported to contain gold.

TOPOGRAPHY The Mulgrave River (NW) and the Russel River (S) form the boundaries. Mt. Bartle Frere North (1,611 m) and Mt. Bartle Frere South (1,600 m) are a few miles apart.

High steep ranges and deep ravines with hundreds of streams characterize the country except for the broad Russel River Valley.

CLIMATE Perpetual heat and moisture prevail but the air is fresher on the mountains. Rainfall varies from 1,270 mm to as much as 4,064 millimeters.

FLORA Many of the forests are primeval. The large number of trees include hoop pine, kauri pine, red cedar, maple, walnut, strangler fig, myrtle, flame trees, umbrella trees, palms (Orania, Linospadix), bamboos, lacewood, teatree, flindersia, Dracophyllum saveri, and others. There are many creepers and climbers like peppers, the matchbox bean, and snakewood.

Treeferns are plentiful. Other ferns grow in the trees, and there are also many arboreal orchids, including various species of Cymbidium, Dendrobium, and other genera (many of the orchid species are apparently endemic for the area).

MAMMALS Most prominent of the mammals are two species of tree kangaroos (Dendrolagus lumholtzi and D. bennettianus). Others at home in this rain forest: long-nosed musk kangaroo and several species of kangaroos and wallabies, ring-tail possums or phalangers (three species), striped possum, two species of cuscus, tiger cat, and giant fruit bats.

BIRDS In rain forests birds are not easily seen but they announce their presence by their songs and calls: for example, spinebill, lesser Lewin honey eater, scrub wren, log runner, gray swiftlet, topknot pigeon, and crested hawk.

There are two other large ground birds beside the flightless cassowary: the brush turkey and the scrub fowl, which are mound-nest builders.

OTHER VERTEBRATES The scrub python (Liasis amethistinus), the largest snake of Australia, is the most impressive of the reptiles. Also prominent is Boyd's forest dragon, (Goniocephalus boydii) with a characteristic dorsal crest.

Gulnare Inlet seen from the peak of Whitsunday Island

GREAT BARRIER REEF N.P. and RESERVES, Queensland
The Great Barrier Reef is the world's greatest agglomeration
of coral reefs and shoals, the work of tiny animals through
eons of time. Lying between 16 and 400 km out from
the mainland, the reef forms an enormous natural breakwater.
with a richness of marine fauna greater than any area of
similar size in the world. Starting in the north off Guinea, it is
2,010 km long, relatively unbroken, compact, and narrow
in the north but elsewhere a collection of coral reefs and
coral islands of various sizes and shapes forming a broad
belt bordering the coast. Some are awash and submerged,
others covered with sand or even with shrubs and trees. The
tide, of course, constantly pulsates back and forth around
these reefs. Eleven of the most important of the hundreds of
islands within the enormous lagoon, the so-called Great
Barrier Reef Channel, will be briefly described below.

It is easy to get to many of these islands and from them
to the reef itself. The living reef is visible only at low tide;
visitors cannot manage more than about two hours of observation on the exposed coral before the tide again covers it.

194

Area: about 30,800 km², includes some 160 islands and cays
Access: most islands reached by launch service from mainland
Accommodation: resorts on most islands

GEOLOGY Some of the reef formations rise 1,830 m above the **ocean floor;** in general the coral rock is about 120 m thick and rests on at least 85 m of sandy pigment, in turn presumably supported by a faulted platform of solid rock.

The greater part of the reef is always submerged. Living reefs seldom occur much below 30 fathoms.

The huge mass of corals of the reef is estimated to be some 30 million years old, starting as a minute marine animal, a polyp. Polyps protect themselves by forming an external skeleton, the coral. As these animals live in colonies, a coral reef grows.

CLIMATE Average temp. of water off Queensland coast does not fall below 60°F., ideal for the growth of coral; the sun's rays penetrate to the depths of the clear seas.

FLORA The largest of the island national parks is Hichinbrook Island (39,378 ha, created 1932) with a spectacular peak, Mt. Bowen, rising to 1,112 meters. Two other island N.P.'s further north: Dunk Is. (731 ha, tourist resort) with rain forest and open woods, and Green Is. (12 ha, guest house, underwater observatory, glass-bottomed boats), NE of Cairns; a cover of damson, beach oak, white cedar, screwpine.

South of Hichinbrook Is. the most interesting island N.P.'s are Orpheus Is. (1,368 ha, tourist resort); Magnetic Is. (2,535 ha, created a N.P. 1954); Long Island (836 ha in the reserve area); Lindeman Is. (park covers 715 ha), with open forests of various species of eucalypts; South Molle Is. (411 ha, tourist resort), with grasslands, scrub, and forests; Whitsunday Is. (10,935 ha), considered the most pictur-

esque, covered by hoop pine; Brampton Is. (2,948 ha, tourist resort), with hoop pine scrub, eucalypts, and she-oaks; Heron Is., a true coral cay, densely wooded.

FAUNA The rich coral growth of about 300 species of coral in all shapes and sizes is, of course, the background of other marine animals. Associated with the coral reefs are many invertebrates like crustaceans and molluscs, from giant clams to the smallest of cowries and of course millions of little fishes attracting larger fishes.

BIRDS Heron Island, surrounded by extensive coral reefs, is noted for its birdlife: waders, terns, gulls, herons, pelicans, cormorants, wedge-tailed shearwater, lesser frigate bird, greater frigate bird, osprey, red-backed sea eagle, and white-breasted sea eagle.

White-capped noddies nest in pisonia trees on many islands. The noddy and no fewer than seven other terns breed on the islands: sooty, roseate, crested, lesser crested, black-naped, bridled, and little tern.

OTHERS The green turtle is another inhabitant of Heron Is.; the dugong inhabits the inner Great Barrier Reef.

Corals and seaweed in the Hook Reef off Whitsunday Island

LAMINGTON NATIONAL PARK (created 1915, modified 1963), Queensland

One of the most interesting bird areas of Australia, with magnificent mountainous forests and waterfalls. This national park includes a section of the rugged McPherson Range.

Location: southeastern Queensland, along the border with New South Wales
Area: 19,631 ha
Protection: strictly supervised; 8 on staff
Access: by road from Brisbane (105 km)
Activities: hiking trails, horses for hire
Accommodation: Binna Burra Lodge and O'Reilly's Guest House

GEOLOGY Essentially a volcanic plateau. Volcanic products (in places more than 1,070 m thick) reflect tremendous activity during three separate periods: the first produced basaltic and andesitic material; the second, agglomerates and viscous lava flows; the third, the most active, filled the valleys and built up an enormous pile extending 50 km or more from the cone.

TOPOGRAPHY The park consists chiefly of mts. with many peaks (highest: Wanungara, 1,196 m). Many streams form more than 500

exquisite waterfalls. Panoramic views are everywhere—of the ocean, the coast, and the Great Dividing Range.

CLIMATE Subtropical but prevailing easterly winds assure high rainfall and moisture, giving a tropical aspect to the vegetation. The moderate elevation makes for a cool, pleasant temperature.

FLORA The park contains some of the oldest trees of the continent, notably Antarctic beeches, estimated to be more than 1,000 years old. Their trunks are covered with hanging mosses and ferns. Other trees: the flame tree, Moreton Bay chestnut, firewheel, giant tristania, hoop pine, several eucalypts.

Ferns of many species abound in the gullies and flowering orchids adorn many trees in spring.

MAMMALS Most of the forests of this park are rain forests of a temperate type, one of the largest such areas still existing in Australia and therefore of extreme importance as a refuge to plants and animals peculiar to this habitat.

One example is the dormouse opossum that has one of its last strongholds in this park (not often observed because nocturnal like most other mammals). Phalangers parachuting about can glide a distance of 100 meters from one tree to another. The koala lives among the eucalypts.

Other mammals: Rock wallaby, tiger cat (*Dasyurops maculatus*), black-tailed phascogale, common possum, short-eared brush-tail possum, rufous ringtail, platypus, echidna, dingo. Flying fox and many other species of bats occur.

Coomera Falls (70 m), Lamington N.P.

A section of the McPherson Mountain Range

BIRDS In the dense rain forests and thick shrubs: olive whistler, rufous scrub bird, riflebird, rufous fantail, Albert lyrebird, regent bowerbird, satin bowerbird, brush turkey, brown pigeon, topknot pigeon, noisy pitta, night heron, wedge-tailed eagle, gray goshawk, black falcon, letter-winged kite, tawny frogmouth, plumed frogmouth, powerful owl, many cockatoos, rosellas and lorikeets.

Other groups of species include broad-billed roller, kingfishers, rainbow-bird, and spine-tailed swift.

OTHER VERTEBRATES Snakes are common but difficult to see: common black snake, green common tree snake, and the carpet python.

Deadly reptiles like death adder and mainland tiger snake occur but are not common.

Many varying groups of lizards like goannas, geckos, skinks, and spiny-scaled lizards. Large species, are the leaf-tailed gecko and the land mullet. Uncommon but spectacular is the rain-forest dragon.

Rain forests are the home of many frogs and toads. The great barred river frog may be seen swimming in these streams.

An orchid (*Dendrobium kingianum*)

KU RING GAI CHASE NATIONAL PARK (created 1894) and MUOGAMARRA SANCTUARY, New South Wales

Much of nature is preserved here intact in spite of the intensive development of recreation areas for residents of nearby Sydney. The Muogamarra Sanctuary, a marvelous reserve for native flora and fauna, lies west of the national park and both are situated on the shores of Broken Bay, south of the Hawkesbury River.

Location: northern suburbs of Sydney
Area: Ku Ring Gai Chase, 15,200 ha
Climate: subtropical, with abundant rainfall at all seasons
Protection: total; numerous visitors
Activities: water sports, camping, sport fishing; recreation center at Bobbin Head
Of special interest: game park (koalas and other animals) in the national park

GEOLOGY The two reserves are both situated in exposed Hawkesbury sandstone tops, with plateaus, ridges, and deep gullies.

FLORA Eucalypt forests cover the broken country of Ku Ring Gai Chase with some areas of open forests and heaths. Both reserves have incredible color effects from masses of wild flowers in the spring, from July to October, with a peak usually in September. Several species of plants that are exterminated elsewhere in New South Wales still exist in Muogamarra, a replica of coastal Australia of 200 years ago.

MAMMALS Some koalas and wallabies can be observed in the forests of Ku Ring Gai Chase, but a small zoological garden near Bobbin Head for native fauna (mammals, birds, reptiles) within the reserves provides easier opportunities to watch the animals closely.

BIRDS The two reserves are particularly rich in birds. Numerous honey eaters pollinate various species of eucalypts, acacias, and banksias. They fill the forests and heaths with their melodious calls (and rather mediocre songs). Among other characteristic birds are shrike thrushes, welcome swallows, laughing kookaburras, fork-tailed and spine-tailed swifts, and boobook owls.

A great many aquatic birds may be seen: royal spoonbill, darter, great jabirus, black swan, and others.

The koala, once nearly exterminated, has recovered through protection.

THE ROYAL NATIONAL PARK (created 1886), New South Wales

This reserve, dating back to 1886, provides a representative series of East Australian coastland habitats from the Pacific seashores to natural forests with their abundant birdlife and contains many species of native flora and fauna. The park adjoins two undeveloped sanctuaries, Garrawarra Park in the south and the Heathcote Primitive Area in the west.

Location: southern shores of Port Hacking, and 12 km of coastline
Area: 14,620 ha
Climate: subtropical, with abundant rainfall throughout the year
Protection: total; staff of 30 guards
Activities: intensive tourism, sports, boating
Nearest city: Sydney (32 km)

GEOLOGY AND TOPOGRAPHY

A part of the Sydney sandstone region and therefore extremely rich in plant species. Rising gradually westward from the coast into a series of ridges up to 240 m, the land is intersected by numerous brooks and creeks.

FLORA The dunes are colonized by salt-supporting grasses constantly washed by sprinkles from the ocean waves. Wind-shaped shrubs crowd together on the dune ridge, beyond which are extensive heaths with dense macchia vegetation, banksia shrubs dominating with a great multitude of plants. In spring—throughout September and October—the heath is in splendid flower with cascading blooms of herbs, shrubs, and small trees.

Westward the heath changes to an open forest of low eucalypts and acacias. Some gullies support temperate rain forests with lilly-pilly trees, sassafras (Doryphora), coachwood, dense growths of tree ferns, hanging vines, and arboreal orchids.

BIRDS Though mammals are rarely seen, birds are very plentiful. Found along the broken shoreline with alternating sandy beaches and flats exposed at high tide: reef herons, sooty oyster-catchers migratory arctic waders, and silver gulls. Sometimes a great wandering albatross, the world's largest flying bird, may be spotted over the sea, as well as white-faced storm petrels.

In the banksia shrubs live numerous birds: lories in blood-red, blue, green and gold, rosellas, cockatoos, parakeets, and other large and small brilliantly colored parrots make extra patches of color. The bush heaths are the haunt of tiny fairy wrens, sky-blue to violet in color, a group of small birds found mainly in Australia.

In the low-growing eucalypt and acacia forest are the mallee fowl and the satin bowerbird, and in the taller and denser forests live the Lewin honey eater, the superb lyrebird, many parrots, and many songbirds.

Rock lily (Dendrobium speciosum) in the rain forest

BLUE MOUNTAINS NATIONAL PARK (created 1959), New South Wales

Resembling a minor North American Grand Canyon, Blue Mountains National Park represents a monumental landscape of eroded rocks, towering cliffs, and deep gorges formed by the Grose River, but unlike the Grand Canyon the park has forest-covered valleys and slopes.

Location: about 96 km W of Sydney
Area: 68,000 ha
Protection: total; staff of four; many visitors
Access: by rail and highway
Accommodation: in neighboring villages

GEOLOGY AND TOPOGRAPHY

The Blue Mountains are of Hawkesbury sandstone formation, probably originating about 190 million years ago. Plateaus and ranges reach 1.070 m, with 180-meter chasms falling away on both sides. Highest cliffs rise bare and multicolored above the forests.

FLORA　Eucalyptus forests and acacias cover lower slopes. Much light penetrates the rather open forest growth, allowing a dense undergrowth where many bushes and flowering plants bring masses of spring bloom of yellow, pink, and white flowers. Above on the plateaus extend vast heathlands with myriads of flowers.

MAMMALS　The great gray kangaroo and several species of brush wallabies, possums, and phalangers may be observed. In undisturbed areas of the Grose River the platypus is common. The wombat goes high up into the mountains.

BIRDS　Masses of flowers in forests and heaths attract many species of honey eaters, found all over the area. Ringing calls of the lyrebird, the notes of the yellow robin and the echoing calls of the coach-whip bird are often heard. Wonga pigeons and crimson rosellas display beautiful color.

OTHER VERTEBRATES　Lizards abound in the bushland and eucalyptus forests; some of these, such as the bluetongue, eat fruit.

Plateaus and steep cliffs of the Blue Mountains N.P.

Geehi Valley, clad in eucalyptus forests, Kosciusko N.P.

KOSCIUSKO NATIONAL PARK (created 1944), New South Wales

This huge area, the Snowy Mountains, contains all the highest peaks of the Australian mainland and affords subalpine and alpine landscape scenery, mainly forested. It is the largest of Australia's national parks, comprising an area the size of the Netherlands.

A federal hydroelectric development on a giant scale with dams, power plants, and tunnels has destroyed and submerged large areas of the park; road construction and a century of grazing have also contributed to the deplorable fact that it would now be impossible to find any large tract in virgin state. Despite these damaged nature areas, however, the park is so large that the reserve is still of great value and provides extensive space giving refuge to plant and animal life.

Location: in the Australian Alps, near Canberra and Sydney
Area: about 600,000 ha (primitive area: 18,130 ha); staff of 26

Activities: many tourist facilities; excursions; winter sports, (ski lifts)
Nearest cities: Canberra 44 km; Sydney, 58 km

GEOLOGY The bedrock is chiefly of granite with two large areas of cavernous limestone. The highlands contain conclusive traces of the presence of former Pleistocene glaciers (of which there are relatively few in the southern hemisphere): U-shaped valleys, cirques, moraines, and glaciated pavements.

TOPOGRAPHY Altitude range: 210—2,130 meters. Swampy plains, valleys, gorges, plateaus, and mountains, glacial lakes, rivers and waterfalls accentuate the topographical variation. Highest mt. is Mt. Kosciusko (2,229 m), named after a Pole, the first European who climbed it. Four other peaks exceed 2,130 meters.

CLIMATE Situated at high elevation on the crest of the Great Dividing Range, the park has low temperatures and high precipitation, including snow.

FLORA The rich flora is remarkably heterogeneous in origin and includes about 700 species of flowering plants, almost 200 species of mosses and liverworts, and more than 24 species of ferns. About half of the plants belong to Australian elements, but the others derive from New Zealand, Antarctica, the Asian tropics, South Africa, South America, and the Northern Hemisphere.

Gum trees *(Eucalyptus)* dominate the forest, with snow gum forming the tree line at about 1,830 meters. Alpine meadows display flowers of many species.

MAMMALS Surprisingly many species of Australia's peculiar animals ascend quite high up on the Snowy Mountains. Some 30 species of mammals include great gray kangaroos, brush-tailed rock wallabies, wombats, possums, spiny anteaters,

Emu, Australia's largest bird

Eucalyptus niphophila forms highest forests (2,000 m) of Kosciusko N.P.

and platypuses, which are common. The koala is slowing recolonizing its ancient habitats.

BIRDS The area has about 150 species of birds; special mention should be made of the emu, lyrebird, gang gang cockatoo, crimson rosella, yellow-tailed black cockatoo, white cockatoo, and the wedge-tailed eagle.

OTHERS In *Sphagnum* bogs above 1,220 m lives the corroboree frog, beautifully patterned in black and yellow.

An extraordinary insect is a colorful grasshopper, *Kosciuskola tristis*, only insect in world known to change color with temperature.

In streams and creeks that are still free from introduced trout occurs a small minnow, *Galaxias findlayi*, extremely interesting zoo-geographically: it has close affinities with species in New Zealand, subantarctic islands, New Caledonia, South Africa, and South America, and is thus a biogeographic parallel to many plants.

Blotched bluetongue (*Tiliqua nigrolutea*)

The tidal river valley with Mt. La Trobe (left) and Mt. Ramsay

WILSON'S PROMONTORY NATIONAL PARK (created 1905), Victoria

Superb coastal scenery, unrivaled elsewhere in Victoria, with beaches and sheer cliffs, and a wide range of habitats with a rich flora and fauna. The reserve comprises 130 km of coastland consisting of sparkling blue bays, long white beaches, dunes, rocky headlands, and rugged mountains with spurs that fall steeply to the sea.

Location: southernmost extremity of the Australian continent
Area: 40,952 ha
Climate: subtropical, with abundant rainfall at all seasons (averages 1,524 mm a year)
Protection: total; many visitors; trails
Access: by rail, road (Melbourne 240 km)
Accommodation: lodges, motels, camping areas

GEOLOGY Approach is by an isthmus formed by the depositing of sedimentation of sluggish tides and windblown sand. Granite mountains of rocks rich in quartz veins dominate the promontory. Coastland features show the results of coastal submergence, which occurred after the last worldwide glaciations began to diminish about 15,000 years ago.

TOPOGRAPHY Mt. Wilson, named in 1798 after Thomas Wilson of London, is 709 m high; the highest mt. of the park: Mt. La Trobe (754 m). Almost all of the land in the interior is mountainous and densely vegetated with numerous gullies and winding streams.

FLORA More than 700 native plants in the park range from dwarf plants such as heaths, everlasting daisies, orchids, golden guineas, blue olive-berry, banksias, and bush peas to mangrove, tea trees, acacias, eucalypts, lillypilly trees, coachwood, antarctic beech, blackwood, giant honey-myrtle, casuarinas, sassafras, honeysuckles, and treeferns like the giant *Cyathea*

204

Australian pelican (*Pelecanus conspicillatus*)

cunninghami. The mountain ash grows to about 60 meters, one of the tallest tree species in the world. Unfortunately, severe bush fires in 1951 destroyed much of the very vulnerable vegetation and the forest fauna. Recovery is rather slow.

MAMMALS The mammals of the park's area were heavily slaughtered before the reserve was established in 1905, and many species disappeared. Since then several species have slowly recovered, and some others have been reintroduced. Now there are koala, wombat, kangaroos, wallabies, bandicoots, possums, and Australian spiny anteater. Among the 36 species of mammals are deer, fox, and rabbit, which unfortunately have been introduced.

BIRDS At least 181 species occur, among them the emu, little pied cormorant, egret, white-breasted sea eagle, brown hawk, Horsfield bronze cuckoo, spotted quail thrush, gray-backed silvereye and the rare ground parrot.

Conservationists were encouraged in 1964 when the rare Cape Barren goose was found to be breeding on the Anser and Glennie Islands off Wilson's Promontory, the first record there since 1910. Black swans may gather in thousands.

OTHERS The clear waters of the sea reveal parrotfishes, sweep, leatherjackets, and southern bream.

Norman Bay, Oberon Range, and Mt. Norgate; Wilson's Promontory N.P.

Tree ferns in King Lake National Park

KING LAKE NATIONAL PARK (created 1928), Victoria
Heavily forested mountain country with deep gullies on the
slopes of the Plenty Ranges along the southern escarpment
of the Great Divide. There are splendid vistas of foothills,
plains, and, on clear days, of Port Phillip Bay. Flora and
fauna are rich and interesting.

Location: about 48 km NE of Melbourne
Area: 5,632 ha, in three sections; open to visitors: Jerorophat Gully, Dame Melba's Lookout, and Mason's Falls (picnic kiosk)
Protection: total; two guards; good network of park roads
Access: from Melbourne
Accommodation: no hotels within park; camping forbidden

GEOLOGY Rock formations are of Silurian age with beds of sandstone and mudstone containing beautifully preserved marine fossils. These rocks were laid down beneath the sea 400—200 million years ago. The seas have receded; upheavals and earth movements have elevated the land far above what is now sea level.

TOPOGRAPHY Steep gullies and valleys have been carved by streams. Highest of the many waterfalls: Mason's Falls on Sugarloaf Creek, where the water cascades 42 m through the bush; the Wombelano Falls are also well worth visiting.

CLIMATE Subtropical-temperate, favoring a lush vegetation, which is typical for the medium wet forests in central Victoria.

FLORA Despite the moisture, the bulk of the vegetation is a tall, dry sclerophyll forest, frequently damaged by bush fires. Narrow-leaf peppermint and messmate (with some trees 30—45 m high) are dominant, shadowing small-leaved understories of common heath, hop goodenia, and sallow wattle.

In gullies are mountain gum and manna gum (45—54 m) over dense blanketleaf, musk, silver wattle, and blackwood.

Treeferns abound; the rare epiphytic butterfly orchid and the elbow orchid may be found; lianas, such as wonga vine and Australian clematis, adorn many trees.

There are over 326 plant species, of which 37 are ferns and 20 are orchids, while nine trees belong to the genus *Eucalyptus* and ten to *Acacia*.

MAMMALS The bush of King Lake National Park supports a wealth of animal species that includes ringtail possum, great gray kangaroo, black-tailed wallaby, wombat, bandicoot, dasyure, koala, echidna, and platypus. (Most of these mammals are nocturnal.)

BIRDS Over 100 species have been recorded including parrots and rosellas with splashes of color, currawongs, magpie larks, mountain thrushes, gray thrushes, coachwhip birds, butcher-birds, cuckoos, cuckoo shrikes, yellow robins, rose robins, fan-tails, honey eaters, wrens, tree creepers, sittellas, whistlers, thornbills, black cockatoos, gang gangs, and lyrebirds.

The wedge-tailed eagle nests in this park and is often seen soaring over the slopes. Owls and the tawny frogmouth (*Podargus strigoides*) can be heard at night.

OTHER VERTEBRATES Among the reptiles, copperhead, white-lipped snake, large skink, and bluetongue may be mentioned.

Tawny frogmouth, a large nightjar

WYPERFELD NATIONAL PARK, (created 1921), Victoria
This reserve in the semi-desert Mallee region, the largest
national park of Victoria, was set aside to protect extraordinary vegetation and wildlife, particularly the mallee hen,
wholly dependent on virgin mallee country (dense, low-
growing eucalyptus thickets). It is situated north of Lake Al-
bacutya (about 450 km NW of Melbourne), on the eastern
margin of the Great Desert.

Location: northwestern Victoria
Area: 56,000 ha
Climate: subtropical; very dry
Protection: total
Access: via Hopetoun, or via Dimboola
Accommodation: in neighboring towns
Best visiting: in the spring (Sept.–Oct.)

GEOLOGY The park lies in the Murray Basin, which consists of Cretaceous sediments covered by Quaternary deposits. In the Upper Oligocene and Miocene periods this part of Australia was invaded by the sea, which retreated in the Pliocene; river silts gradually produced the alluvial plain and a complex pattern of dry lakes and lagoons.

TOPOGRAPHY The area consists of undulating wind-blown sandhills, often over 45 m high (probably formed within the last 10,000 years). Despite its aridity, the reserve is by no means a desert.

FLORA Central part of park dominated by dense mallee *(Eucalyptus gracilis, E. leptophylla, E. incrassata)*, the sandhills to the E and W being lightly covered with heath and dwarf shrubs. In spring the semi-desert bursts into a blazing patchwork of yellow, white, pink, and violet flowers.

Despite the arid climate there are at least 348 species of flowering plants in the park, including six orchids. In 1959 almost all of the area W of the dry lake region was destroyed by fire, and 24,300 hectares of mallee were razed. This is now steadily regenerating.

MAMMALS Black-faced kangaroos roam in hundreds, the commonest but also the wariest of native species. Brush-tail possum is at times very common. The spiny anteater also occurs. Rabbits and foxes are introduced exotics here as they are all over Australia.

BIRDS abound with at least 196 species. The mallee hen, has a good population—its "incubating" mounds of debris may be seen here and there. The pink cockatoo and the regent parrot, two of Australia's finest birds, occur in this park.

Other species: emu, goshawk, wedge-tailed eagle, tawny frogmouth, tree martin, eastern whiteface, 12 species of honey eaters, and black-winged currawong.

OTHER VERTEBRATES Western bluetongue lizard and Gould's sand goanna are common.

Mycromyrtus ciliatus. Wyperfeld

Panskiri Bluff at Lake Waikaremoana, Urewera National Park

NEW ZEALAND

Area: 269,714 km^2 Population density: 10/km^2

New Zealand, ornithologically famous, has ten national
parks, of which eight are described here. (The other two are
Mt. Aspiring National Park, 199,232 ha, and Nelson Lakes
National Park, 57,112 ha, both on South Island.) The native
mammals of N.Z. are Forster's fur seal and two bats; other
mammals seen in parks are exotics. Hunting and fishing
are authorized in most parks (controlled by a permit system)
and the shooting of introduced species that are creating
considerable damage, such as red deer, chamois, opossum,
is encouraged. The National Parks Authority, Department of
Lands and Survey (P.O. Box 8003, Wellington) issues information and excellent booklets.

UREWERA NATIONAL PARK (created 1954), North Island
Urewera National Park contains the largest remaining area
of unspoiled mountain forest in the North Island and includes Lake Waikaremoana, which belongs to the Maori
people. The region abounds with historic Maori places, and
there are pocket areas of Maori land inside the national park.

209

Hopuruahine Cascades, Urewera N.P.

Location: central North Island
Area: 199,523 ha
Protection: total; personnel of six; well-marked trails; trout fishing
Accommodation: hotel and motor camp at Lake House camping grounds

GEOLOGY In the distant past, the mts. of Urewera were many miles deep under the ocean. Basement rocks are generally Urewera greywacke, overlaid by mudstones and sandstones of Lower Cretaceous Age (argillites). There is also a Quaternary volcanic belt in W part of park.

TOPOGRAPHY Bush-covered ranges are dissected by numerous streams with many waterfalls. Altitudes: from 152 m in the Whakatane River Valley to 1,366 m in Maungaphohatu range and 1,402 m at Manuoha.

The park includes the catchment basins of Lake Waikaremoana and Lake Waikareiti and the headwaters of the Whakatane and Waimana rivers.

CLIMATE Summers are mild and pleasant, winters stormy with biting frosts and snow at higher elevations. Annual rain exceeds 2,500 mm.

FLORA At lower levels, luxuriant kohekohe and large rimu and northern rata stand above the tawa. Damp gully sites have been colonized by dense treeferns, fuchsia, wineberry, and mahoe.

With a rise in elevation various species of antarctic beeches take over. In general silver beech continues alone above about 1,157 m up to the timber line.

MAMMALS Regrettably, this park contains noxious exotic mammals: pigs, goats, red deer, and possum.

BIRDS A wide variety of sheltered: passerines like gray warbler, whitehead, tui, kaka, New Zealand pigeon, shining cuckoo, and others. On lakes and rivers: paradise duck, blue duck, gray duck and blue-winged shoveler.

Paradise duck (*Tadorna variegata*)

Ngauruhoe, Tongariro N.P., is New Zealand's most active volcano.

TONGARIRO NATIONAL PARK (created 1887), North Island

New Zealand's first park came into being by the generosity of the chief Te Heuheu IV and his family, who gave a 6,500 acre area around the summits of the three sacred volcanoes Tongariro, Ngauruhoe, and Ruapehu "as a gift for ever from me and my people." Now ten times larger, the park still has the three sacred mountains as its central area. The park occupies the heart of the North Island, an area with many surrounding minor volcanic cones, lakes, streams, waterfalls, forests, grasslands, subalpine vegetation, and a desert-like lava plain. Six glaciers hang on the flanks of the volcano Ruapehu, the highest of North Island's mountains.

Location: central North Island
Area: 67,405 ha
Protection: two areas set aside for strict protection; personnel: 13; buses for trips in and around park; well-marked hiking trails
Access: by road from Hamilton and Rotorua; by rail from Wellington (325 km) and Auckland
Accommodation: first class hotel, Chateau Tongariro; motels, huts, motor camps

GEOLOGY The old volcano Ruapehu (height: 2,796 m) has been intermittently active for more than half a million years (the latest eruption occurring in June 1969). Tongariro (1,968 m) is also an old volcano with numerous craters. The young Ngauruhoe volcano (2,291 m) has grown up in an old crater

211

New Zealand pigeon

TOPOGRAPHY The lower areas of the larger volcanic plateau are about 600 m above SL. Glaciers on Ruapehu feed rivers that have cut deep gorges into the volcanic slopes. Crater Lake, near the summit of this volcano, usually contains hot water though surrounded by snow and ice. Tongariro has hot springs and a sulfur lagoon on its southern slope. A barren area east of Ruapehu is the Rangipo Desert, stripped of vegetation by volcanic mud flows, floods, and wind erosion.

CLIMATE Mountainous, with rapid and extreme changes. Warmest month: February. Average temp. 53°F; mean temp. of winter months: 36°–37°F. All months are rather wet. Ground frosts have been recorded in all seasons; the area is entirely covered by snow in winter.

FLORA The 470 or so plants of this N.P. represent various highland communities: below 914 m are forests of rimu, matai, kamahi, miro, silver beech, and red beech; at 914–1,200 meter levels: mountain totara and mountain beech; at 1,200–1,520 meters: red tussock communities dominate. Still higher: herb and rock fields, alpine meadows and bogs with *Senecio bidwillii*, and mountain toatoa.

Lodgepole pine and heather are rapidly invading the area.

of Tongariro and now reaches higher than the mother mountain. It is New Zealand's most active volcano, erupting with clouds of volcanic ash and steam every few years. (Violent eruptions occurred in the years 1869, 1949, and 1954–1955 with resulting lava flows.)

Underlying sedimentary rocks are hard sandstones and mudstones, with overlying younger marine sediments such as limestones, siltstones, and sandstones.

MAMMALS Exotic mammals in the park: red deer, pig, ermine, possum, cat, rabbit, hare, rats, mice.

BIRDS Most of the birdlife is in the mixed forest on the lower mountain slopes: New Zealand pigeon, fantail, rifleman (New Zealand's smallest bird), gray warbler, tui, and morepork. The brown kiwi exists in this N.P., as do the weka, a flightless rail, and the kaha. Upper slopes have banded dotterels.

Introduced birds include blackbird, chaffinch, and skylark.

The weka, a flightless rail

Mt. Egmont seen from about the 800-meter level, where the forest gives way to a scrub belt of many subalpine plants

EGMONT NATIONAL PARK (created 1900), North Island

In the history of the Maori, Mount Egmont with its Fuji-like, snow-covered volcanic dome was a sacred place. The park protects Mt. Egmont, and the Pouakai and Kaitake ranges, all remnants of volcanic activities and now clothed in beautiful forests. The area shelters a rich and varied birdlife.

Location: Taranaki Province, western North Island
Area: 33,377 ha
Protection: total; personnel of five; well-marked paths; guides available
Access: good roads from the nearest towns: New Plymouth and Stratford
Activities: skiing and climbing
Accommodation: Dawson Falls Hostels, North Egmont Chalet, Stratford Mountain House; lodges, huts, camping sites

GEOLOGY About 3–5 million years ago volcanic action extended on a large scale along a fault line running through the Kaitake and Pouakai ranges to Egmont. Kaitake (682 m) and Pouakai (1,399 m) have long been extinct. Egmont, although at present dormant, has been active since the human occupation of New Zealand. A series of eruptions about half a million years ago shaped the present symmetrical cone. All the volcanoes are composed of andesite.

TOPOGRAPHY Mt. Egmont rises straight out of the plain, dominating the landscape. Smaller cones are scattered around the main volcanoes. Water from melting snow is channeled by a network of streams, cascading in waterfalls through gorges to the arable valleys below.

213

New Zealand kingfisher

From 550 to 765 meters: a mixed forest zone of totara, rimu, miro, kamahi, and northern rata. Farther up, Hall's totara replaces kamahi and is joined by mountain cedar. About 50 species of ferns occur in these moist forests; a profusion of mosses and lichens covers almost every part of the trees.

A belt of scrub with many subalpine plants is found up to 1,370—1,430 m, and above this are tussock grasslands to about 1,675 m, and then mosses, lichens, and many species of flowering plants. At 2,286 m, ten flowering plants remain and at 2,438 m, only one (Colobanthus). Mosses and lichens alone reach the crater limit.

CLIMATE High rainfall and moisture; many summer storms. Mists often cover the forests, but the cone of Mt. Egmont is usually free. Winter snow accumulates and creeps down to about 1,200 meters.
FLORA Magnificent dense virgin rain forests of an almost subtropical appearance grow on the lower slopes of Mt. Egmont. The absence of antarctic beeches is remarkable.

MAMMALS A depressing fact, from the conservationist's point of view, is that a high number of introduced exotic mammals occur in the national park: feral cat, ermine, opossum, cattle, sheep, goats, hares, rabbit, rats and mice. The battle against them is intensive, but the elimination is costly.
BIRDS The rich birdlife includes a number of rare birds though the denseness of the vegetation means that birds are not easily seen.

Along the streams in the lowland forest is the New Zealand kingfisher. The comparatively rare kokako inhabits lower-level forests, particularly where there are tawa trees. Whiteheads and moreporks are common up to about 915 meters. Birds that do not ascend above 1,065 meters: tomtit, fantail, and shining cuckoo.

Silvereye goes up to about 1,220 m, and the New Zealand pipit frequents tussock land and alpine meadows to levels of about 1,830 meters.

Rare birds on Mt. Egmont include kaka, North Island robin, and brown kiwi.

Morepork (Ninox novae-seelandiae)

The rocky and cliffy coast of Abel Tasman National Park looks much today as it did when Tasman anchored there in 1642.

ABEL TASMAN NATIONAL PARK (created 1942), South Island

A botanist's paradise with rich birdlife, including the blue penguin. The reserve comprises an unspoiled broken coastland with a variety of islands, rocks, reefs, beaches, coves, and precipitous cliffs, as well as uplands with mountains and valleys extending inland about ten kilometers.

The national park is named for the Dutch navigator who "discovered" New Zealand in 1642. He anchored that year in the vicinity of the Tata Islands within the national park.

Location: at Tasman Bay, northern South Island
Area: 18,265 ha
Protection: total; personnel of three; roads and paths within park
Access: by boat and by road (nearest city: Nelson)
Accommodation: camping grounds; huts

GEOLOGY Granite composes the major part. In the SW of the reserve is Takaka Hill, the very ancient rock (400 million years old) with strangely eroded outcrops and caves of exposed marble. The Tata Islands, however, are of Tertiary limestone.

The attractive golden sand of the beaches is largely quartz and feldspar from the weathering of granite. Small amounts of gold, silver, lead, copper, scheelite, and molybdenite appear in a large reef crossing the summit of Mt. Evans.

Forster's fur seal

TOPOGRAPHY There is an extraordinary variety of maritime and forest scenery: from the cliffs and rocks flanking the sandy beaches and dunes to landscapes with marshes, bush-clad headlands, and heavily forested mts. with cascades and waterfalls. The land rises steeply from the coast to 1,130 m.

CLIMATE Temperate. Average temp. at nearby Wellington is 54° F.

FLORA A century ago the area was forested. Cultivation and fires changed much of the lower vegetation, but today the hills are being allowed to return to something like their natural state. The higher slopes and ridges are occupied by antarctic beech forests. It is unusual to be able to find all of New Zealand's five species of antarctic beeches in one restricted park area: red beech forests, mountain beech, silver beech, hard beech, and black beech.

At about 975 m, an open tussock area, Moa Park, is completely surrounded by stunted silver beeches.

The two remaining patches of rain forest, consisting mostly of rimu, are on the road to Totaranui and in the Falls River Valley. Epiphytes, climbers, and orchids live on almost every tall tree.

In more sheltered gullies there are northern rata with scattered totara, matai, miro, and hinau.

MAMMALS A native mammal of the national park is Forster's fur seal, which is joined infrequently by sea lions and sea bears.

Unfortunately here, as in all the rest of New Zealand, earlier introductions of red deer, goats, pigs, and opossum are a menace to indigenous plants and animals.

BIRDS Seabirds abound along the rugged coast: southern black-backed gull, red-billed gull, Caspian tern, oystercatchers (*Haematopus finschi* and *H. reischeki*), reef heron, spotted shag, black shag, several petrels, and the blue penguin.

Swampy areas have white-faced herons and brown bitterns and the very rare fernbird.

Bush and forest birds include South Island robin, bellbird, and tui.

The weka prefers drier scrubs or the edge of the forest. Pigeons of various species are numerous. In higher beech forests occur parrots (such as yellow-billed parakeet and others), the kaka, and the kea.

OTHERS Skin divers may meet with butterfish, cod, (a grouper), snapper, sharp-beaked gurnard, stingaree, and other fish. A giant land snail occurs above 600 meters.

Blue penguin

A winter scene in the Arthur's Pass National Park

ARTHUR'S PASS NATIONAL PARK (created 1929), South Island

The park extends on both sides of the Main Divide of the Southern Alps between the Waimakariri and Taramakau rivers, an area of snowy mountains, broad valleys, forest slopes, and waterfalls. The reserve has been notable for its alpine flora.

On the northern side of the divide in Westland, the Otehake Wilderness Area has been set aside within the national park (access allowed only on foot). A scenic gem in this area is Lake Kaurapataka at an altitude of 415 meters.

Area: 98,371 ha
Protection: total; six guards
Access: by road (152 km from Christchurch), and by rail
Activities: tramping, climbing, skiing (July–October)
Accommodation: motels, huts

GEOLOGY The area lies within a region in which the crust of the earth is not yet at rest and earthquakes, landslides, and movements of the riverbeds' whole mass of gravel and sand occur.

Dominating rocks in the Arthur's Pass N.P. are gray sandstone, called greywacke, of sedimentary origin.

Glacial actions of the past have modeled the mountain slopes, moraine deposits dotting the surface with irregular and rocky mounds.

About 10,000 years ago, Arthur's Pass was covered in ice to a depth of more than a hundred meters. The mts. in the vicinity form the present northern limit for true glaciers in South Island.

TOPOGRAPHY Altitudinal range: 548–2,271 m (height of Mt. Rolleston). Arthur's Pass is at 923 meters.

The Otira Gorge and the Devil's Punchbowl waterfall, nearly 150 meters high, should be mentioned. There are also cirques, bogs, meadows, forests, and alpine heaths.

CLIMATE Variations are pronounced, since the park is on both sides of the Main Divide. Prevailing NW winds are laden with moisture that condenses on passing over the Southern Alps. Climate to the

Kea (Nestor notabilis)

east much drier. In winter the park is covered with snow.

FLORA Vegetation reflects the climatic variations: there are at least 13 main plant communities, of which some of the more important are river terraces with tussock grasslands; bogs and margins of tarns with sedge cushions, bog moss turfs, bladderwort, and mountain gentians; antarctic beech forests of mt. slopes on east side up to 1,372 meters, the trees decorated with lichens, mosses, climbing plants, the scarlet mistletoe and a yellow-flowered mistletoe; at higher elevations, subalpine plants: tree daisies, tree groundsels, mountain cedar, and Hall's totara; bog forests of pink pine; above timber line: snow totara, snow grass, mountain daisy, and many others.

The wet Westland area forests are quite different from those on the east side of the Main Divide: red beech the main species, with silver beech, white pine and rimu, black pine, southern rata and totara. Farther up, kamahi becomes more common and orchids are plentiful. In summer the slopes burn red when the rata trees bloom. The upper forest zone is dominated by Hall's totara, the big grass tree, and mountain cedar.

MAMMALS Introduced deer, chamois, and possum destroy much of the native vegetation.

BIRDS The most famous birds of this park are the great spotted kiwi and the kea.

Other noteworthy species: bellbird, rifleman (so called because of its voice), gray warbler, tomtit, silvereye, rock wren, morepork, New Zealand falcon, harrier, paradise duck, blue duck, black-fronted tern, and weka (reintroduced in 1966).

Canada geese, chaffinches, thrushes, goldfinches, and other exotics are, of course, introduced.

Mt. Cook lily (Ranunculus lyalli)

Glaciers and permanent snow, Mt. Cook seen from Hooker Valley

MOUNT COOK AND WESTLAND NATIONAL PARKS, South Island

The Cook National Park is chiefly mountainous with 27 peaks above 3,048 meters, snowfields, glaciers, and little forests of silver beech; Westland National Park ranges from sea level to 3,497 meters and its mountains, swept by moist winds, are clothed by dense forests up to the snow line. The ridge of the Main Divide in the Southern Alps forms the common boundary of the two parks.

Location: New Zealand's Southern Alps
Area: Mt. Cook N.P., 70,002 ha (created 1953); Westland N.P., 91,804 ha (created 1960)
Protection: total for the two contiguous areas; personnel: 18
Access: by rail and car, by road, and by air from Christchurch to Ross and Hoikitika, nearest cities
Activities: skiing, tramping, climbing; ski-equipped air strip with year-round scenic trips
Accommodation: Hermitage Hotel and Lodges (Mt. Cook); two hotels in Westland; huts, camps

GEOLOGY Mt. Cook National Park contains mts. of intensely folded greywacke sandstone, argillite, and other sedimentary rocks deposited on the sea floor some 150–200 million years ago before they became schists and gneiss; the present peaks and valleys were sculptured by glaciers and streams during a late stage in New Zealand's geology.

219

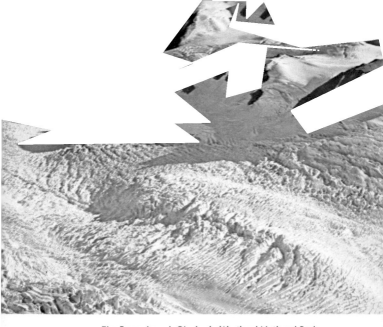

The Franz Joseph Glacier in Westland National Park

In Westland N.P. the alpine fault is well defined and forms an impressive boundary between the Southern Alps and the lowland.

TOPOGRAPHY Over a third of Mt. Cook N.P. is made up of permanent snow and glaciers. Within the park are the majority of New Zealand's great mountains; the highest is Mt. Cook (3,764 m). Other striking massifs: Mt. Sefton (3,157 m), Mt. La Perouse (3,079 m), Mt. Hicks (3,183 m), Mt. Dampier (3,440 m).

Westland National Park's highest mt. is Mt. Tasman (3,498 m), which forms the summit of the boundary with Mt. Cook N.P. The large Fox and Franz Josef glaciers descend, passing luxuriant bush, to within 300 meters above SL. Other features are Lake Matheson, Lake Mapourika, and Lake Wahapo, rivers, waterfalls, and hot springs.

CLIMATE The nearby sea, west winds predominating, influences the climate of Westland National Park. Rainfall, 3,000 mm a year near the coast, probably exceeds 7,500 mm in the mts., mostly falling as snow above 2,134 meters. Snow line in winter and spring: 1,220–1,525 meters; in summer and autumn: 2,135–2,440 meters.

Mt. Cook N.P., less exposed to the sea, has a more rigid climate, with severe winters and less rainfall.

FLORA Both parks represent a spectrum of vertical botanical zones: black pine, white pine and totara in the lower valleys (with the conifers miro and rimu in river terraces) give way to thick shrubs and mountain cedar above 1,000 meters. Ferns are characteristic of Westland N.P.

In Mt. Cook N.P. over 300 species of native plants have been found, chiefly alpine species, with a flowering season from October to January. Edelweiss, gentians,

New Zealand snowberry
(*Gualtheria depressa*)

mountain buttercups, daisies (silvery *Celmisia coriacea* and dull green *C. petiolata*) are conspicuous.

MAMMALS A great number of introduced exotic mammals exist in the two N.P.'s: tahr, chamois, red deer, goat, opossum, ermine, weasel, and ferret.

A native mammal, however, is Forster's fur seal, which may be observed at Gillespies Beach.

BIRDS of both parks differ through the wide range of vertical habitats. Along the beaches, coastal lagoons, and estuaries: black-backed gull, banded dotterel, New Zealand kingfisher, three species of shags, among many others. In swamps: harrier, bittern and pukeho; along river beds and on flats: paradise duck, blue duck, and South Island pied oystercatcher; in lakes: gray duck, little shag, white heron, and crested grebe; in forests and bush: gray warbler, tui, rifleman, fantail, yellow-crowned parakeet, N.Z. pigeon (also seen in townships), shining cuckoo, and morepork; on the alpine tussock and rocky plateaus: N.Z. pipit, rock wren, kea (often coming down to township areas), and N.Z. falcon.

Fox Glacier gliding down through a lush green valley

Long seawater fiords penetrate mountainous inland of Fiordland N.P.

FIORDLAND NATIONAL PARK (created 1904), South Island

The largest national park of New Zealand, and one of the world's largest, is an immense fiordland with a spectacular seacoast where bays and sounds penetrate deep into the high mountains, which display lakes, rivers, waterfalls, forests, and glaciers. The park gives protection to several very rare birds and is the area in New Zealand where visitors have a chance of seeing most of the species that have made New Zealand's birdlife so famous.

In the heart of the region a special area protects the flightless takahe, thought to be extinct until rediscovered in 1948. (This is its only known locality.) Special permission is required to visit the area. Another wilderness area is Secretary Island between Doubtful and Thomson sounds.

Location: southwestern South Island
Area: 1,223,654 ha (wilderness area of 11,664 ha)
Climate: temperate, with an average rainfall of about 5,000 mm
Access: by boat and by road
Activities: mountaineering, deer stalking, tramping, skiing, water sports
Accommodation: Milford Hotel, Cascade Creek, and Lower Hollyford camps
Nearest large town: Queenstown

GEOLOGY The oldest rocks of the area were originally sandstones and limestones laid down on the sea bottom 400–300 million years ago. Present Fiordland comprises schists and gneisses. Granites and diorites, as well as volcanic rocks, also exist.

Tui (Prosthemadera novaeseelandiae)

TOPOGRAPHY Milford Sound, most striking of New Zealand's fiords, mirrors the mountain slopes and peaks parading on both sides (Mitre Peak, 1,695 m, and Mt. Pembroke, 2,045 m). Te Anau is the largest lake of South Island, Mt. Tutoko the highest peak (2,756 m). Outstanding features are Sutherland Falls (580 m), one of the highest in the world, and the chasm of the Cleddau River that tumbles into the depths of the immense cavern it has carved (with a wonderful view from the chasm of Mt. Underwood and the snow domes of Mt. Tutoko).

FLORA Beech forests (silver beech and mountain beech) extend along the shore line and climb to about 915–1,070 meters. In lower parts, southern rata, mountain ribbonwood, rimu, miro, and broadleaf are typical—all thickly coated with moss; also several species of treeferns. In the upper forests grass trees are typical. Above the timber line, alpine scrub and grasslands with mountain daisy, New Zealand edelweiss, and spaniard merge into lichen-covered rocks and snowfields.

MAMMALS The native mammals are the Forster's fur seals, which used to be common along the coast before the sealing trade. Sea lions may also be seen. Many introduced mammals include ermine, possum, wapiti, red deer, axis deer, moose, chamois, goat, pig and rats.

BIRDS The park is a refuge for many New Zealand birds not seen elsewhere. All three species of kiwis—great spotted kiwi, little spotted kiwi, and brown kiwi—occur. So do the kea and the flightless kakapo, takahe, and weka. The only known remaining habitat of the kapapo is the Tutoko Valley near Milford Sound, while the takahe is confined to an area in the Murchison Mountains.

Species often observed: bush robin, bellbird, tomtit, tui, silvereye, yellow-crowned parakeet, kaka, New Zealand pigeon, rifleman, rock wren, New Zealand shoveler, gray duck, paradise duck, blue duck, crested grebe, pukeko, and the Fiordland crested penguin.

Many introduced birds in New Zealand have infiltrated the park: blackbird, greenfinch, dunnock, California quail, and spur-winged plover (introduced from Australia).

OTHERS Species like Atlantic salmon, rainbow and brown trout have been acclimatized to encourage fishermen.

Brown kiwi (Apteryx australis)

Area: 18,343 km²   Population density: 22/km²

Two reserves on the Fiji Islands are effectively protected: Nandarivatu, described below, and Ravilevu (3,972 ha on Taveuni Island). There are also some very small reserves and protected areas. The Ministry of Natural Resources, Suva, is in charge of their administration.

NANDARIVATU NATURE RESERVE (created 1956, 1958) The name applies to three neighboring reserves, which are from one to six miles apart: Tomaniivi, Nagaranibuluti, and Nandarivatu. These are connected by a little winding road controlled by forest guards. A mountainous region, clad in rain forest, which protects several rare bird species. The reserve lies up on the mountains 27 km from the town of Tavua, which is about 96 km from Nandi International Airport.

Location: northern Viti Levu, the largest island
Area: 1,674 ha in three neighboring reserves
Protection: strict supervision by forest guards; road and paths to major points of interest
Access: by a small winding road
Accommodation: none in the park

GEOLOGY Hundreds of millions of years ago volcanic upheavals rent the bed of the Pacific Ocean. Some of the undersea mountains thrust their tops above the ocean surface and became exposed to sun, winds, and rains. This was the genesis of the Fijis.

TOPOGRAPHY The reserve comprises an upland valley; altitude: about 820 meters with surrounding mountains from 910 to 1,323 meters (the height of Mt. Victoria, a mountain of two peaks connected by a saddle, and usually covered by clouds).

CLIMATE Tropical, but without extremes of heat and humidity. Temperatures: in the lowland range from 60° to 90°F, but temperatures in the reserve always about 10°F cooler.

The hottest, wettest, and most humid period is from December to February; the coolest and driest

months are from May to November, when southeastern trade winds blow.

FLORA The reserve is densely wooded by rain forests, where the indigenous kauri pine *Agathis vitiensis* occurs. Other spectacular trees are *Triocularis vitiensis* and *Geissos superba*.

Above 760 meters, there are three species of particularly beautiful orchids: red dendrobium, white dendrobium, and pink dendrobium.

BIRDS The bird fauna is very rich and includes the rare golden dove, as well as many other pigeons and doves.

Peregrine, swamp harrier, and the endemic Fiji goshawk may be seen. The red-throated lorikeet is also peculiar to Fiji, where it occurs in mountain forests on at least three islands.

OTHER VERTEBRATES Among reptiles, a Pacific boa *(Enygrus)* occurs, as well as some lizards. There is also a tree frog. The boa and the frog are interesting to naturalists because the Fiji Islands are the most remote point reached by truly native snakes and frogs in the Pacific.

The Palihea stream near timberline on the slope of Haleakala N.P.

Area: 16,770 km^2 Population density: 35/km^2

Hawaii has two national parks (both described here) and several protected areas.

HALEAKALA NATIONAL PARK (created 1916)

Haleakala, a big dormant volcano occupying the entire eastern end of the island of Maui, is one of the earth's largest craterlike depressions, comprising, like a lunar world, numerous multicolored cinder cones with bowl-shaped craters, peaks, canyons, and valleys. From many beautiful overlooks, particularly from Kalahau, the true dimensions of the huge volcano can be realized: 12 km long, 4 km wide, 30 km in perimeter, and 910 m deep with cinder cones rising 300 m above the crater floor.

In clear weather the peaks of Mauna Kea and Mauna Loa on the Island of Hawaii are visible.

Location: Maui Island
Area: 10,560 ha
Protection: total; no roads leading into the crater; well-marked trails provided
Access: by sea or air; daily scheduled flights from Honolulu; taxis meet planes and ships; road to park entrance; summit can be reached by car
Activities: hiking, horseback riding possible in the crater
Accommodation: three cabins within crater; closest lodge is 19 km.

GEOLOGY   Haleakala represents three great periods of activity, the first less than 20 million years ago, the later two separated by a long quiescent interval but with intense erosion by running water that has excavated four large valleys nearly a thousand meters deep, and has worn away parts of the summit ridge. The most recent volcanic activity, according to Hawaiian legend, occurred about 1750.

The Haleakala "crater" has been interpreted in many ways by geologists, some claiming that the depression is a crater, some believing it to be a collapsed caldera, a deep gorge, a mt. ripped apart by mighty convulsions, or the result of erosion—this latter hypothesis at present thought to be the most likely, although several of the factors mentioned are probably involved.

TOPOGRAPHY   Elevation of the national park ranges from 1,172 m above SL in Kaupo Gap to 3,055 m at the summit of the mt., the highest point of Maui. The road enters the N.P. at an elevation of 2,054 meters.

CLIMATE   Mornings give the best possibilities of fine weather but around noon clouds often gather. The area is tropical but up on the volcano often windy and cool. Rainfall: 400—1,250 mm a year.

FLORA   The most extraordinary plant of Haleakala N.P., found in the wild state in the world only here on Maui and on Hawaii, is the silversword that grows mostly in the dry cinder areas of the crater and on the outer slopes of the volcano above 2,130 meters. A fenced area close to the road protects it from the feral goats that together with man have almost exterminated this plant. Before flowering, silversword grows from four to 20 years as a round mass of silvery stiletto-shaped leaves. The flower stalk, up to 3 m tall, develops rapidly from May to November, and produces hundreds of purplish blooms like a giant hyacinth; the plant dies after the seeds have matured.

Moonlike landscape in Haleakala Volcano's immense caldera

Silversword shortly after flowering

Other locally common plants are the yellow kupaoa and the puke-awe with white to reddish berries. In moister parts of the crater (such as Paliku), there is a forest of native trees: olapa, ohia, kolea, and manono, with thickets of Hawaiian raspberry.

In general, however, the crater area is bare or only thinly covered by vegetation. The outer slopes are very different with a large number of shrub species; on the NE slopes of the volcano are beautiful rain forests. In Koolau Gap (outside the national park) vegetation is lush, becoming junglelike and almost impenetrable.

MAMMALS The only native mammal species is a bat, but there are many introduced rats, mice, mongooses, feral pigs, and goats.

BIRDS As it is for the silversword among plants, Haleakala National Park is also famous for a bird: the Hawaiian goose or the nene, the world's rarest goose, which was near extinction during the second and third decades of this century. Nenes reared in captivity have been reintroduced in Haleakala. These occur seasonally in the crater at Paliku, but there is no evidence of breeding. They breed on the Island of Hawaii, where the same operation of reintroduction has been successful.

Other birds include scarlet-red iiwi and the crimson-red apapane. Both belong to Hawaii's famous honey-creepers, associated with ohia trees, seen at altitudes up to 2,590 meters. The green amakihi feeding on mamani blossoms and the olive creeper are found up in the alpine zone.

The Hawaiian short-eared owl hunts over grasslands and heaths. White-tailed tropicbirds occasionally soar around the cliffs inside the crater.

Most birds seen at Haleakala, however, are introduced species,

as is true through much of the Hawaiian Islands. Skylarks sing almost anywhere over open country up to the alpine zone. Japanese white-eye, mynah, California quail, and pheasant are some other exotics met with in the national park.

Hawaii Volcanoes N.P. has Hawaii's only active volcanoes.

HAWAII VOLCANOES NATIONAL PARK (created 1926)

This national park, on the largest and youngest of the Hawaiian Islands, consists of the much-studied volcanoes Mauna Loa and Kilauea, representing one of the most spectacular volcanic areas of the world. Many of the frequent eruptions are announced in advance by remarkably successful predictions. Active craters may be approached with reasonable safety even when they are erupting.

The most varied vegetation offers much of interest, from the coconut groves of the coast to the stunted ohia trees near the timberline.

Location: Island of Hawaii
Area: 88,137 ha
Protection: total; park open year round; paved road and trails within the park
Access: by road and by scheduled flights to Hilo from Honolulu; cars can drive to the volcanic center and even down into the Kilauea Crater
Accommodation: one hotel, Volcano House; camp grounds; hikers' cabins
Of special interest: museum; research observatory

GEOLOGY All of the Hawaiian Islands are volcanic, but today the only active volcanoes of the islands are Mauna Loa and Kilauea, both in this national park. They are, in fact, two of the most active volcanoes in the world.

The enormous Mauna Loa, whose summit caldera and part of the NE rift are included in the reserve, extends from the ocean bottom, 5,-500 m below SL, to its highest point, 4,207 m above SL, which means that it is the tallest mountain in the world.

It is intermittently active with eruptions within the caldera or on the outer slopes of the volcano. One of its most voluminous lava flows occurred in 1950, when the lava advanced with an average speed of 5.8 mph and reached the sea in less than three hours.

Kilauea is the more active of the two volcanoes. Its summit has collapsed to form a depression, a caldera called "Kilauea Crater." Within this caldera is the most active real crater (Halemaumau) of Kilauea. Its probably most spectacular eruption in historic times began in November 1959, when fountains of molten lava reached a height of 580 meters.

CLIMATE Horizontally there is local variation in the climate: a few hundred meters can separate an area of heavy rainfall from one of extreme dryness. Near the park headquarters, the annual rainfall averages 2,540 mm, while the tree forest below has 4,570 mm of rain a year. Climate of higher levels of the N.P. is semi-tropical. At Kilauea, about 1,200 m above SL, weather can be cool at any time of the year. June—August tend to have the best weather.

FLORA Many forests and bushes have come and gone, burned and buried by lava and volcanic fallout. The pioneer plants are lichens, first to colonize ash beds and lava, and ferns follow soon. Around Kilauea with its many trails, vegetation is remarkably varied, from lush jungle with treeferns and ohia forests to the sparse vegetation of the dry Kau Desert.

About 70 species of ferns have been found, and five of these are treeferns. Below the true fern forests, magnificent tropical rain forests cover some of the lower slopes of Kilauea and Mauna Loa; the upper slopes support more open forests, chiefly ohia, the commonest native tree in the Hawaiian Islands, with scarlet blossoms in late spring.

A forest of tree ferns

Other common trees are the mamani with yellow flowers and the koa, dominant on the slopes of Mauna Loa. Berry bushes are ohelo with edible berries and akia with poisonous berries.

Few Hawaiian plants are more spectacular than the tall and slen-

Ti (*Cordyline terminalis*)

MAMMALS A bat, Hawaii's only native mammal, may be seen occasionally; all other mammals in the national park are the result of earlier introductions: rats came from the ships, pigs were brought by the Polynesians, goats by the British, and mongooses from India to get rid of the rats (but they turned instead to the native birds).

BIRDS Many species of birds occur in Kipuka Pereiau; for example, elepaio, apapane, amakihi, and iiwi. Hawaiian short-eared owl, white-tailed tropicbird, and Hawaiian hawk may be observed in the national park (the latter occurring nowhere else in the world). The American golden plover, which nests in Alaska, is common in barren areas from August to May. Hawaiian geese, which breed on Mauna Kea, may sometimes be seen flying over the slopes of Mauna Loa.

der ti, a lily whose leaves are much used for many purposes by the Polynesians. White strawberries grow in moist forests on both Kilauea and Mauna Loa.

The Kipuka Paulu area by the road on the Mauna Loa slope contains over 20 species of trees and a rich flora of other plants.

Many species in the reserve represent birds that were formerly introduced in Hawaii: mynah, Japanese white-eye, cardinal, house finch, skylark, California quail, Chukar partridge, and pheasant.

The Hawaiian goose or nene, a bird peculiar to Hawaii

PHOTO CREDITS
Unless credited below all photographs are by Kai Curry-Lindahl

14 P. C. Thresher
16 P. C. Thresher
17 Animals-Animals
19 Animals-Animals
22 G. Morel
23 Animals-Animals
24 J. Verschuren
25 Animals-Animals
26 (t) Ministry of
    Information,
    Broadcasting and
    Tourism
27 M. Condamin
29 J. Verschuren
33 (tb) P. Flizot
34 Service du Tourism,
    Banqui, Central
    Africa
35 G. Coleach
37 Animals-Animals
43 G. Shaller
46 (b) Animals-Animals
47 Dept. of Tourism
    Rhodesia
48 Ministry of
    Information
    Broadcasting and
    Tourism
49 (b) J. Verschuren
50 G. Shaller
51 (t) G. Shaller
    (b) A. Root/Grimez
52 P. J. Meyer
54 (t) P. J. Meyer
55 (t) Animals-Animals
    (b) Ministry of
    Information,
    Broadcasting and
    Tourism
62 (b) A. Singer
63 (t) World Wildlife
    Fund
    (p) P. C. Thresher
64 Animals-Animals
67 Animals-Animals
68 (t) P. Thresher
    (b) A. Singer
71 (t) Animals-Animals
    (b) G. Shaller
72 (t) P. Thresher
    (b) J. Verschuren
78 Animals-Animals
79 P. Thresher
80 (b) J. Verschuren
84 World Wildlife Fund
85 P. Thresher
91 Dept. of Tourism,
    Rhodesia
92 Dept. of Tourism,
    Rhodesia

93 J. B. Shenton
95 Dept. of Tourism,
    Rhodesia
96 A. Singer
97 Animals-Animals
98 Animals-Animals
100 F. Vollmer
104 (t) F. Vollmer
108 P. Flizot
111 C. Niloticus
112 C. Niloticus
122 G. Shaller
126 P. Géroudet
127 P. Géroudet
128 O. Aktar
129 A. Aloa
130 A. Aloa
131 E. P. Gee
132 E. P. Gee
133 E. P. Gee
135 (t) G. Shaller
137 G. Shaller
138 G. Shaller
140 (tb) G. Coleach
141 E. P. Gee
142 G. Coleach
143 E. Hosking
144 E. Hosking
145 (tb) E. Hosking
147 (tb) G. Coleach
148 (tb) G. Coleach
151 (t) G. McKay
    (b) G. Coleach
152 (tb) G. Coleach
154 (t) A. Singer
    (b) G. Coleach
156 (b) G. Coleach
157 D. Banisbatana
158 D. Banisbatana
161 World Wildlife Fund
162 World Wildlife Fund
163 A. Singer
164 J. Verschuren
165 (t) G. Coleach
    (b) P. Pfeffer
166 P. Pfeffer
167 (t) P. Pfeffer
    (b) G. Coleach
168 J. Stern
170 (tl) A. Singer
    (tr) G. Coleach
    (b) A. Singer
172 (tb) B. E. Weber
174 A. Singer
175 G. Coleach
176 T. Senge
178 T. Senge
180 T. Senge
181 T. Senge
184 T. Senge

185 (t) Animals-Animals
    (b) A. Singer
186 O. S. Pettingill
189 Animals-Animals
190 M. Rosalsky
191 Alice Vrbsky
192 (t) World Wildlife
    Fund
    (b) Animals-Animals
194 E. Kemp
195 E. Kemp
196 E. Kemp
197 (b) E. Kemp
198 Animals-Animals
199 C. Sainty
200 M. Rosalsky
201 M. Waugh
202 Animals-Animals
203 (t) M. Waugh
204 L. H. Smith
205 (t) A. Singer
    (b) L. H. Smith
206 D. Saunders
207 (tb) D. Saunders
208 L. H. Smith
209 National Publicity
    Studios,
    N. Zealand
210 (b) M. F. Soper
211 M. Rosalsky
212 (t) O. S. Pettingill
    (b) M. F. Soper
213 National Publicity
    Studios,
    N. Zealand
214 (tb) G. Moon
215 M. F. Soper
216 (t) M. F. Soper
    (b) G. Moon
218 (t) O. S. Pettingill
219 National Publicity
    Studios,
    N. Zealand
220 M. Rosalsky
    (t) M. F. Soper
221 (b) O. S. Pettingill
222 National Publicity
    Studios,
    N. Zealand
223 (t) M. F. Soper
    (b) O. S. Pettingill
225 H. Hale
228 R. Wenkam
230 (t) R. Wenkam
    (b) A. Singer

INDEX to VOLUME II

This index is divided into two categories of listings: (1) parks and reserves, and (2) common and scientific names of plants and animals.

INDEX to VOLUME II

233

235

A   B   C   D   E